W9-AQS-780

THE COPYRIGHT BOOK

The Copyright Book

A Practical Guide

Fifth Edition

William S. Strong

The MIT Press

Cambridge, Massachusetts

London, England

This book was printed and bound in the United States of America.

Library of Congress Cataloging-in-Publication Data

Strong, William S.
The copyright book : a practical guide / William S. Strong. — 5th ed.
p. cm.
Includes bibliographical references and index.
1. Copyright—United States. I. Title.
KF2994.S75 1999
346.7304'82—DC21 99-22332
CIP

Periodic updates to this edition will be posted on the book's website:
http://mitpress.mit.edu/book-home.tcl?isbn=0262194198

For my parents

Contents

Appendixes

Preface

At their best, our laws embody our deepest assumptions about human beings and what proper relations among human beings ought to be. Copyright is such a law. It springs from the belief that those who try to contribute to our always inadequate store of information and inspiration ought to be paid for their pains. This seems a very creditable attitude.

My purpose in writing this book has been to make available to people whose lives and work are affected by the laws of copyright an understanding of their rights and responsibilities. However, I hope that in doing so I have also managed to communicate some of my own fascination with the subject.

I have found it useful to write much of this book as though from the standpoint of the creator of a work—be it a novel, a painting, a blueprint, a dance. But whatever is not kept safe for the artist is given to the public; if you are a would-be user of an artistic or other creative work, you will know your boundaries by the boundaries drawn for the creator of it.

I have tried to gather material and organize it in a way that will tell the story simply. This has not proved possible in all respects; parts of the law are so complex that no amount of pruning and rearranging could make them any less dense. Nor has it proved possible at every point to avoid technical language and terms whose legal definition differs from their ordinary meaning. In such places I have given examples to try to make clear what is being said.

Two further comments about organization are in order. First, because the copyright law that went into effect on January 1, 1978, governs all works created after 1977 and many aspects of works created earlier, I have used this law as my guide for most of the book. If you are concerned with pre-1978 works, you should be sure to read chapter 9, which deals with these works. Second, although many rules differ from one art form to another, it became apparent that to deal with various art forms individually would create a great deal of needless repetition. Instead, therefore, I have treated the various aspects of the law as units and within each unit discussed the exceptions pertaining to one art form or another.

Space does not permit me to acknowledge adequately the encouragement that family and friends have given me to write and later revise this book. However, I do want to take the occasion to thank two people, Evie Hanlon and Michelle Kincade, who have given new meaning to the word *secretary* and without whom all encouragement would have been in vain.

THE ©OPYRIGHT BOOK

The Subject Matter of Copyright

Copyright law is essentially a system of property. Like property in land, you can sell it, leave it to your heirs, donate it, or lease it under any sort of conditions; you can divide it into separate parts; you can protect it from almost every kind of trespass. Also like property in land, copyrights can be subjected to certain kinds of public use that are considered to be in the public interest. I shall explain these various aspects of copyright property through the course of this book.

The province of copyright is communication. It does not deal with machines or processes—those are governed by patent law—though it has been stretched, with a bit of sophistry, to cover computer software. It does not deal with titles, slogans, and the other symbols that businesses use to distinguish themselves in the public eye, for that is the stuff of trademark law. Works of art and literature are what copyright protects, no matter what the medium, and works whose purpose is to convey information or ideas. In the words of the statute, it protects "original works of authorship fixed in any tangible medium of expression, now known or later developed, from which they can be perceived, reproduced, or otherwise communicated, either directly or with the aid of a machine or device."[1]

This seemingly simple bit of language incorporates three of the fundamental concepts of the law, concepts whose meaning must be clearly grasped before all else: fixation, originality, and expression.

FIXATION

Fixation is the act of rendering a creation in some tangible form in which, or by means of which, other people can perceive it. Even the word *perceive* has its own special legal meaning; in the law's definition one "perceives" a work of choreography, for example, or a work of music, by seeing on a piece of paper the notation that enables a performer to reproduce the work. Thus a musical work may be fixed in sheet music, as well as on tape. On the other hand performing the musical work, without taping it simultaneously, does not fix it because the performance is not tangible. It is heard and is gone.

The great importance of the act of fixation is that it marks the beginning of your federal copyright. You obtain copyright under the federal law as of the instant that you fix your work in tangible form. Fixation also draws the boundary line between federal copyright protection and so-called common law copyright, which is largely the prerogative of the individual states. (*Common law* is the term for law that is built up over the years by judicial opinions; in the copyright field there has not been a great deal of variation from one state to another.)

Until January 1, 1978, common law copyright protected all unpublished works except those that were registered with the U.S. Copyright Office; now it protects only works that have not been fixed in tangible form.[2] If, for example, you have developed a pantomime in your head, but have not written any notes about it that would enable another performer to reproduce it, your unfixed work falls under the protection of common law copyright. You may perform it as often as you like, or you can let others perform it for a fee, and no one else may copy it. Presumably also you can bequeath the right to perform it to your children, and they to their children. After your death, though, it will grow increasingly difficult to prove just what your common law copyright consisted of and who owns it.

Not much more of substance can be said at this point about common law copyright. Rights in works that have not been fixed are difficult to prove and difficult to protect; it is not even easy to prove what the work is if there is no tangible copy of it. Because the expanded federal law has so severely restricted the operation of the common law, this book is devoted to works that are fixed and thus governed by the federal law, except where I specifically state otherwise.

ORIGINALITY

A work must be the product of your own mind in order to be copyrightable. Originality is not by itself sufficient; facts, even if they are facts that no one else has ever discovered, are regarded as the common property of all of us, as are scientific discoveries, mathematical equations, and historical theories.[3] Facts are not copyrightable because they are not human inventions; theories are not copyrightable because they are ideas, not expression. But although originality is not sufficient in itself, it is essential all the same.

The law follows a highly subjective theory of originality that often surprises, and sometimes shocks, those encountering it for the first time. If asked whether a person can get a copyright for something that has been created by someone else, most people would answer "no," but that answer would not always be correct. It is true that you cannot get a valid copyright in material that you have taken from someone else's work. But if you have recreated a preexisting work without having had access to it or knowledge of it, you are entitled to your own copyright. The logical extension of this is that you can enforce your copyright against anyone who has actually copied from you, regardless of the fact that that person might have copied with equal ease from the preexisting work. "If by some magic," one distinguished judge has observed, "a man who had never known it were to compose anew Keats's *Ode on a Grecian Urn,* he would be an 'author,' and... others might not copy that poem, though they might of course copy Keats's."[4] This is said to illustrate the difference between copyright and patent (which is based on objective originality), and indeed it does on a somewhat impractical level. The likelihood of someone's recreating Keats is vanishingly small, but lesser works—fabric designs, simple tunes, and the like—are often reinvented. Copyright's subjective approach to originality allows them all to flourish, in whatever soil they can find.

That elements of your work may be in the public domain does not invalidate your entire copyright. It only limits your copyright to what is original with you.

An original exposition of public domain material may take the form of arrangement. For example, *The Waste Land* is clearly a copyrightable poem, even though many of its lines are taken from works that are in the public domain. Eliot's originality lies (partly) in the juxtaposition of these public domain elements, and his copyright extends only to the limits of his originality. Similarly, a collage made of newspaper clippings is a copyrightable arrangement.

DERIVATIVE WORKS

Of a slightly different nature, but copyrightable on the same basic principle, are works the law calls "derivative works." Derivative works are those in which someone else's creation is "recast, transformed, or adapted."[5] Translations, sound recordings that transform musical or other works into magnetic notation, movie versions of plays or stories, orchestrations of melodies, and dolls based on cartoon characters are all obvious examples of derivative works. Others are less obvious but equally common, such as art reproductions. A lithographic reproduction of a painting might seem to be a copy rather than a derivative work entitled to a protection in its own right, but in fact it is regarded as a derivative work. The reasoning behind this is that the manufacture of an art reproduction in a medium different from that of the original requires the reproducer to contribute some measure of his own special skill, and that contribution is entitled to protection. In fact it has even been held that an exact reproduction of a piece of sculpture, substantially reduced in scale, can be copyrighted as a derivative work if the making of it requires great artistic skill and effort.[6]

A derivative work may be made of a copyrighted work or of a work in the public domain. If it is of a copyrighted work, and if the artist or author has not authorized it, the work will constitute an infringement of the artist's or author's copyright. In any event the protection afforded to a derivative work extends only to the original contribution of the maker.[7]

Would Eliot's *The Waste Land* be regarded as a derivative work? Would *West Side Story* be regarded as a derivative work of *Romeo and Juliet?* Would Moussorgsky's *Pictures at an Exhibition* be regarded as a derivative work of the pictures that inspired him? The answer to all three of these questions is "no." It may be helpful to analyze why.

Partly the question is one of motive. Eliot's use of preexisting poems was intended not to recast those works in another medium but to use them, through parody and juxtaposition, as building blocks for a message uniquely his own. It was not Eliot's intent, nor was it his achievement, merely to create a new version of Marvell's *To His Coy Mistress* when he wrote

---

But at my back from time to time I hear
The sound of horns and motors which shall bring
Sweeney to Mrs. Porter in the spring.

Similarly, *West Side Story* is not based on *Romeo and Juliet* in the way that the movie *Gone with the Wind* was based on Margaret Mitchell's novel; it attempts not to tell Shakespeare's story in another medium but to tell its own story, which resembles Shakespeare's play in many important respects. (If *Romeo and Juliet* were still under copyright, *West Side Story* might be an infringement, but that is another matter.)

Partly too the question is one of recognizability. Quite simply one does not recognize particular pictures in Moussorgsky's composition. Recognizability is not perhaps a firm and reassuring principle, but it is nonetheless an important one in determining derivativeness.

Another category of derivative works that deserves mention is that described in the statute as works "consisting of editorial revisions, annotations, elaborations, or other modifications which, as a whole, represent an original work of authorship." What the law protects here is the original contribution of the editor or annotator. The law will not protect trivial modifications, but it will protect modifications that are sweeping enough to constitute a "new version" of the preexisting work. The protection given a revision would cover only the work of the editor's own creativity. If a scholar, on the basis of research, revises the text of, say, a poem by Spenser, he cannot get a copyright in the new text because what he has done is to restore Spenser's own words.

The amount of originality required for a derivative work to be eligible for copyright is not clear-cut. Despite the efforts of courts to formulate rules, actual decisions tend to be ad hoc, driven by their particular facts. For example, the Second Circuit Court of Appeals struck down the copyright of an Uncle Sam mechanical bank that was a smaller-scale version of earlier, public domain models but with certain features altered, because (in part at least) it found that most of the variations from the public domain were dictated by plastic molding technology, which reduced the claimant's creativity to near zero. Another federal court (the Seventh Circuit) adopted a needlessly strict stance when it denied copyright to paintings that were based on but noticeably different from movie stills. Although early cases required only that the author have contributed a "distinguishable variation," now, for some courts at least, the variation must also be "substantial." Such a requirement seems out of sync with the general standard of originality that applies elsewhere in the law.[8] The substantiality doctrine would, if taken too far, make it impossible for one who adapts a work to a new medium to get a copyright without making changes in the content of the work as well.

Those judges who have taken a more restrictive view seem particularly worried that a looser standard will make it difficult in litigation to determine which work was being copied, the original or the derivative. Also they seem to fear the creation of traps by those who slyly place copyright notices on works to which they have made covert alterations. These fears seem exaggerated. If we apply the "distinguishable variation" test, it will be easy to know whether a defendant has copied the original or the derivative work by whether the variation appears in the defendant's product. As for traps, two things can be said. First, if the variation is truly distinguishable, forcing the would-be copyist to go to the original source does not seem all that oppressive.[9] Second, those who set such traps can always (and usually should) be punished by the courts when the traps are sprung in litigation, by granting attorneys' fees to the defendants.

Authors should always bear in mind that the right to create derivative works is part of copyright. Thus, if an author transfers all rights in a work to someone else, this right goes with the rest. The author would no longer be able, for example, to create new versions of his work. This is often an important negotiating point in copyright agreements.

When a derivative work gets its own copyright, this copyright is limited, like all other copyrights, to whatever material is original with the creator. An English translation of *Anna Karenina* is a derivative work, and it can be copyrighted, but the copyright will be narrowly defined to avoid giving the translator any kind of rights in what was actually created by Tolstoy. The translator will be protected against someone who copies his translation but not against someone who makes a similar translation by independent effort. Another example is the musical version of *Oliver Twist.* Without doubt the musical *Oliver* is copyrightable, but only to the extent that its characters, its plot, and its dialogue differ from Dickens's novel and are the original creation of its authors. You are at liberty, if it strikes your fancy, to write another musical based on *Oliver Twist,* but you cannot use the variations from Dickens's story that the authors of *Oliver* created, unless they are absolutely necessary to the task and unavoidable.

If the derivative work you make is of a work still subject to copyright, much the same rules apply. Your copyright in your derivative work covers only your own inventions, variations, and additions. You have no right to authorize someone else to use those parts of your derivative work that you have taken from the original, beyond whatever right your license agreement gives you.[10] Furthermore, when the copyright term of the original work runs out, everything in your work that you took from the original goes into the public domain, and only what you yourself have created will remain protected. The converse is also true: if a derivative work loses its copyright, the copyright of the original remains unaffected.

Tracing a work through its derivative forms can be like tagging migratory animals. Take the example of the movie *South Pacific*. It started out as a collection of short stories by

James Michener. Next, several of the stories were combined and adapted into a musical by Rodgers and Hammerstein. Then the musical was rewritten as a screenplay, and the screenplay was made into a movie. There were thus three layers of derivative works, each cutting old material and adding new. And the movie producer had three different copyrights to worry about: the short stories, the musical, and the screenplay. The movie could not be made without derivative work licenses covering all three previous forms.

The law regards an object code version of a computer program as a copy of the program, not a derivative work. (See below in this chapter.) The same rationale applies to the making of a computer-readable version of any work. For example, inputting an English-language directory into a computer database would be copying it, not "translating" it into a new language. Thus no one who makes a computer-readable version of any public domain work would have any copyright in it, unless some new elements are added. On the other hand, translating a computer program from one computer language to another *would* create a derivative work—assuming of course that anything survived the process other than the ideas or algorithms of the original.

COMPILATIONS

The other category of work in which copyrights can become layered is what the statute calls "compilations." This term covers two very different types of works: so-called "collective works," which are collections of things that could be copyrightable on their own, and databases, in which facts or other uncopyrightable things are collected. I use the computer-age term "databases" for convenience only; databases may in fact be fixed in print and other media as well as on computer tapes and disks.

The original authorship that the law protects in compilations is the selection, coordination, or arrangement of items. This is a separate copyright from any that may exist in the underlying material. The author of the compilation may be the same, but need not be the same, as the author of the component parts.

Anthologies are an example of the type of collective work that is made up of preexisting copyrightable works. Magazines, newspapers, and encyclopedias are examples of collective works that pull together the fresh labors of numerous writers and photographers. The author of a collective work will often add new material of an editorial or descriptive nature. For example, a coffee table book of Monet's paintings might contain text supplied by the person who chose what paintings to include. Technically, the copyright in that editorial text is separate from the copyright in the collective work, although they are rarely separated in practice. The presence of some small embellishment of text would not affect the "compilation" nature of the work. By contrast, though, a scholarly study of Monet that happened to be illustrated with reproductions from his work would not be thought of as a collective work. Why the difference? The pictorial elements in the scholarly study are subservient to the text, whereas in the coffee table book the compiling of images, and their arrangement in the book, is what gives the book its shape.

The other kind of compilation is the database. Databases are all around us: telephone books, medical records, sports statistics, mailing lists. In all of these, facts or other data have been assembled, whether through careful thought or sheer drudgery. Not all of them are copyrightable.

Until very recently drudgery (if great enough) sufficed to secure copyright protection in some courts. Judges responded to the perceived unfairness of allowing people a free ride on other people's work, and upheld copyright in things as menial as the telephone white pages. In 1991, however, the

Supreme Court lowered the boom on this practice. In *Feist Publications, Inc. v. Rural Telephone Service Co.,*[11] the Court held that industrious labor by itself was not enough; some "spark of creativity" is needed. The Court even went so far as to say that it is constitutionally required. It held that the mere assemblage of people's names, addresses, and phone numbers, and their arrangement alphabetically by name, lacks that necessary spark.

By this long-overdue and potentially far-reaching opinion, the Supreme Court reasserted the importance of originality to copyright. But what kind of originality? Owners of properties once considered valuable are now worrying whether their value will disappear.

If selection, coordination, and arrangement are to rise to the level of originality, they must have some degree of arbitrariness. The very word "selection" implies a range of choices, all of which may be equally valid. No one, for example, could challenge the copyrightability of a listing of "America's Most Eligible Bachelors." But where a selection is either right or wrong—say, "America's 100 Largest Cities"—the necessary scope for originality is lacking.[12]

What about mailing lists, which are the livelihood of much of America's retail commerce? They, too, present difficult issues. From one point of view, they are (unlike telephone directories) entirely random, consisting of the names and addresses of those who happen to order a company's products. But where is the spark of creativity?

These are issues certain to see a great deal of litigation, and perhaps legislation, in the future. Information has become critical to our economy, and the struggle between those who have it and those who want it is certain to intensify. It is easy to characterize one side as the hardworking, the diligent, and the other side as freeloaders. European countries, in this spirit, have been enacting laws protecting databases that copyright cannot protect. The U.S. Congress has been under pressure to follow suit. It should resist. The very premise of our copyright system is that what is not protected is free for all to use, and that society benefits by not forcing people to reinvent such things as the telephone book.

EXPRESSION

The third requirement of copyrightability is that the work be "expression" and not "idea." It is an old truism in copyright law that you cannot copyright an idea but only your expression of it: ideas, like facts, are in the public domain. For example, a literary critic who publishes a new theory of the structure of the novel cannot obtain a copyright in that theory; he can copyright only his written expression of that theory. A thief may steal his theory with impunity if the thief expresses the theory in his own words, and the thief, scurrilous though he may be, can obtain a new copyright in his own written work. Perhaps the first author should have an action for unfair competition if no attribution is made, given the nature of scholarly competition. But such a doctrine, which would be separate from copyright, has yet to develop.

A simple example like this one of literary criticism may make the rule itself seem simple. It is not. In fact it is riddled with ambiguities. What, for example, is a musical "idea" and how is it separable from musical "expression"? How basic must a plot become, how stripped of embellishment, before it ceases to be the writer's own copyrightable expression and becomes mere "idea"? No one really knows the answers to these questions, though many a court has formulated an all-embracing theory, only to see it discarded by the next court.

The rule that an idea cannot be copyrighted has an interesting corollary: copyright in the expression of an idea will not be enforced so as to prevent other people from putting the idea to practical use. This principle was first stated in the last century, in the case of *Baker v. Selden,* which involved a book on accounting techniques.[13] The book described a system of bookkeeping and, as illustration of it, contained a page ruled into columns appropriate for the system. When another publisher, impressed by the system, printed and sold copies of the ruled page—without any explanatory material—the original author brought suit.

In a decision that has continued to reverberate through the case law ever since, the Supreme Court held for the defendant. It said that if a copyrighted work describes a system or process, copyright does not prevent anyone else from making whatever printed works are necessary to use that system. To hold otherwise, the Court said, would be to treat the copyright like a patent.

It is important to understand the limits of this principle. *Baker v. Selden* does not stand for the proposition that blank forms can never be copyrighted. It does mean, though, that forms will not be protected if protection would prevent other people from using the system they embody. Nor does *Baker v. Selden* apply to forms that are purely arbitrary in their content, such as the answer sheets for copyrighted tests.[14]

A closely related doctrine provides that if a certain order of words is the only reasonable way, or one of only a few reasonable ways, of expressing an idea, that precise order of words will be protected narrowly or not at all.[15] This is called the "merger doctrine" because idea and expression are seen as merged. It has been applied not only to insurance contracts, sweepstakes rules, and other works of a business or commercial nature but also to simple artistic works such as certain pieces of jewelry. It could and probably should have been applied in the *Feist* case: surely there is no scope of expression for the idea of organizing a particular phone book alphabetically by name?

Under certain circumstances an idea may be protected before publication by an agreement to treat it as confidential. (Confidentiality is part of the law of trade secrets and is not a part of the copyright law.) If you wish to submit an idea for a work or an advertising program or something of the sort, make every effort to get a written or at least oral agreement in advance from whomever you wish to submit it to that it will be treated in confidence and paid for if used. In the absence of such an agreement, the other person will probably not be obligated to pay you. You will have only yourself to blame if you blurt out your idea without getting this protection.

If you are submitting an idea to your employer, the nature of your job may determine whether you have any rights in it. Try to clarify this in advance with the employer. When submitting an idea, whether as an insider or an outsider, be sure also that it is worked out in reasonable detail and described clearly in words or pictures. The vaguer or more general the idea, the less likely will courts be to impose liability on the user.

SCOPE OF COPYRIGHT

Once the three basic requirements of fixation, originality, and expression are met, the law's protection, though not universal, is extremely broad. Almost any kind of artistic work or work that communicates a message in any tangible medium can be copyrighted. The statute specifically lists literary works, musical works (including accompanying words), dramatic works (including accompanying music), pantomimes, choreographic works, "pictorial, graphic, and sculptural works" (in other words any visual work, whether two- or three-dimensional), sound recordings, motion pictures and all other audiovisual works, and architectural works—and this list is not complete.[16] None of these categories implies artistic merit; the yellow pages are a "literary work," and road maps are "graphic works."[17] The term "literary work" is hopelessly anachronistic, given that it now includes computer programs. A more accurate if cumbersome phrase would be "works fixed in letters or other symbols other than works intended for performance."

Although the law does not require that a work have artistic merit, certain works nonetheless do stand outside its shelter, in the cold drizzle of uncopyrightability. They are excluded for one of two reasons: either they are trivial, or they are utilitarian.

In the first category fall, for example, titles and slogans, simple designs, and minor variations on works already in the public domain.[18] Titles and slogans can be protected to some extent by federal trademark law and by state laws against unfair competition and misappropriation; a title, for example, will be protected by those laws if it has acquired such a reputation in the public mind that the use of it by someone else would amount to taking a free ride on the first user's popularity.[19] This protection, though, exists entirely apart from copyright and is not available for most items that are excluded from copyright on the grounds of triviality. Ballroom or discotheque dance steps, for example, are not considered to rise to the level of choreographic works within the meaning of the copyright statute and are unlikely to find protection under any other legal doctrine.[20]

The exclusion of utilitarian works is considerably less simple a concept. The threshold question is what the term "utilitarian" means in a copyright context. Some answers to that will seem obvious, others less so. Toys and games have been found not to be utilitarian. They serve a function, it is true; they enable a child to play. But playing is not in essence a utilitarian thing to do, and toys and games are routinely given copyright provided they meet the other relevant standards. On the other hand, items of clothing—even strikingly original creations by great designers such as Chanel—are considered utilitarian in the United States (but, unsurprisingly, not in France), and their designs are not copyrightable. Between these two fairly obvious propositions lies a gray area that has caused some trouble. What is one to do, for example, with Halloween and masquerade costumes? Some designers of costumes have tried to obtain copyright by referring to their work as "soft sculpture." The Copyright Office accepts registrations for certain fanciful kinds of costumes. Yet a case decided in late 1998 may, unless overturned on appeal, put paid to that. It found that masquerade costumes are essentially useful articles because they enable the wearer to masquerade. This seems clearly wrong. Granted one cannot masquerade without a costume, but on what theory is masquerading a *useful* function? How is it any more useful than playing a game with a toy? Going from bad to worse, the court went on to say that the artistic elements of the costumes in question—the elaborate headpieces, the masks, and so on—were not separable from the utilitarian function of the costumes and therefore not protected. In the end, it threw out the entire copyright claim, and in the process appeared to set itself at odds with Copyright Office practice and common sense.[21]

Another interesting conundrum concerns typefaces. Digital fonts—the compilations of data that map the bit points of a letter in a computer font such as the one on this page—are considered copyrightable, on the theory that in data form they are not useful but merely descriptive. However, the designs of the letters themselves are not protectable; no typeface however fanciful has ever obtained copyright, because Congress regards typefaces as fundamentally utilitarian.

Defining a work as utilitarian does not necessarily end the discussion. The law holds that the design of a useful article may be protected as a pictorial, graphic, or sculptural work if the purely artistic elements of the article can be "identified separately from, and are capable of existing independently of, the utilitarian aspects of the article." The statutory history says that this language permits copyright to those design elements that are "physically or conceptually separable" from the utilitarian aspects—an explanation that has served to complicate, rather than simplify, the matter.[22] One almost needs training in Platonic philosophy to tell when a design element is "conceptually" separable from its utilitarian element. One is being asked, in essence, to discuss the lampness of a lamp, the tableness of a table. I bid you look up from this book for a moment at the lamp beneath which you are reading and identify those parts of its design that may clearly be segregated from its functional requirements. If your lamp is by Tiffany, your task will be relatively easy; if, on the other hand, it is made in the Scandinavian style, the problem is rather more challenging. One court has suggested that design elements that are influenced to any degree by utilitarian considerations should be denied copyright.[23] This is an effective, if draconian, resolution.

Does this mean that if a lamp cannot be copyrighted, a drawing of it cannot be either? Not so. Even a drawing by a lamp designer, made not as an end in itself but solely as a prelude to manufacture, is copyrightable as a pictorial work because it is not in itself a useful article but only teaches how to make one. No one may publish copies of the drawing without the designer's permission. However, the copyright does not prevent someone from actually making a lamp that embodies the functional parts portrayed in the drawing. (Here again you hear the echo of *Baker v. Selden.*) The designer's right to control manufacture based on his drawing extends only to those parts of his drawing that depict nonfunctional things.[24]

ARCHITECTURAL WORKS

Architectural works present special complications. An architect's plans, like any other drawings, have long been copyrightable as pictorial or graphic works. No one may copy or publish those drawings without the architect's permission. However, until July of 1991 U.S. law did not protect buildings from being copied, or prevent anyone from erecting a building from copyrighted plans, except insofar as an unauthorized building might copy "nonfunctional" or "monumental"—i.e., nonutilitarian—features.[25] (In practice this exception was rarely if ever invoked.)

As of July 1991, copyright has been extended to the architectural design as such, with the result that plans are now protected against unauthorized construction, and buildings against unauthorized reproduction. Of these two protections, the former is likely to be of greater significance. It gives architects a stick to wield against deadbeat or unscrupulous clients. Formerly, if a builder failed to pay his bill, the architect's sole remedy was to sue for breach of contract. Now, if the copyright license to build has been made contingent on payment in full, the architect can sue for copyright infringement, with the possibility of recovering attorneys' fees. The same will apply if a builder tries—as many do—to reuse plans without paying the architect a new fee for the privilege.

We may safely predict that the builder's principal defense to such suit will be that the architectural design was dictated by functional considerations. For though the statute is silent on this point, the Congressional report on the bill states that copyright should be denied where form is dictated by function.[26] Technically, this is different from the "separability" analysis regarding designs of utilitarian objects, and it is clearly intended to be a looser standard. In practice it may prove just as difficult to apply.

The very definition of an "architectural work" presents some puzzles of its own. That definition is:

. . . the design of a building as embodied in any tangible medium of expression, including a building, architectural plans, or drawings. The work includes the overall form as well as the arrangement and composition of spaces and elements in the design, but does not include individual standard features.[27]

According to the statutory history, the word "building" includes any "habitable structure."[28]

No sooner had this definition been enacted than the question arose whether it included habitable structures that are divorced from the real estate on which they sit, such as tents, recreational vehicles, and mobile homes. The Copyright Office has opined that it does not, because, in its view, a structure must be both permanent and stationary to qualify as a "building."[29] This view sounds comfortably definitive, and yet it may not prove so in practice. The permanence requirement, for example, is more subjective than it may at first appear. Presumably, it excludes any structure (such as a fair pavilion or a movie set) that is erected with the intent that it be dismantled shortly thereafter. And yet, some famous movie sets from decades ago are still on the lots in Hollywood, more permanent probably than the houses of those who made them. The "stationary" requirement, too, while not subjective, is flawed in its own way. Things that their owners called "mobile homes" are probably just that, but what about the nearly identical things that other owners call "prefabricated housing"—built to be movable, but in practice never moved once installed? At what point, if at all, do they become architectural works? Or are they to be denied protection merely because at one point in their careers they drifted from one spot of earth to another?

The statutory history also says that "building" includes any structure "used by" human beings, and suggests that the term includes houses, office buildings, churches, gazebos, and garden pavilions, but excludes "purely functional structures" such as bridges, cloverleafs, dams, or walkways. But what does "used by" mean? Does copyright cover structures such as the Washington Monument (leaving aside the fact that that monument is now in the public domain) or the Vietnam War Memorial that serve no definable useful function? Is the presence of interior space enough to make a structure a "building"? The Hoover Dam has extensive habitable space inside its massive walls, but would that be copyrightable given that the exterior is an uncopyrightable dam?

What about "individual standard features"? Are we really excluding "standard designs of individual features"? If so, why was such an exclusion thought necessary, given that originality is a prerequisite of copyright and the word "standard" as good as presumes lack of originality? There is a general principle that statutes should not be interpreted so as to render them irrelevant. Yet that is precisely what the Copyright Office has done, and, given the Copyright Office's close involvement in developing the architectural work provision of the statute, its interpretation is probably definitive. In its final regulations on registration of architectural works, the Copyright Office has not only interpreted the phrase in question to mean "standard designs of individual features," but compounded the redundancy by adding solemnly that copyright does not extend to "standard configuration of spaces."[30] While engaged in these platitudes, it might have added that standard configuration of *features* (as distinct from spaces) is also not copyrightable, but for whatever reason, it did not. However, we should infer nothing from this silence. Whatever is standard, be it features, spaces, or arrangements of features and spaces, is no one's property, except in those rare cases where an original work by luck or genius becomes the standard that everyone must buy to stay in the game.

Does copyright extend to individual features of a building, provided they are not standard? Logically, the implication seems unavoidable. This would mean, if true, that once a building design as a whole is protectable as an architectural work, that protection extends to the design of individual features, quite apart from the architectural work as a whole. Thus, if a house contained a window of particularly interesting and original design, the copyright would protect not only the house as such against piracy, but also the design of the window. And thus, no competitor could copy that window without permission even if the window is the only part of the architectural work that the competitor copies.

This result, while perfectly logical, would create an odd tension. It would mean that we would apply one standard of copyrightability to features in an architectural context and a different standard to identical features that are developed independently. (For remember that a window or fountain standing alone is a "useful article," and only those elements that can be "identified separately" from its utilitarian features are copyrightable.) And the door, if you will, would thus open to abuse. The shrewd manufacturer would have its new line of faucets designed as part of a "dream house," copyright the dream house as an architectural work, and thus get a copyright in features it might otherwise not be able to protect. This is probably a *reductio ad absurdum*. The statute and its history seem to suggest that an architectural work arises from the selection and arrangement of features, not from any particular individual feature. If this is the case, then the design of those features is no more protected by the copyright in the architectural work than a scholarly article is protected by the copyright in the journal—the collective work—in which it appears. The individual feature should be judged on whether it has artistic merit that is "separable" from its utilitarian function, just as the individual scholarly article is judged on the originality of its own expression. And yet one wonders if courts will be able to keep this fine distinction always in their minds.

Must an architect be wary of too much success? What if a copyrighted feature becomes "standard" in the industry—does the statute intervene at that point to strip it of protection? Surely not, or we have stepped through the looking glass. Copyright exists to reward, not to punish, success.

PLOTS AND CHARACTERS

In works that tell stories, the coverage afforded by copyright is broader than one might think, primarily because more and more things that long ago were considered merely ideas have come to be regarded as expression. For example, the plot of a novel is covered by the novel's copyright, at least to the extent that it is original with the author. The courts have developed the ingenious theory that a plot is an "arrangement of ideas" and that an arrangement of ideas amounts, magically, to "expression."[31] From a philosophical or logical point of view, this is probably a falsehood, but nonetheless it is the law.

What about characters? Here again the law gives protection to what might at first seem to be an idea. Indeed similarity of characters is often the principal battleground when one author sues another for plagiarism. But there is one unusually perplexing problem with characters: who owns them? (You may as well resign yourself early to one of the facts of life of copyright law: no principle is fixed or firm, self-defining or self-limiting. If you are commonsensical, this will cause you frequent exasperation, but on the other hand common sense will also tend to get you out of the mazes into which pure logic leads.)

This problem of characters arose in a case involving *The Maltese Falcon*.[32] After selling the story to Warner Brothers, Dashiell Hammett wrote several more stories about his detective hero, Sam Spade. Warner Brothers took him to court, claiming that he had violated the terms of his contract of sale and that the character, Sam Spade, was their exclusive property.

It might have been enough for the court to construe the contract in Hammett's favor and to hold that he had not in fact sold Warner Brothers his rights in Sam Spade. The court did this, but it did not let the matter rest there. It went on to consider whether a character, as such, could even be copyrighted, and concluded that it could not, unless it constituted the story being told. (Emma in Jane Austen's novel might be an example of the latter case.) Its opinion was that characters like Sam Spade are a writer's stock-in-trade and that the activities or words of a character in a particular story are copyrightable but not the character as such. The court characterized an author's ownership of a character as property of a different sort—property that is protected by ordinary legal rules, not by copyright law.

This case has been nothing if not controversial. Commentators note that courts have often found (or denied) infringement of literary works by comparing their characters, thus suggesting that characters are indeed covered by copyright. And yet on closer analysis perhaps these characters fit the formula of the Spade case, as the story (or elements of the story) being told. The character who stands apart from the story, however, has an ancient lineage. From Genji to Sherlock Holmes, the world's literature is rich with heroes (and with villains like Professor Moriarty) whose identity builds over the span of many tales. Can there be any doubt that if Conan Doyle were our contemporary he could sue someone who created a detective with Holmes's characteristics, even if the new detective had a different name? And yet the character of Holmes does not reside in any one of Conan Doyle's stories. Assignment of copyright in any one of them would certainly not assign the rights to Holmes the character.

In the practical world people need not agonize over this issue. Publishers and movie producers who want the rights to characters usually include them specifically in their contracts. And conversely people who wish to retain the rights to their characters should specify as much in their contracts.

Nonetheless, if the Sam Spade case is still good law, its implications are far-reaching. How long does this unusual property right in characters last? Does it vanish when the author dies, or can he bequeath it to his children? Can he bequeath it to someone who has no connection at all with his copyrights? Could Hammett, for example, have bequeathed his rights in Sam Spade to Lillian Hellman, and would Hammett's children and publishers then have been powerless to stop her from writing books about Sam Spade? (The court never faced these problems; I would not venture to guess how a court might decide them in the future.)

The final problem of this case is that it may mean that a sale by an author of his "property" in a character is not protected by the provision in the copyright law that permits an author to terminate (revoke) a transfer of copyright. I shall deal with termination at length in chapter 3; I raise the point now only to underscore the dangers presented.

I should add that most of these issues do not arise where cartoon or other visual characters are concerned. Mickey Mouse and his colleagues are clearly protected by copyright as works of visual art.

COMPUTER PROGRAMS

Many principles of copyright are being put to the test as courts struggle with questions concerning computer programs. Programs are eligible for copyright, but there is considerable confusion about what such a copyright protects or should protect.

One important doctrine is that a computer program is protected not only in source code form but in object code form as well. This is true even if the object code is embedded in the computer, as is the case with operating system software.[33] (Source code is the version of a program that is written in FORTRAN, PASCAL, C, or any of the other so-called computer languages. The source code of a program is not intelligible to a layman, but can be easily read and understood by experts. Object code, on the other hand, is the machine-readable form of a program, whether in tape, disk, or other form, and is intelligible for the most part only to the machine it is put into, not to humans. Operating system software is the set of instructions that governs the computer's thought processes, so to speak.) Though this doctrine is the cornerstone of practical copyright protection for software, it is by no means self-evident.

At the time that this sensitive area was being studied by the National Commission on New Technological Uses of Copyrighted Works (CONTU), most Commission members felt that object code was merely a copy of the source code and should be protected by copyright. In a vigorous dissent, however, the novelist John Hersey and others protested that an object code, although it is an embodiment of the source code, functions solely as a part of the computer, is not intended to communicate to human beings, and should not be protected by copyright.[34] Thus the dispute centered on what the copyright law means when it defines a "copy" as "a material object in which a work is fixed by any method now known or later developed, and from which the work can be perceived, reproduced, or otherwise communicated, either directly or with the aid of a machine or device." The majority of the Commission took the view that the object code of a program was a copy because, theoretically, the source code could be printed out from it. The fact is, however, that that is not the purpose of object code, and indeed the last thing any program vendor wants is for his program to be deciphered; most try (however futilely) to encrypt or otherwise protect their object codes from ever being "read" and understood.

In my opinion the dissent held the higher ground, so far as logic is concerned. But logic was not the only force at work here; CONTU and later the courts acted, whether consciously or not, partly out of fear that not to extend copyright protection to object code would open the gates to the Japanese or Taiwanese invader. Certainly that fear was and is widespread in the computer industry. Many computer people will, if pressed, admit that copyright doesn't fit very well onto object code, but, they say, patent protection is expensive and time-consuming to obtain, and most programs have only a short commercial life.

The problem with the current state of the law is that granting copyright protection to things like operating system software—to pick the most blatant example—is in effect granting a long-term patentlike monopoly in the machine itself, without requiring the inventor to meet the standards of patentability. This is not healthy for the economy, nor in the long run for the law either. A better solution might have been to enact a special statute for software, combining elements of patent and copyright.

Accepting, though, that copyright applies to software, we must somehow distinguish the "expression" in a program from the "idea." A program is fundamentally a series of instructions directing a computer to perform certain analytic or other functions. If the problem to be solved is a difficult one, writing the program requires great skill and creativity, and, we say at a gut level, this effort deserves protection. But how do we protect those instructions without actually protecting the process they embody? In the precomputer age instructions for doing something, even something as arbitrary as playing a game, were narrowly limited in their copyrights.[35] CONTU considered this question and decided that for any given data-processing problem there were a great number of possible programming solutions. At a certain level of specificity, they said, the choice of computer instructions constitutes the "expression" of the general solution or algorithm, which in turn constitutes the idea.[36]

If this strikes you as disingenuous, I am inclined to agree. A process is no less a process just because it is set out in more detail or is chosen from a group of processes that have the same end result. CONTU's analysis likens a program to the plot of a novel, in which the arrangement of ideas can constitute expression. But the specifics of a plot are themselves a commentary on human life and as such constitute part of the novel's end result; it cannot be said that two plots, in their details, are merely two ways of getting from A to B, because the author's choice of details helps define and describe the world he is writing about. Furthermore, the novelist's choices are arbitrary, dictated only by imagination. A computer programmer, on the other hand, cannot choose details at random but must always have his eye on B, and his skill is judged by how quickly and efficiently he gets there. ("Efficiently"—is that a word compatible with copyright?) Still the CONTU theory has some validity, if only because there is no clear alternative.

Some courts in their eagerness to wed copyright to software have overlooked the more cautionary parts of the liturgy. An early and controversial case was *Whelan Associates, Inc. v. Jaslow Dental Laboratories, Inc.,*[37] in which it was held that the "overall structure" of a computer program could be protected by copyright. Addressing the idea-expression dichotomy, the court said that the "idea" concerned was the idea of running a dental laboratory by using a computer, thus implying that everything in the program more specific than that constituted copyrightable expression. But if copyright protects the "overall structure" of a program, is it not protecting the algorithm? Is it not protecting the process or method of the program, both of which are specifically excluded from copyright by statute?

Fortunately, a more recent case in a different federal circuit has expressly rejected the teaching of *Whelan.* In a technically sophisticated and tightly reasoned opinion in the case of *Computer Associates International v. Altai, Inc.,*[38] the Second Circuit has laid down principles for software copyright that are becoming the model throughout the country. Returning to a more traditional copyright analysis, and specifically citing *Baker v. Selden,* the court emphasized the need to draw the line between a program's idea and its expression so as not to prevent use of the processes embedded in the program. This, the court said, requires analyzing the various modules of a program and sifting out what is not copyrightable. It is in its analysis of what is not copyrightable that the *Altai* opinion gives its clearest and most desperately needed guidance. It reaffirms what some of us feared had been utterly lost sight of: that insofar as program structure is informed by concerns of "efficiency," the scope of expression is narrow and there is, in that narrow range, likely to be a merger of idea and expression, in which case the expression will not be protected. It reaffirms what should have been obvious: that copyright must not protect program elements that are dictated by external factors, such as the demands of the task to be performed, or the compatibility requirements of other programs in conjunction with which a program is intended to run. Finally, it warns against inadvertent protection of programming that is common coin in the software industry. Having sifted out all these unprotectable elements we are left, in the court's colorful phase, with the program's "golden nugget" of copyrightable expression. Significantly, the court does not attempt to define what that is, though we may presume it is the programmer's own creative and somewhat arbitrary way of accomplishing the task before him. That nugget, like the gold in a prospector's pan, can only be arrived at by reduction, not assumed or defined a priori.

The effect of *Altai* will likely be a general narrowing of the scope of copyright protection for computer code, as opposed (perhaps) to the screen displays that it may generate. For the broader promise of protection held out earlier by *Whelan,* one should look to patent. Some software developers already have. In fact, many in the software industry believe that the only really valuable part of a program is its algorithm—and for that, only patent will suffice. The Supreme Court has upheld the issuance of a patent where a computer program is the key part—indeed the only novel part—of a mechanical process.[39] Patents of this type are now granted without much controversy. Patent thus appears well suited to robotics, expert systems, and the like. Furthermore there appears to be a trend in the U.S. Patent Office toward granting patents to algorithms, even where there is little if any connection to patent's traditional realm of processes, devices, and machines. For example, a patent has been granted to the algorithm developed at Bell Labs that can be used for optimal routing of everything from telephone calls to airline flights.[40] But patents are time-consuming to obtain and may turn out to have a high mortality rate in the courts. For many applications only copyright is appropriate.

Some who secure patents for their programs also secure copyright. The apparent conflict can perhaps be resolved by saying that patent protects the algorithm and structure of the program, whereas copyright protects the program at a more specific level. Thus when the seventeen-year patent term ends, copyright would continue to protect the specific instruction sequences of the program.

Yet for many software producers neither patent nor copyright is desirable. In fact, anyone planning to distribute software by one-on-one licensing would do well to follow common industry practice and rely primarily on trade-secret protection. This involves placing tight restrictions on the uses that the customer can make of the software, prohibiting disclosure to persons other than the licensee and its key employees, and requiring return or destruction of the software if for any reason the license is terminated. If you are marketing your software over the counter, trade-secret protection is of course not appropriate. In such a case copyright is probably the only alternative now available.

Another area of controversy in the application of copyright to software is the protection of the "look and feel" of a program. At issue is the user interface of a program, which consists primarily of the menus and other displays that appear on the screen and the order of keystrokes by which a user inputs and manipulates data.

Popular software begets imitation, and clever imitators can copy the user interface of a program without copying any underlying code. Such was the case with Lotus Development Corporation's popular spreadsheet program 1-2-3, which had become the industry standard for financial spreadsheet software. In 1990 Lotus won a suit against a leading "clone" producer.[41]

The threshold question presented by this and other look-and-feel cases is whether the screen displays are a separate work from the underlying code or both are parts of one unitary work. The U.S. Copyright Office has taken the position that if both the code and the display are produced by the same persons, they should be treated as two parts of a single work. In this the Office expressly disagreed with a prior District Court case on the point.[42]

Assuming the Copyright Office view prevails, it nonetheless seems likely that courts will judge the copyrightability of screen displays separately from that of the code. At least one court has already done so.[43] This means that a court may acknowledge copyright in the unitary work as a whole but still find that the screen display element is not copyrightable, just as it might find a novel to be copyrightable as a whole but deny copyright protection to various scenes or plot sequences. What sorts of screen displays, then, may be protected?

There can be little doubt that video game screens are copyrightable, provided they contain a minimal level of original expression. They are, in essence, animated cartoons.

But what about spreadsheet displays? Clone manufacturers argued that spreadsheets and accompanying menus, like the accounting sheets in *Baker v. Selden,* cannot be given copyright without granting a monopoly to Lotus in the financial planning techniques that the spreadsheets embody. The court disagreed, finding the screen displays to be copyrightable expression in most though not all respects.

A related issue raised in the Lotus and other look-and-feel cases is the copyrightability of the keystrokes required of menu structure, command hierarchy, and, in general, a program's user interface. The trial court had held that Lotus's copyright in its interface was valid. It found, moreover, that Borland International's Quattro Pro software, which copied none of Lotus's source code but was designed to be compatible with 1-2-3, using a so-called "Lotus Emulation Interface," infringed the copyright in 1-2-3 by copying such things as menu commands and macros.

The First Circuit Court of Appeals reversed this finding on appeal. Contrary to most people's expectations, it did not engage in an "abstraction, filtration, comparison" analysis such as the Second Circuit (and many other circuits since) adopted for comparing one piece of software to another. It found that test not applicable to the fundamental question of whether a menu command hierarchy is copyrightable per se. Nor despite the urgings of Borland did it find *Baker v. Selden* especially helpful, although its analysis of that case strikes this observer as being rather oversimplified. Instead, the First Circuit found the menu command hierarchy at issue to be a mere "method of operation" and therefore ineligible for protection under the explicit wording of the Copyright Act, which denies copyright to any "method of operation."[44]

The Supreme Court agreed to hear the appeal of this decision. It was widely expected to use the case as a jumping-off point for a more far-reaching exploration of copyright as applied to computer software, as it had done for the "sweat of the brow" doctrine in *Feist Publications v. Rural Telephone Co.* But again the smart money was disappointed, because one judge ending up having to recuse himself and the remaining eight split down the middle. At the end of the day the First Circuit's decision was left undisturbed, but its value as precedent was seriously undermined because we all know that half of the Supreme Court thought it was bad law and, for all anyone can tell, a 5-4 decision could well have gone against it. Even more disappointing for those keenest to know where the Supreme Court stands on these issues, no opinions were issued by either side and the "pro" justices and "con" justices were not identified, so there is no way of telling along what fault lines, if any, the Court split, and no way of predicting what will happen when they finally take, and decide, a software copyright case.

Although the First Circuit got where it got by an uncharted route of its own making, its decision strikes me as sound. Granting copyright to the menu commands that a program user must employ to make the program run has always seemed overreaching. Certainly in past years, before this decision, it had a chilling effect on the development of products that could compete on efficiency and price for the loyalty of customers who have an investment in existing data files and staff training.

Is "look-and-feel" copyright dead? The trial court's views of the case had no doubt extended the reach of look-and-feel copyright. But I do not read the First Circuit's opinion as undercutting look-and-feel except where the fundamental method of using a program is at stake. Other, equally questionable (to my thinking) claims to copyright for some sort of nebulous overall impression of a work remain undisturbed.

As the foregoing discussion may suggest, where computer software is concerned, we are dealing with something suspiciously like new wine and old bottles. The Lotus decision has proved controversial among copyright scholars, suggesting that outside the easy cases there is no consensus on where the boundaries of copyright should be drawn.

WORKS CREATED WITH THE AID OF COMPUTERS

Can a work created by applying a computer program to a database receive a copyright? A typical work of this sort might be a biblical concordance, created by feeding the Bible into a computer bank and then applying to it a program designed to locate and arrange word correspondences. Although no case has yet raised the issue, there seems to be no reason why a work of this type should not be entitled to a copyright. Admittedly the computer is doing the bulk of the legwork, but this is only at the guidance of a human being. It is a tool, no matter how creative it may be. A certain degree of human will and intellectual labor is present in any computer product.[45]

As intellectual production of this type becomes more and more common, some unusual problems of ownership will emerge. I shall deal with these in greater detail in the next chapter.

MASK WORKS

By an amendment to the Copyright Act in 1984, Congress granted a truncated form of copyright protection to the masks, so called, that are used to create semiconductor chips.[46] It was felt that these masks, being essentially utilitarian works, would not receive protection without specific statutory language.

A mask lies somewhere between a design and a stencil, or perhaps more accurately it is both. In it the intricate circuitry of a semiconductor chip is cut, and through it laser light etches the circuitry design onto the chip's silicon. Because of their inherently utilitarian character, Congress has granted mask works a shorter term of protection and a narrower scope of rights than other works. And, interestingly, Congress has specifically authorized anyone to use the technology contained in a mask work, provided he obtains it by reverse engineering and does not merely copy the mask.[47]

PERFORMANCES

Performances of works are not regarded as works themselves until they are fixed, on tape or film, as sound recordings or audiovisual works. They are therefore not protected by copyright law until that time. This does not mean that someone can film or record a performance without the performer's permission. That used to be forbidden by state law, if at all. Now, for musical performances, it is forbidden by federal law as well.

As of December 8, 1994, the date on which GATT-implementing legislation passed into law, federal law grants limited protection to unfixed live musical performances. Although aimed particularly at the growing market for bootlegged CD-ROMs and music videos, the new Section 1101 of the Copyright Act makes it illegal to fix the sounds and images of a live musical performance in any medium, or to make, transport, or sell copies of phonorecords that duplicate any fixation, unless authorized by the performer(s). The new law also makes it illegal to "transmit or otherwise communicate to the public," by cable, broadcast, or otherwise, any live musical performance without the performer's permission. The remedies for a violation of this law are the same as for copyright infringement, but there is no requirement that anything be registered (indeed, what is there to register?) in order for the aggrieved performer to sue or to obtain any of the special benefits that timely registration confers on a copyright plaintiff. (See chapter 5.)[48] Furthermore, if the offender has acted with a motive of financial gain, he is guilty of a criminal offense and may be both fined heavily and imprisoned for up to ten years.[49]

The sweep of this new law is hard to overstate. It prohibits unauthorized distribution in this country even if the unauthorized fixation occurred outside the United States. And even, apparently, if the fixation occurred in a non-GATT country. It has no cutoff date. As far as anyone can tell, the performer's right continues to be protected indefinitely; there is no "life-plus-seventy" or other fixed term. This raises interesting Constitutional problems, for the U.S. Constitution says that copyright may last only for "limited times."[50] Perhaps, if challenged, the provision may be defended by reference to the so-called commerce clause of the Constitution, which gives Congress broad power to regulate interstate and international commerce. But whether defensible or not on Constitutional grounds, the absence of a cutoff date will create havoc unless corrected.

Furthermore, the statute can be read as preventing distribution of (for example) bootlegged CDs even if the unauthorized fixation occurred before the statute was enacted. Nor is the performer's right subject to any third-party right of "fair use." The statutory history suggests that the statute may not be enforced in such a way as to conflict with First Amendment rights of free speech, but this is a more narrow and even less clear limitation than fair use. (See chapter 8.)

Note that every performer has the right described here, no matter how insignificant his or her contribution to the performance. Every performer in a band or orchestra must consent or the fixation or broadcast is unlawful. In contrast to a copyright license, a license to fix a performance cannot be granted by just one of the group of right holders; it must be granted by all.

Nothing in the statute appears to prevent a performer from delegating his right of consent, so presumably orchestras and bands will obtain from their members the necessary authority to act for everyone in the group. What is less clear is whether the right can be assigned outright. The statute does not say. For example, what happens to the right of consent when the performer has died? If after a singer has died someone starts selling copies of a bootleg recording of one of her concerts, who can sue the bootlegger? Is this right of consent a personal right, to be exercised only by a performer's family, or is it a commercial right that can be freely assigned? In contrast to copyright rights, the statute provides no rules or even guidelines for how the right can be transferred, and there is no registry where the right can be recorded. It is conceivable that the Copyright Office could record claims of ownership of this right, but its current procedures are not geared to do so and there are no implementing regulations in the offing. It is not even clear that the right survives the performer's death, although the failure to specify a cutoff date for the right probably implies, as I have said, that it does survive.

Another problem that the statute finesses is how "consent" is to be determined. There is no requirement that it be in writing. If the unauthorized fixation or transmission occurred in a foreign country with different legal customs as to what constitutes "consent," will U.S. courts defer to that law or judge the facts under American contract principles? There is no way to predict.

Just to make things more interesting, a treaty whose adoption is pending as this book goes to press would require the United States to prohibit unauthorized fixation of *all* aural performances, not just musical ones.

Whether authorized fixation, when it occurs, will protect a performer's interpretation, voice, or style is a matter on which the courts have not agreed. In one case on the subject, Bette Midler was able to stop the use of television commercials in which another singer imitated her voice and style.[51] But in general, performers seeking to protect these elements should look to the "right of publicity" laws of the various states.

VESSEL HULLS

Under pressure from industry, Congress agreed to adopt statutory protection for the hull designs of yachts and ships. Contrary to good sense, and apparently for want of any better place to stick such protection, Congress inserted it into the Copyright Act, where it stands out in all its bizarre incongruity. This is the first sort of industrial design protection the United States has ever enacted on the European model. European law has long protected the nonpatentable, noncopyrightable but original designs of ordinary commercial goods: a sleek new toaster, for example, or an aesthetically pleasing ball point pen would be given protection in most European countries for a decade or so against slavish copying. American industry has always, until now, resisted such doctrine. Whether this new vessel hull design law will prove to be the camel's nose in the tent, or will pass out of history unmourned, remains to be seen.

Essentially, the new law protects vessel hull designs that are original and different from public domain designs in some significant way, and that are not staple, commonplace, or dictated solely by utilitarian function. To obtain it, one must apply for it within a year (or perhaps two years; the statute seems to contradict itself) after the design is made public. It is not available to designs already publicly known as of the date the new law went into effect in late 1998. Although protection is theoretically good for ten years, in fact it is subject to a two-year sunset provision in the law, and if the law is not extended at the end of that initial two-year period the law's protection will drop away.

Because of this sunset provision, and because the entire subject is so far removed from true copyright, I will say nothing more about it here. Interested persons should refer to Chapter 13 of the Copyright Act, as amended in late 1998.

NATIONAL ORIGIN

The United States will honor the copyright of any unpublished work, regardless of the nationality of its author. Its protection for published works is only marginally less broad. It will protect any published work if, on the date of first publication, one or more of the authors is a national or domiciliary of the United States, or is a national, domiciliary, or sovereign authority of a foreign nation that is a party to any copyright treaty to which the United States is a party, or is a stateless person. The protection of works of foreign governments is worth noting, particularly inasmuch as the United States does not grant copyright to any work of its own federal government.

U.S. law will also protect any work first published in the United States or in any foreign country that is party to a copyright treaty, or is first published by the United Nations or any of its specialized agencies, or by the Organization of American States.

Given the ambiguity of whether buildings are "published," it is worth noting that U.S. copyright also extends to any pictorial, graphic, or sculptural work incorporated in a building or structure, and to any architectural work embodied in a building, if the building or structure is located in the United States or in the territory of one of its treaty partners.

There is also a special rule for sound recordings. Any sound recording first fixed in a foreign country that is party to a copyright treaty with the U.S. will be protected in the U.S., regardless of whether it meets any of the other tests listed above. I should add that two of the copyright treaties in question are limited to sound recordings. If a country is party to one of these but not to any other copyright treaty, the protection extended to its works and those of its nationals, etc., is limited to sound recordings.

Finally, there is a provision for copyright to be extended to the works of a foreign country by Presidential proclamation. Given that most if not all countries now belong to one or more copyright treaties, this provision is no longer of much relevance.

In chapter 11, I discuss some of the interesting problems that arise in international copyright protection. What I have to say in the intervening chapters will be limited to U.S. law, and based on the assumption (largely but not wholly correct) that U.S. law will apply, within the borders of the United States, to any foreign work just as it applies to any native work.

2 Ownership

Copyright comes into existence at the moment of a work's creation, just as, in some theologies, the soul enters the body at birth. At that time ownership vests in the author or authors.

The word *author* has a special meaning in the copyright law. It is used regardless of the kind of work; writers, painters, sculptors, and composers are all authors. This usage indeed is almost universal—in other countries as a matter of convenience and in this country as a necessity. The Constitution, from which Congress derives its power to establish copyrights, speaks specifically of "authors" and "writings," and to extend the law's protection to nonliterary works, the courts have had to interpret these words broadly. However, *author* is not synonymous with *creator,* for in certain circumstances a person, or company, will be considered an author without lifting a creative finger. So what seems at first almost a frivolous question—Who is the author?—is in fact both complex and important.

Authorship

Only in a work by one individual acting on his own behalf is the answer to the question obvious. In the case of, say, a poem written by one person and set to music by another, it is anything but obvious. Three different relationships can exist between that poet and that composer. The first, in which the words and music are considered separately, can hardly even be called a relationship. The poet is the author of the words and may do what she likes with her poem; the composer is the author of the music and may do with the music anything that he pleases. In the absence of some exclusive licensing arrangement, the first composer cannot prevent another from making a new musical setting for the poem, and the first poet cannot prevent another from writing new words to fit the music. A singer who wants to perform such a song would have to acquire the performance right in the poem from the poet and the performance right in the music from the composer.

It is also possible, and more common, for the poet and composer to be "joint authors," and for the song to be a "joint work." Joint authorship ranks among the more slippery principles of copyright law, and many courts and commentators have grappled with it without achieving a clear victory. Intuitively we all know what a joint work is; it is, just as the statute says, a work "prepared by two or more authors with the intention that their contributions be merged into inseparable or interdependent parts of a unitary whole."[1] But what do these words mean? Do they mean that for a work to be a joint work, all of the authors must agree among themselves before any of them begins creating any part of the work? That would violate good sense. As one court said in a case under the old law,

---

Suppose, for example, that after Burnett had composed the music, expecting his wife to write the words, she had died or changed her mind about writing the lyrics, and Burnett had gone to [his publisher] and asked him to find someone to write the words. We submit that no court would hold that the fact that when Burnett composed the music he expected his wife to write the words, would make the actual song any less a "joint work" of Burnett and the lyricist found by [his publishers].[2]

The force of this reasoning cannot be denied, and there seems no reason not to apply it to the new statute. As the House Report accompanying the new statute makes clear, the "intention" on which the law is focused is the intention with which the author's contribution was created.[3] And as the Burnett case holds, the intention need not be *mutual* among the authors; it is sufficient that each author have intended that his product be merged with others. Thus even if a lyricist dies before finding a composer, when a composer is finally found, the resulting work will be a joint work.

What is less clear is whether anything is gained by focusing on intention where the contributions are inseparable. Take, for example, the case of a mystery writer who, when she is halfway done, decides to bring in a collaborator to finish her newest work. Their contributions are inseparable, and the work is inescapably a joint work; no possible alternative designation exists. Now suppose instead that the first writer dies, leaving an unfinished manuscript. Her executor finds another writer willing to finish the book. Should not the resulting work be considered a joint work? The deceased author certainly intended that there be only one work, yet technically she did not intend that her efforts be merged with those of any other writer. The alternative is to consider the unfinished manuscript a completed work for copyright purposes and the finished product a derivative work with separate copyright. This seems absurd, but one cannot be sure it is incorrect.

Although the intention the statute requires is that the contributions be merged, some recent court decisions have put a different spin on this language. Instead of asking what was the parties' creative intent, these decisions ask whether the parties intended to create the legal relationship of joint authorship. For example, the Second Circuit opined that while an editor at a publishing house may make substantial and inseparable contributions to a work, neither author nor editor intends to create a joint authorship arrangement and thus the editor is not a joint author.[4] This reasoning is seductive, because the example is so compelling; to side with the author seems like only common sense. The editor is a craftsperson, performing a function that editors have always performed, without ever expecting or being given any rights. An editor is an employee of the author's publisher, and the publisher, bound by age-old custom and needing to keep good relations with its authors, is never going to raise the issue. The fact that the publisher never has raised the issue may help explain why the court found it so easy to assume that the publisher has no legal interest. So a straw man was set up and knocked down.

But the precedent set in that case is in fact quite dangerous, as the same court demonstrated more recently in a case involving a dramaturg. Dramaturgs are typically brought into theatrical productions when it is clear that a script is not going to work. They are freelance "editors," so to speak, who sometimes become deeply involved in the plays they work on. One such person was responsible for extensive rewriting of the script for the Broadway musical *Rent*. Her role was so great that she was even given credit as "Dramaturg." But when she—breaking from the age-old custom of *her* industry—sought to establish joint ownership of the copyright, the original playwright refused. He said he had never intended that she be treated as a joint author—and indeed, in his dealings with third parties, he had acted as if he owned the whole play. The Second Circuit upheld his contention, based on evidence that he had never demonstrated any intent to share *authorship* with the dramaturg.[5]

This may make for predictable commercial transactions, but it plays fast and loose with the language of the statute. And it leaves some troubling questions unresolved. For if the editor's or dramaturg's work is not a contribution to a joint work, what is it? If the "author" is lucky, it may be work made for hire (see below) of which he is the owner by dint of control. But if not, what is it? A separate work? A gift to the author? The court overlooked the fact that unless the editor/dramaturg/whatever is an employee for hire, the material that he or she creates cannot be owned by the "author" in the absence of a written instrument. We may not have heard the last of this problem.

An important but not always understood requirement of joint authorship is that there be authorship on all sides, i.e., that every contributor's input be copyrightable expression. Thus, the "idea person" cannot claim joint authorship simply on the basis of having contributed ideas, no matter how original or how critical to the work's success.[6] To hold otherwise, it is said, would impede the free exchange of ideas by creating fear that the use of those ideas would subject the author to claims upon his copyright.

Where joint authorship exists, it creates a hybrid sort of ownership. Joint authors are not like joint owners of a house, with the last survivor taking the whole title. Instead they are regarded as "tenants in common." This means that each of them owns an undivided share of the entire work and can bequeath that share to his own heirs. This share is not necessarily equal, for the authors can slice the pie unevenly if they so choose.[7] However, unlike someone who owns land as a tenant in common, a joint author cannot force a division of the property as such. Instead, because ownership is theoretically undivided, each joint author can grant rights in the entire work without consulting the others. (If he does so, he will have to account to his fellow authors for their shares of the profits.) Yet by the same token a grant by any one joint author will not prevent any of the other joint authors from making an identical sale to someone else. For this reason purchasers generally insist on getting all of the authors to sign the contract.

Outside the United States the rule is stricter: to be effective, even a nonexclusive license must be signed by all joint authors. Anyone contemplating foreign distribution of a work should insist on obtaining all signatures.[8]

WORKS MADE FOR HIRE

I have discussed so far two possible relationships between persons whose creative efforts are in some manner connected. The first is that they are merely independent authors combining their independent creations; the second is that they are joint authors. A third possible relationship is that one of them is an employee of the other, in which case the resulting work is a "work made for hire." Works made for hire have a different copyright term from that of most other works, and they are the only works for which an author has no statutory right to terminate a transfer. (See the discussion of termination of rights in chapter 3.) The author of a work made for hire is the person who does the "hiring"; the creator has no rights whatever in the work.

The most obvious examples of works made for hire are newspapers, movies, dictionaries, and other works that we think of as created, in a sense, by the companies that publish them. These companies have staffs of full-time writers and artists who work specifically on these products.

The rule is broader, though. An employer is considered the author of anything written by an employee within the scope of his or her employment. Thus when a scientist in a research laboratory writes a report on her work for her supervisor, the laboratory is the author of the report.

Determining whether a person's authorship is within the scope of his employment is not as simple as it may sound. Courts look not only at the nature of the work but also at whether the work is done within the limits of time and space authorized by the employer. Where these factors do not yield an easy answer, they will inquire whether the authorship is motivated, at least in part, by a desire to advance the employer's interests. The outcome of this analysis can be surprising. Courts have even gone so far as to find that an employer owned copyright in a scientific article written by its employee at home after hours.[9]

Even more open to argument than the "scope of employment" is the question of who is an "employee." The clear-cut example is the full-time staff writer, who is an employee in every sense of the word. But what about someone who is commissioned to create a specific work, is paid by the job—or not paid at all—and then moves on? The Supreme Court has attempted to answer that question, with results that may not be entirely desirable.

First, a word of background. Under pre-1978 law it was generally held that one who commissioned a work became the "author" and copyright owner. This was largely a judge-made rule, based on what courts perceived as the legitimate expectations of the parties. For example, commissioned portraits were works for hire, and the copyright belonged to the purchaser instead of the painter.[10] Where a company paid someone to develop an advertisement, a court would grant copyright to the company, believing that any other result would be unfair.[11]

The old statute was rather cursory on this question of what constitutes "for hire." By contrast, the new statute goes into it at some length. It sets up two categories of work for hire: on the one hand, work created by an employee "within the scope of his or her employment"; on the other hand, a specifically ordered or commissioned work if it falls within one of nine clearly defined categories and if the parties have agreed in writing to treat the work as made for hire.

The question then arose whether by this new language Congress intended to limit the work-for-hire doctrine, in cases of commissioned materials, exclusively to works that fall within the nine defined categories and are the subject of written agreements, or whether in some cases a commissioned person could still be viewed as, in some broader sense, an employee.

The first major case on this point came up from New York to the Second Circuit. It involved authorship of certain statuettes, and the evidence showed that the people who commissioned the work had actively participated in its creation, giving detailed instructions on various design issues. The Second Circuit held that even though the commissioned artisans were not employees in the legal sense, they had acted under the "direction and control" of the commissioning party and thus should be regarded as employees for work-for-hire purposes.[12] This rule was subsequently followed by a number of other courts and was extended to cases where a commissioning party had the *right* to supervise and control, even though the right might never have been exercised.[13]

All was tranquil, then, until the Fifth Circuit rejected this doctrine in the case of *Easter Seals Society for Crippled Children v. Playboy Enterprises*.[14] The facts are less titillating (and less one-sided) than the name of the case might suggest; at issue was ownership of some film footage of jazz musicians that had been made at the request of the Easter Seals Society for use in a promotional broadcast.

The Fifth Circuit carried out what might be termed archaeology on the statute, interpreting it in the light of the various drafts it had gone through, remarks of legislators, and the like. It decided that although "employee" did not mean only persons on a payroll, the term did exclude independent contractors who were merely subject to direction and control. An "employee" had to be either an employee in the strictest sense or at least someone so nearly like that as to be considered an "agent" of the other party. (At common law, contrary to popular usage, an "agent" is neither a spy nor a broker but any person who acts on another's behalf, rather than his own.) To determine agency, the court suggested looking to the law of personal injury: if one would be held liable for a physical injury caused by a commissioned artist, one would be that artist's employer for copyright purposes.

Following this reasoning, the District of Columbia Circuit held, in the case that ultimately went on to the Supreme Court, that a statue belonged to the sculptor even though the charity that commissioned the sculpture had contributed portions of it and made far more than cursory stipulations about its design.[15] The D.C. Circuit Court went so far as to suggest that the commissioning charity and the sculptor might be joint authors—an idea neither party had suggested or, we may suppose, would happily endorse.

Not to be outdone, the Ninth Circuit, sitting in California, subsequently held that only works produced by actual salaried employees could be works made for hire, unless they fell within one of the nine special categories and were subject to written agreements.[16]

The end result of all this judicial activity was that, as of 1989, who owned copyright in a commissioned work depended on what circuit's jurisdiction you were under. At this point the Supreme Court stepped in and delivered a definitive ruling, endorsing the approach taken by the Fifth and District of Columbia Circuits.[17]

Though it may be idle now to complain, all sides in this dispute have been guilty of the kind of entrail reading, known euphemistically as "statutory history," that other countries do not allow courts to indulge in when interpreting a law. All sides are victims of a Congress that seems incapable of saying what it means.

All sides have also overstated the virtues of their positions. The Fifth and D.C. Circuits, and now the Supreme Court, have claimed that their agency-based rule will promote certainty by adopting a "bright line" definition of employee. But nothing could be further from the truth. As I have noted, the D.C. Circuit and the Supreme Court suggested that joint ownership should apply where an artist is not an employee but the commissioning party makes substantial input into the work. Of what benefit is such a Solomonic decision? Neither the artist nor the patron can grant an exclusive license to a publisher, and no one in the real world will ever pay much for a nonexclusive license. The result is not certainty but stalemate. Perhaps parties who find themselves in such a situation will settle their differences and work out some *modus vivendi.* But perhaps they will not, and the work will never see the circulation it deserves. The law should avoid violently yoking together people who do not intend to be yoked.

Some groups representing the interests of authors have hailed the Supreme Court's decision as a great victory. I am not convinced. It does unquestionably place on commissioning parties the burden of obtaining written agreements. An advertiser, for example, will need a written assignment of copyright to own the ads it commissions. Many deals that have traditionally been done on a handshake will require new legalisms. Those already consummated are now open to revision, because the Supreme Court's ruling is retroactive to January 1, 1976.

But if the commissioning parties have the bargaining power, they will usually manage to extract by contract what the old law gave them by right. The only right an author cannot contract away is the right of termination after thirty-five years (discussed in chapter 3); this right is meaningful only to the most significant works of art or letters. It has no relevance in the fields where the work-for-hire rules actually operate: commercial photography, computer software, and so forth. So what the new rule has accomplished is, where commissioning parties are alert, to stimulate a lot of new paperwork, and where they are not alert, to create a trap into which they can stumble.

Even on its own terms the "bright line" rule adopted by the Supreme Court is anything but self-defining. As noted, it imports into copyright the law of agency, a strange new bedfellow. Treatises have been written about agency; treatises are not written about things that are neat and thoroughly predictable. In the income tax arena, Congress and the IRS have for years wrestled inconclusively with the problem of when A should be treated as an employee of B, and when as an independent contractor. The same issue has led to years of litigation over who can claim the benefits of collective bargaining. How then are we to know whether someone fits the employee/agent profile? The test, as described in older noncopyright cases cited by the Supreme Court, is whether the hiring party has the right to control not merely the result, but also the manner and means by which the result is accomplished. The Supreme Court specifically invokes this language and then states that the following factors (and perhaps others as well) should be assessed when determining whether someone is *de facto* an employee and thus an agent of the hiring party in the creative process. I list these factors with some observations as to their application:

- *The skill required.* A highly skilled artisan is less likely to be an employee than a mere paper pusher.
- *The source of the tools and materials used to create the work.* This factor reflects the general truth that one in business for oneself has one's own tools; employees use their employers' tools.
- *The duration of the relationship.* A one-shot job is less likely to be a for-hire relationship than a job of long standing in which various works are created.
- *Whether the commissioning party has the right to assign additional projects to the creative party.* The right to say, "Hey, you. Put down that paintbrush and shovel the driveway" (to give a perhaps extreme example), will clearly weigh for the hiring party. On the other hand, it has been held that a software designer is not an "employee" just by virtue of

being the hiring party's "regular troubleshooter," called in whenever the hiring party has computer problems.[18]

- *Who determines when and how long the creative party works.* Control of one's own working hours tends to indicate independent contractor status.
- *The method of payment.* A flat fee (or better yet a royalty) will be most favorable to the creative party, and an hourly fee will be most favorable to the commissioning party.
- *Who decides what assistants will be hired, and who pays them.*
- *Whether the work is in the ordinary line of business of the commissioning party.* The doll factory that commissions a new doll will fare better than the automobile dealership that commissions a music video.
- *Whether the creative party is in business on his own.*
- *Whether the creative party receives employee benefits such as health insurance from the commissioning party.*
- *The tax treatment of the creative party.* For example, if the commissioning party pays FICA and withholding on an artist's earnings, it is more likely to be the copyright "author" than if the artist pays self-employment taxes.

The Supreme Court gave no indication of how these factors should be weighed: should each be given equal weight, and whoever gets the most points wins, or are some of these more important than others?

It is somewhat in the nature of Supreme Court opinions to be Delphic, and this case is an example. But some lower court attempts to fashion clear and useful rules out of it have, by contrast, not been Delphic enough. A tendency has emerged to ignore the dynamic creative process and focus exclusively on the static relationship of the parties. Likewise, courts have given, in my judgment, far too much weight to the tax treatment of the hired party and whether the hired party receives employee benefits.

The Second Circuit has recently ruled that different factors will be more or less important depending on the context, but that some are significant in nearly every case and are usually "highly probative" of the true nature of the relationship. These "highly probative" factors are: the right to control the manner and means of creation (here is a typical instance of doctrinal confusion in this field: what the Supreme Court described as the overarching inquiry is described by the Second Circuit as just one of many questions), the skill required, whether the hired party receives employee benefits, the tax treatment of the hired party, and whether the hiring party has the right to assign other projects to the hired party.[19] The court went beyond this to state that failure to provide employee benefits or pay payroll taxes (Social Security, etc.) for the hired party will weigh heavily against the hiring party because they indicate that for purposes other than copyright the hiring party is treating the hired party as an independent contractor. The opinion seems to view a claim of work-for-hire in these circumstances as attempting to keep one's cake while eating it.

A major problem with the Second Circuit's analysis is that these tax and benefit arrangements are the standard indicia of ordinary, quotidian employment: the very sort of relationship that the Ninth Circuit had said the law requires and that the Supreme Court expressly said it does not. If we give too much weight to these factors, we will end up closing the door that the Supreme Court went to some pains to keep open. Of the two cases cited with approval by the Supreme Court in its discussion—both of which arose in the field of collective bargaining law—one found an employment relationship to exist even though the hired parties paid their own income taxes, and the other found no employment relationship even though the hired parties were on the hiring party's payroll. Thus, the Second Circuit's recent approach seems at odds with precedent.

Another problem with focusing too much on the static relationship of the parties is that we may fail to see "agency" in the truest sense of the word. One may imagine instances where the entire creative process is closely guided by the hiring party, or where the hiring party sketches the entire work and leaves the details to a hired draftsman. Fairness ought to favor the hiring party in such situations, but I would hesitate to say that the law will too. Fortunately, a recent decision in the Third Circuit seems to take a more flexible and realistic approach,[20] but it is too early to tell which view of the law will prevail.

Whichever prevails, we cannot escape the fact that future determinations are going to be to some degree ad hoc, and thus potentially unpredictable. This underscores the desirability of reducing every deal to writing, and specifically of allocating copyright ownership in that writing. Indeed, at one level or another the parties' rights are always going to be ad hoc unless *everything* is written down. This is good for the legal profession but not the polity. An example may help to illustrate.

The example is unfortunately a common one. Suppose Green commissions Brown to create a work of some sort, and it does not qualify as a work made for hire. What rights do Green and Brown actually have in the work? If it is a portrait, for example, Green obviously has ownership of the portrait itself and thus has a limited right to display it publicly.[21] Green does not own any other rights in it.

Suppose, though, that the work is something Green intends to use, such as advertising material. Fairness would dictate that Green have a nonexclusive license to publish the work, to display or perform it, and to make new versions or other derivative works based on it.[22] However, does Brown have to give Green access to the printing plates and negatives, or master tapes, so that Green can reproduce the work conveniently? The statute does not say so, and neither does any reported case. The question is not a copyright question, strictly speaking, but a question of contract or of equity. A commissioning party in these circumstances might have some right of access, either expressly in its contract with the hired party or implied as a matter of equity. So might a joint author whose collaborator refuses to share possession of the work. So might an artist who has sold a painting and wants the collector to let her photograph it for reproduction. But if such rights exist—and it is not at all clear that they do—they exist outside copyright. Odd or counterintuitive as it may sound, copyright is the right to prevent others from copying, not an affirmative right to copy. In the case of the artist who has sold a painting, there may be an equitable answer, as I will discuss under the topic of "divisibility," later in this chapter.

Would Brown, the commissioned creator of the ad, be at liberty to revise the same advertising materials for the use of another client? As a matter of copyright law he ought to be, but that might well violate the customer's expectations. Contract law might seek to imply a restriction on Brown's exercise of his rights, but this would be problematic, given the primacy of the copyright law over state law doctrines of equity.[23] So we are back to where we started, with an emphasis on the parties' states of mind—the very thing the bright liners claim to be avoiding.

Therefore it bears repeating: reduce your deals to writing. Try to be explicit about copyright ownership and about any uses or restrictions on use that might some day become important.

If you are considered an employee, however that term is defined, can you arrange for a specific work not to be considered "for hire"? Unfortunately not. The most you can do in advance is agree either that certain types of work will not be in the scope of employment or that even if the employer is to be the author, you will still own the rights, or certain specific rights, in the work. This amounts to a transfer in advance of copyright ownership. The first type of agreement—defining the scope of employment—may be written or oral, but written is more reliable. The latter type must be in writing and signed by both the employer and you; otherwise the agreement will be only a nonexclusive license to you the employee.[24]

Under the old law this was not so. Before publication an author's entire copyright could be transferred orally, and this applied in the work-for-hire context as well.[25] By a handshake an employer and employee could effectively waive the work-for-hire rule. Even now the formality of requiring *both* signatures applies only to agreements between an employer and employee made in advance of creation of the work. After the work is in fact created, the normal rules for transfer of copyright apply. (See chapter 3.)

Returning to the subject of specially commissioned works, the law provides, as noted, that certain types of commissioned works may be treated as works made for hire, regardless of the lack of supervision and control. These are:

- A contribution to a movie or other audiovisual work.
- A contribution to a periodical or other collective work.
- A translation.
- A supplementary work, that is, a work that is somehow auxiliary to the main work—for example, an illustration, an illustrative map or chart, editorial notes, a musical arrangement, a bibliography, a foreword, an index, and so forth—but only if it is subordinate to the main work. For example, illustrations that are of equivalent importance to the text will not qualify as subordinate works.

- A compilation, that is, a work created by collecting and assembling data or preexisting materials; an example would be an anthology, a hotel guide, or a racing chart.
- An instructional text.
- A test.
- Answer material for a test.
- An atlas.

For any of these commissioned works to be a work made for hire, the creator and whoever commissions the creator must agree that this will be so. The agreement must be in writing and signed by both of them. The law does not require in so many words that the contract has to say, "This work will be a work made for hire," but there is little doubt that that is what it means. A court is likely to interpret any language less explicit than this in the opposite way. Even if the contract says "A hires B to do such-and-such," a court may well believe that the word *hires* was used loosely as a synonym for *commissions*. The phrase "work made for hire" is a legal term and ought to be used wherever that is the intent.[26]

By the same token, if the hired party in these circumstances is to have any exclusive rights in that work, that understanding must also be in writing and signed by both parties.[27]

To be commissioned, a work must be done at the request of the person for whom it is done. Nevertheless some magazine publishers send, to authors who have submitted unsolicited manuscripts, contracts that say "This work will be a work made for hire." This is illogical and ineffective; at most, such a contract will be interpreted as a transfer of copyright ownership from the author to the magazine.[28]

Assuming that a work truly is commissioned, the question has arisen whether the written work-for-hire agreement may be signed after the work is done, or whether it must be signed in advance. Although the statute is not explicit on this point, the Seventh Circuit has held that the written agreement must precede creation of the work.[29] This is an impractical and needlessly rigid decision. The court said that its rule was necessary "to make ownership of property rights . . . clear and definite, so that such property will be readily marketable." Although it did not say so, the court may have been swayed by the fact that the commissioned party, a photographer, had already sold his business, including whatever copyright he owned, by the time he got around to signing a work-for-hire contract, so that validating the retroactive work-for-hire contract would have unfairly prejudiced the purchaser of his business. On its facts, the decision was clearly the only fair one. We can hope that future cases limit the advance-writing requirement to such circumstances. Indeed, the Second Circuit in a more recent case has specifically validated retroactive work-for-hire agreements, allowing them to be created by language included in the endorsement of the checks that paid for the work.[30] Only by referring to the very different situations involved can these two decisions be reconciled.

There is another interesting and potentially important twist in the law governing these special categories of commissioned works. The statute permits them to be considered works made for hire only if they are "specially ordered or commissioned for use as" a contribution to a collective work, a translation, or whatever. What if the commissioned work is not used in the way originally intended? For example, suppose that a drawing is commissioned to be used as a contribution to a periodical, but the publisher decides instead to use it for a poster advertising a book. Will the publisher still be considered the author? The issue has not yet arisen, but it is a possibility to consider. People commissioning works should specify in the contract that those works may be used in any way the commissioning party thinks appropriate, or avoid specifying at all how they are to be used.

OWNERSHIP OF WORKS CREATED BY PARTNERSHIPS

Partnerships make each partner a co-owner, as a matter of law, of all property created to further the business of the partnership. This makes partners co-owners, but not coauthors, of any one partner's copyrightable works.[31] But it is not clear that the rights of a partner in partnership copyrights are quite the same as the rights of a normal co-owner. For example, the typical co-owner of a copyright—such as a child of an author who has inherited her father's copyrights in common with her siblings—cannot give anyone an exclusive license or transfer of the copyright. In a partnership, though, each partner is bound by the actions of the other partners. Does this mean that one partner can make an exclusive grant of copyright without the written consent of his partners, who may happen to be the authors? There is simply no law on this point, one way or the other.

U.S. GOVERNMENT WORKS

One special variant of the work-for-hire rule relates to works of the U.S. Government. The law denies copyright to works "prepared by an officer or employee of the United States Government as part of that person's official duties."[32] (These works may nonetheless receive copyright protection in other countries.)[33] By implication it seems possible that if a government officer or employee, working within the scope of his official duties, jointly authors a work with a private citizen, the private citizen could own the entire copyright and have no obligation beyond the terms of his contract to share any of the profits with the government.[34] Will the government or the public have any rights? It is impossible to say, for the issue has never been tried.

Problems arise in defining a person's official duties. The well-publicized lawsuits involving President Nixon's and Henry Kissinger's tapes and memoranda are only the most sensational. By and large the "scope of employment" test will work here as with other works for hire.

AUTHORSHIP OF COMPILATIONS

As discussed in chapter 1, compilations can be and derivative works always are layered works. The author of a compilation is the person who does the compiling, and copyright in a compilation covers only the arrangement and selection of material. The underlying material may be separately copyrightable, as in an anthology, in which case the copyright in the compilation is separate from each underlying copyright. Or the underlying material may be uncopyrightable facts, in which case the only copyright is that arising from the "selection, coordination, or arrangement" of those facts. In the same manner, a derivative work may be based on copyrighted material or on material in the public domain. In either case, the compilation or derivative work is owned separately from the underlying material.

If the underlying material has not been lawfully used, copyright will be denied to those parts of the compilation or derivative work in which the unlawful use occurs.[35] This acts, and was intended, as a severe penalty for unlawful use.

DIVISIBILITY

The principles of authorship determine who owns copyright at the time a work is first fixed in tangible form. At that point a property right comes into being and may be transferred to others. At that point also the principle of divisibility comes into play.

A copyright is in reality a bundle of rights, each of which may be exploited separately. These rights are to reproduce the work, to distribute it to the public, to perform it publicly, to display it publicly, and to create derivative works based on it. The author may transfer any one or more of them without transferring the others. The owner or exclusive licensee of any of these rights is, with respect to that right, a "copyright owner." He is like a tenant who can sublet to a third person and collect rent from the subtenant.

The divisibility principle goes further than this, though, for each of these five rights can in turn be carved up in a hundred ways. A novelist need not give a publisher the entire publication right to her novel. She may give one publisher the hardcover rights and another publisher the paperback rights. A playwright need not sell to a producer his entire performance right; he may give the stage right to one producer and the television right to another. Rights can be carved up geographically and chronologically as well. There is in fact no end to the number of possible subsidiary rights, although some of them are more appropriate to certain kinds of work than to others. And any licensee, such as the television producer, is considered a copyright owner of the work, to the extent of his license, as long as the license is exclusive.[36]

It is important to remember that copyright in a work is separate from the physical object. The person who owns a work of art, for example, does not necessarily own copyright in it.[37] All he owns is the right to display it publicly, and even that right does not extend to display by means of television broadcast. Furthermore, if the object is a movie or other audiovisual work, he can display publicly only one frame at a time.[38]

In short, the author of a work retains copyright even if the work itself is sold or given away. There is one major gap in this rule, however. Although the author theoretically owns the right to copy the work, nothing in the law requires the owner to give the author access to the actual object. An artist who has sold a canvas may find the right to copy it a rather empty privilege.

To deal with this apparent inequity, one court has fashioned, out of whole cloth, what it calls an "implied easement of necessity." On this basis it has compelled the owner of a work to give the artist sufficient access to enable him to copy the work.[39] This new doctrine, while laudable in many ways, creates peculiar conflicts between copyright and the laws of private property. Whether and how it evolves will be interesting to watch.

COMMUNITY PROPERTY

A special problem of ownership affects those who live in states that treat property acquired during marriage as belonging equally to husband and wife. Is a copyright acquired after a marriage subject to this so-called "community property" rule? One state court, in California, has so held, reasoning that although federal law vests copyright in the author of a work, state law is free to transfer a share of that ownership to the author's spouse. More recently, a federal court in Louisiana has held exactly the opposite. Time will tell which view prevails.[40]

DURATION OF COPYRIGHT

Authorship determines not only ownership of a copyright, but also its duration. The regular term is life of the author plus seventy years. In the case of a joint work, though, it is life of the last joint author to die plus seventy years. In either case the copyright runs until the end of the calendar year seventy years after the author's death. (Special rules apply to works created before 1978; see chapter 9.)

Suppose you do not know if or when an author might have died. Does the copyright go on and on forever, sheltered by public ignorance? No; the law provides that if, ninety-five years after first publication of a work or one hundred twenty years after its creation, the records of the Copyright Office contain no information as to the author's being alive or as to when the author died, the author will be presumed to have been dead for seventy years. Anyone who in good faith relies on this presumption may not be held liable as an infringer. The only requirement is that he must obtain from the Copyright Office a certified report that it has no information on the subject. Presumably he will be able to continue using the work even if he subsequently learns the author has not been dead for seventy years, although the statute is not explicit on this point.

Anyone who has a stake in the copyright can file a statement with the Copyright Office, indicating that the author is still alive, or died on such-and-such a date. This may or may not be desirable, of course; it would actually shorten the copyright term if the author dies fewer than forty-five years after publication of his work or in some cases fewer than seventy years after its creation.

There are exceptions to the life-plus-seventy rule. Mask works receive only a ten-year term, measured from the date of registration or from first commercial exploitation, whichever occurs first.[41] The most important exception, however, is that for works made for hire. Copyright in a work made for hire lasts for ninety-five years from the date of first publication or one hundred twenty years from the date of creation, whichever is the shorter period. Suppose, for example, that in 1978 a publisher of a children's story commissioned someone to illustrate it as a work for hire, and the story, complete with illustrations, was published in 1979. The writer has a copyright in the story for her lifetime plus seventy years, but copyright in the illustrations, which are made for hire, lasts for ninety-five years (that is, through December 31, 2074). However, if the book is not published until 2012, copyright in the illustrations would expire in 2099 (one hundred twenty years from the date of creation) rather than in 2107 (ninety-five years from the date of publication). These provisions also apply to any joint work if any contribution to it is made for hire.[42] Thus if the story and illustrations I have just described were considered parts of a joint work, the work-for-hire duration rules would govern.

The term for a work that is authored anonymously or under a pseudonym is much the same as for a work made for hire. If the records of the Copyright Office contain no information as to the true identity of the author, the copyright term, like that of a work made for hire, will be ninety-five years from first publication or one hundred twenty years from creation, whichever period expires first.

At any time up to the expiration of this period, anyone who has a stake in the copyright can file a statement in the Copyright Office revealing the identity of the author.[43] As of that moment the copyright term becomes life plus seventy years (unless of course the work is also a work made for hire). This may not be desirable; if the author died, say, five years after publishing the work, revealing the author's identity will actually cause the copyright term to be shorter than it would have been if he had remained incognito. This situation creates an opportunity for the unscrupulous. Suppose that a movie producer owns the movie rights to a novel written under a pseudonym and has made a film that still, seventy years after the author's death, continues to produce yearly revenues. A rival film company, by buying up some other right in the novel, could obtain a stake in the copyright and be entitled to file a statement revealing the author's identity. The work would then be in the public domain, and the rival would be able to make a film of its own.

There is no way to avoid this result. However, if you are publishing a work under a pseudonym, you should require in every contract by which you transfer any interest in your copyright that the purchaser promises not to reveal your identity unless doing so will lengthen your copyright term. You should also require every purchaser to make the same demand of everyone purchasing from him. In this way you will preserve a right to sue for damages if a statement is filed to your detriment.

The last and newest exception to the basic rules of copyright duration is for "architectural works" (as distinct from blueprints and drawings protectable as pictorial works). Since these were not eligible for copyright before December of 1990, any earlier architectural work has, as such, no copyright, unless as of December 1, 1990, the work had not been built and existed only in unpublished plans or drawings. In the latter case, copyright will expire at the end of 2002 unless the work is constructed before that date, in which event the usual term of copyright (e.g., life of the author plus seventy years) will apply.

3 Transfers and Licenses of Copyright

An argument can be made that the word *property* refers not to possession of a thing but only to the right to use or dispose of it. It is this, I think, that underlies our use of the word *property* for so intangible a thing as copyright.

Because copyright is property, it can be sold, given away, donated to charity, bequeathed by will, or rented out on whatever terms the owner desires. And the same is true of any subsidiary right, such as the right to publish, the right to perform, and so on. However, copyright differs from most other kinds of property in two important respects:

First, the property of individual authors (as opposed to corporations that are authors of works made for hire) is immunized in an unusual way from government interference. Until an individual author has made at least one exclusive license or grant of his copyright, or of some part of it—for example, the right to perform the work publicly—no part of that copyright can be expropriated, transferred, or confiscated from the author by any court or other governmental body for any purpose or any reason, except in the context of bankruptcy.[1] This special immunity was originally intended to prevent communist governments from appropriating the U.S. copyrights of dissident authors, but it has possible impact closer to home. Although the issue has not been decided, it seems that this immunity ought to override the power of divorce courts to partition spouses' property. Presumably, also, it insulates unpublished works from seizure by the tax authorities.

Second, a sale or license that appears to be absolute and irrevocable may be revoked (or "terminated," to use the language of the statute) by the author or by his heirs, provided that certain procedures are followed. This is a statutory right and does not affect any right of termination that the author may have reserved by contract.

Of these two special rules, the second is likely to be the most important in years to come. It was enacted to prevent a recurrence in the future of the sad tales we know so well, in which the hero signs away his copyright for a pittance only to see the villain reap enormous profits. The new rule will have little practical value for the average work, as will be seen.

MAKING A TRANSFER OR LICENSE

First, a word about nomenclature. The term "license" means a conveyance of copyright rights that is limited in duration, or is subject to being revoked if the licensee fails to make royalty payments or otherwise breaks the contract. A sale or "assignment" of copyright is a transaction in which outright ownership of the copyright—or some right comprised in the copyright—passes from one person to another. The term "transfer" refers to any assignment or exclusive license. The term "grant" includes both transfers and nonexclusive licenses. Nonexclusive licenses tend to be for limited periods of time; for example, a high school theater company needs no more than a nonexclusive license for its spring play. A book publisher, on the other hand, will insist on getting at the very least the exclusive publication right in a manuscript in its principal territory.

A nonexclusive license can be as informal as a handshake. It can be inferred from the conduct of those involved. But can it be imposed on someone who would otherwise be merely the buyer of a copy? That is the issue presented by the kind of "license" often used on over-the-counter software. This "shrink wrap" license, so called because of the kind of plastic wrapping used on the software package, purports to change what would otherwise be the sale of an object into a license of copyright by saying, "By opening this package you will be indicating your consent to the following terms." The legal validity of this approach has been a subject of much debate. Congress has implicitly approved unilateral licenses in the context of shareware, which admittedly is made available to users at a reduced price compared to ordinary retail software.[2] More recently the Seventh Circuit gave its blessing to the practice of shrink wrap licensing.[3]

An exclusive license or other transfer—be it a mortgage, sale, gift, or bequest—must be in writing and must be signed by the person making it. With regard to unpublished works, this did not use to be so. The old rule was that common law copyrights could be transferred orally or even by implication.[4]

The only instance in which an exclusive grant does not need a signed instrument is where it comes about by what is called "operation of law." For example, if an author dies without a will, the law of the state where she lives will give her copyright to her heirs, and no written instrument is needed.[5]

"Exclusive" is not so broad as it seems. You can give an exclusive license to perform a play in Alaska if you put the agreement in writing and sign it. You can give an exclusive license to perform a play for a limited period of time, say, five years. You can give one person an exclusive license to distribute a work by mail and another person an exclusive license to sell over the counter.

Any limit on a license must be expressly stated.[6] If the license is in writing, the limitation should be as well; if the license is by word of mouth, the limitation must be clearly understood by both parties.

Sometimes, though, even written limitations on a license are less clear than they seem. For example, did a grant of "motion picture rights" back in the 1930s include or exclude television broadcast of the movie? (The source of the contention is that television did not become a standard means or place of showing a movie until a decade or two later.)[7] Cases arising from technologies unforeseen by the contract drafters have gone both ways, depending on minor differences in wording. This and similar problems of interpretation underline the need for careful drafting of licenses. The particular problem of unforeseen technologies can be avoided by a clause something like, "The producer will have the right to perform and display his motion picture in any manner and by any means now known or later developed." But, of course, the licensor is always inclined to resist such a sweeping grant.

The only clear exception to the rule that limitations on a license must be expressly stated is for contributions to collective works. Here the statute reverses the general rule. It provides that if you contribute, say, a poem to an anthology, the owner of the anthology can publish it only in that anthology, revisions of that anthology, or later works in the same series, unless you give a broader license. A contribution to a magazine would be another common example; the publisher is presumed to acquire only the right to publish it in issues of that magazine. This is a major departure from pre-1978 law.[8] A court has recently held that the publisher's right extends to including the contribution in electronic versions of the original periodical issue.[9]

Can a license be transferred? In other words, can a licensee give someone else part or all of his license? Here too the law has changed since 1977. Under the old law, sublicensing, as this is called, was not allowed unless the licensee was clearly given that right.[10] Under the new law the answer depends on whether the license is exclusive or nonexclusive. It is fairly clear under the new statute that an exclusive license can be transferred unless the copyright owner has specified otherwise.[11] However, nothing in the new law seems to have changed the old rule with respect to nonexclusive licenses.

COPYRIGHT LICENSES DISTINGUISHED FROM SALES OF OBJECTS

As has been mentioned, copyright in a work exists separately from the tangible forms in which it may be fixed. Transferring ownership of a painting, therefore, does not transfer copyright in it. And the reverse is also true: transferring copyright does not give the new copyright owner any right to possess the actual painting or other work.

In this respect the law has changed dramatically in favor of authors. Prior to 1978, explicit written instruments were necessary to transfer federal copyright, but not state law rights in unpublished works. State common law would often infer a transfer of copyright from transfers of the physical object, if the work were unpublished.[12] In essence the law assumed that if you were parting with the means of reproduction—be it a painting, photographic negative, in some cases even a manuscript—you intended to empower the new owner to reproduce the work.

Under the new federal regime, transfer of the means of reproduction may possibly be evidence of a nonexclusive license, or of a waiver of rights by the creator, but that would be the extent of it.

A friend of mine in the profession once told me that at cocktail parties—those wonderful clearing houses of free legal advice—the question he is most often asked is, Who owns copyright in letters? Why does this question seem to trouble so many apparently respectable citizens? Whatever the reason, the answer will comfort them, for it is the writer who owns copyright unless there is some clear indication to the contrary. However, the recipient would have the right to make the letter public if it were necessary for some reason—to his defense against a libel action, or to clearing his character, or something of that sort.[13]

DRAFTING A TRANSFER AGREEMENT

The written instrument necessary for a copyright transfer can come in many shapes and sizes. A written memorandum of the transfer will suffice if it is signed by the transferor. A letter from an author to her mother describing the transfer could satisfy the requirement if a court found it to be adequate evidence. If you are getting a license and are afraid that someone will try to question its existence—for example, by claiming that the author's signature is forged—have the instrument of transfer notarized.[14]

The instrument of transfer may be executed at any time, even retroactively, although a retroactive instrument will presumably not be enforceable against a third party who acted in reasonable reliance on its absence.[15]

For the benefit of all concerned, any copyright transfer should clearly state, in addition to royalty provisions, warranties, and so on, the answers to the following questions:

1. What rights are being transferred? If the entire copyright is transferred, a clause often used is "X hereby transfers to Y all right, title, and interest, including copyright, in and to a certain work entitled *Mud Wrestling for Fun and Profit.*" Otherwise be quite specific; for example: "X hereby transfers to Y the exclusive right to perform publicly a certain work entitled *Mud Wrestling for Fun and Profit*"; or "X hereby licenses to Y the exclusive right to make audiovisual works based on X's work entitled *Mud Wrestling for Fun and Profit.*"

2. How long is the transfer to last? What other limitations are there?

3. When, how, and for what reasons can the transfer be terminated? If not at all, nothing needs to be said on this point, but cautious drafters will often add the word "irrevocable." Typical reasons for revocation are failure to pay royalties, the making of unauthorized alterations, failure to meet agreed sales objectives, and so on.

4. Whose name will be placed in the notice on any published copies? Every contract concerning publication should require that the person receiving the grant place proper copyright notice on all published copies.[16] (See chapter 4 for a fuller discussion of copyright notice.)

5. Who will bear the cost of prosecuting or defending any infringement suit?

6. How will damages won in any such suit be apportioned?

7. Who will pay if someone wins an infringement suit against the work?

To keep their dealings with their authors private, many publishers limit their instruments of transfer to a brief description of the transfer and deal with the other issues (points 3 through 7) in a separate contract. Thus when they record with the Copyright Office, they file only a single sheet of paper. This is a practice I recommend to anyone drafting a copyright agreement. If you follow this practice, your separate contract should state, "The instrument of transfer concerning this work is incorporated in this contract by reference and made a part of this contract." Your "short form" transfer should make reference to your contract, but *without* incorporating it by reference. In this way the two documents are tied together for all purposes other than recordation.

RECORDING THE SALE OR LICENSE

The written evidence of a copyright grant—be it a contract, a memorandum, or a letter—may be recorded in the Copyright Office. When recordation has been completed in the Copyright Office, the person who records will receive a certificate of recordation. See appendix F for the fees charged by the Copyright Office for these services.

In an effort to eliminate the time formerly spent by its staff in reading documents and extracting from them the necessary indexing information, the Copyright Office now requires with every document submitted for recordation a "Document Cover Sheet," in duplicate. On this form, which is available from the same address as registration forms (see chapter 5), you must state the following information: the parties to the document; the nature of the document; its date of execution and/or effective date; the titles, registration numbers, and author of the works dealt with in the document; and any other identifying information you consider relevant. You must also state whether the document is complete in itself or, in effect, can only be properly understood by reference to other documents or to facts not recited in the document. If the document is not complete in itself, you are not required to supply the missing pieces, but you are obliged to acknowledge the incompleteness. Finally, you must sign an "Affirmation" that the information submitted on the Document Cover Sheet is true and correct.

Recordation that clearly identifies the work will give general notice to the world at large of the facts set forth in the recorded document. Other people are presumed to have notice of all the information recorded, regardless of whether they have actually seen the document. For this to be so, however, the work must also be registered (see chapter 5).[17] Recordation of a transfer cannot be used as a substitute for registration of the underlying work.

Copyright owners of computer shareware may also wish to record with the Copyright Office the terms of the general license they give to users. The Copyright Office maintains a separate Computer Shareware Registry, and any document intended for it should be clearly labeled a "Document Pertaining to Computer Shareware." The fee for recording is computed in the same way as the recording fees. Submission of the license document in hard copy is required, but additional PC-compatible copies are encouraged.

TWO PEOPLE CLAIMING THE SAME RIGHT

One important effect of recording a transfer is to establish priority of ownership. Suppose that a novelist sells dramatization rights in his novel to Smith on April 1 and then on April 2 sells the same rights to Jones. Smith has a one-month grace period in which to record the transfer (two months if the transfer is executed outside the country). After that time it is a horse race: Jones will be regarded as the legal owner of the copyright if he records before Smith, even though the transfer to him took place later than that to Smith, provided Jones was unaware of the deal with Smith.[18]

But again this is true only if the work has been registered. Thus we see the lengths to which Congress has been willing to go to induce people to register copyright claims. If the work is not registered, or until it is registered, no one has priority over anyone else, and neither Smith nor Jones may sue the other for going about his business. It is therefore in the interest of anyone who is recording a transfer to ensure that the work is registered.

There are two important circumstances under which these rules of priority do not apply. First, if the later transfer is a gift or bequest it cannot take precedence over a sale that preceded it, no matter when the sale is actually recorded.[19] This result seems only fair; it would be hard to justify a law that gave precedence to someone who had paid nothing for a right over someone who had paid. Second, if the person who received the second transfer actually knew of the first transfer, he cannot take precedence over the earlier purchaser by beating him to the Copyright Office. This too seems only fair.

The question of priority occurs not only between one transfer and another but also between a transfer of ownership and a nonexclusive license. Suppose, for instance, that a playwright sells performing rights in her play to a Broadway producer and later in the week gives permission to a local troupe to perform the same play. If the nonexclusive license was taken by the local troupe without knowledge of the prior transfer and before the transfer was recorded, the troupe has the right to perform the work within the limits of its license without regard to the rights of the producer. This is so provided the nonexclusive license itself is in writing, but regardless of whether it is recorded.[20]

Suppose in another instance that the nonexclusive license is given before the sale of rights is made. Here again, the nonexclusive license, if in writing, takes priority over the transfer, regardless of whether or when either of them is recorded. The nonexclusive license in such a case is like a right-of-way over a piece of land: any purchaser of the land is obligated to honor the right-of-way.

In no instance does it matter whether the nonexclusive license was paid for or was a gift or bequest. In this the law with respect to nonexclusive licenses differs fundamentally from the law of transfers.

These priority rules have proved to be of major importance in the context of bankruptcy. Many banks have lent money to movie producers and other copyright-centered businesses, taking as collateral general security interests in all the debtors' property, copyrights included. Some have failed to ensure that the copyrights were registered and that their security agreements were recorded in the Copyright Office, and have found themselves holding worthless paper after the debtors have sold their copyrights and the purchasers have recorded the sales in the Copyright Office, thus gaining priority of claim. The special copyright regime takes precedence over ordinary commercial rules, which permit filing of security agreements with state and local authorities.[21]

RECORDATION OF LICENSES FOR PUBLIC BROADCASTING

If you give any public broadcasting station or network a license to perform or display a published musical work or to display a published work of art, whether or not you also give it the right to tape the performance or display, you should require it to record the license within thirty days. If the license is not recorded, you will be bound by the terms of a compulsory license created by statute (see chapter 7).

TERMINATION OF GRANTS

In addition to any termination right an author may reserve in a contract, the author and his heirs have a termination right under the copyright statute. The statutory right of termination, unlike the copyright itself, cannot be contracted away, given away, or bequeathed. No agreement that anyone can persuade an author to sign will diminish his right or the right of his heirs to terminate a grant of copyright.[22] For this reason a contract clause requiring the author to pay the other party money if he exercises his termination right would probably be held invalid under the new law. In short, the right to terminate is not a property right but a privilege under the law. It extends to all works other than those made for hire and to all grants except those of rights in foreign countries.[23]

In general, only grants made by a living author, and made after December 31, 1977, may be terminated. Other grants, including those made by the author in his will, are not subject to termination.[24] An exception for certain pre-1978 works is discussed in chapter 9.

After termination, the person who once owned the right or license cannot exploit the work further in any way. There is one exception: if someone has made a derivative work under a grant permitting him to do so, he can continue to exploit this work, because the derivative work has a separate copyright. Termination prevents him only from making or authorizing further derivative works. Moreover, any royalty income from that derivative work will continue to be paid as it was before termination, even if this means that an intermediary, rather than the terminating author, receives the benefit.[25]

The statutory termination right is open to authors, their widows or widowers, and their children and grandchildren (whether legitimate or not and whether natural or adopted). If all of these persons are deceased, the author's "executor, administrator, personal representative, or trustee" owns the termination right. This language, added in 1998, creates a new fiduciary obligation for those who administer certain authors' estates. The inclusion of "trustee" in the list is presumably intended to give the termination right to trustees who succeed to the bulk of an author's estate. However, the statute gives no guidance for situations where the author has left two or more different trusts with different trustees.

No statutory termination right exists for anyone else. Someone outside the author's line of descent who has received a right from an author, or even the entire copyright, and transferred it to a third person, has no termination right.[26]

The right is also limited in time. Termination may be made only in a five-year period beginning thirty-five years after the date of the grant and ending forty years after the date of the grant. The only variation from this rule is the case of a publication right. The five-year period in which a grant of a publication right may be terminated can begin at one of two times: either forty years after the date of the grant or thirty-five years after the date of first publication, whichever is earlier.[27]

Certain procedures must be followed in exercising this right. These procedures apply whether the original grant or license was exclusive or nonexclusive; even a word-of-mouth license cannot be terminated except by following the rules:[28]

If the work is a joint work, and two or more of the joint authors execute a grant, termination may be made only by a majority of those authors who executed the grant. The law does not require a majority of the interest in the work, only a numerical majority of the authors who made the grant. Because nonexclusive transfers of copyright in a joint work can be made by one joint author without the others' consent, the termination rules focus on who made the grant, not who owns the copyright. In other words, even if one of three joint authors is entitled, by agreement with the others, to 60 percent of the royalties, he cannot single-handedly terminate a grant unless he alone made it. The majority requirement also means that if only two authors executed the grant, they must both join in the termination for it to be effective.

Just what obligations one joint author has to another in this respect is unclear. Co-owners are liable to each other for profits and, in many cases, for loss they may cause to the income-producing ability of what they own. Will joint authors be liable to each other for loss of revenues if the loss is caused by termination of a grant? My guess is that they will not be, because the termination is a legal right created by statute.

If an author or a joint author is dead, his right to terminate or to join in a termination may be exercised by his surviving spouse (regardless of whether the spouse has remarried) and his children or grandchildren. The spouse controls half of the right and the children or grandchildren the other half. If there are no children or grandchildren, then the spouse controls the entire right, and if there is no spouse, then the children and grandchildren control the entire right. The statute makes no provision for more distant generations, but it does pass the termination right to the author's fiduciaries if there is no surviving spouse, child, or grandchild living.

If children or grandchildren own the termination right, or one-half of it, what they own is to be divided among them in equal shares. This division into shares is a *per stirpes* distribution. This means that if, for example, an author's daughter is living, her children (grandchildren of the author) have no share. But if the daughter is dead but has surviving children, her share belongs to her children and may be exercised only by a majority of them. If all of an author's children are dead, the surviving grandchildren do not take equally; each set of grandchildren takes the share that would belong to their parent if he or she were alive.

The required percentage: The termination right of a deceased author may be exercised only by persons owning, among them, over 50 percent of the termination right. For example, if there are a widow, one child, and three grandchildren of a deceased child, then the widow owns 50 percent of the right, the child owns 25 percent, and the three grandchildren among them own 25 percent, but can exercise their 25 percent only if a majority of them agree. In such a case termination can take place only if the child or two of the grandchildren agree with the widow to terminate. If there are a widower, one child, and two grandchildren, then either the child or both grandchildren must join with the widower. If there is no spouse, but there are three children, then two of the children must join together.

Notice of termination must be given in advance. This notice must be in writing and must be signed by the necessary persons or their authorized agents. It must specify the exact date on which termination is to become effective. That date must be within the appropriate five-year period. Notice itself must be given at least two years before that date, but not more than ten years before it. Notice must be recorded (for a fee; see appendix F) in the Copyright Office before that date, or it will be invalid. The notice must be served, in person or by first-class mail, on "the grantee or the grantee's successor in title," that is, on the person who originally received the transfer, or on anyone who has obtained it from him.

This language is anything but self-explanatory. Suppose the grantee (the person who received the transfer) has sold it to someone else without your knowledge. If you serve notice only on the grantee, will that terminate the rights of the person he sold it to? If we say "yes," we are perhaps creating hardship for the second purchaser. If we say "no," we are perhaps creating hardship for you, the author.

Neither the statute nor the regulations of the Copyright Office shed much light on this problem. It will be one for the courts to clarify. My guess—or, more accurately, my hope—is that the terminator will be held only to his own personal knowledge of what subsequent transfers have been made and to a knowledge of any transfers recorded in the Copyright Office. If the author is a composer whose work is handled by ASCAP, BMI, or one of the other performing rights societies, he will also have a duty to check the society's records. If his search reveals no "successor in title," it will be enough that he has served notice on the original grantee. This puts the burden on the successors in title to record the instruments by which they obtain their rights, and that seems not only a fair allocation of the burden but one in keeping with the law's general policy of encouraging recordation.

COPYRIGHT AFTER TERMINATION

As of the date that notice of termination is served, the right or rights that are to terminate become vested in the persons who own the termination right.[29] For example, as of the date that a playwright's widow and children terminate his grant of the performance rights, the performance right vests in them. Vesting means entitlement, not actual possession; what happens is that the rights that will eventually revert, when the termination takes effect, are allocated before that time, and are a limited kind of property interest.

The rights vest in everyone who could have joined in the termination, regardless of who actually did take part in it. If, for example, an author's son did not take part in giving notice of termination, he will still get his proportionate share of the right when it reverts. If the termination is made by the family of a deceased author, the rights vest in the same *per stirpes* manner described previously. In the case of a joint work, nothing vests in an author (or the family of an author) who did not join in the original grant, because he did not own a termination right with respect to that grant.

MAKING A NEW TRANSFER

Because vesting is less than actual possession, the rule that the rights vest as of the date notice is received does not mean that the new owners can make a new transfer immediately. They cannot make a new grant of any kind, exclusive or nonexclusive, before the date of termination; not even the author can do this. Moreover, with one exception, those in whom the right vests cannot even make a commitment to make a grant before the date of termination. And because selling the right to make a grant is tantamount to making a grant, it is probable that even someone who receives the entire right, when that right vests, cannot sell his right to make a new grant until the date the termination takes effect.

The exception to this rule is that the people terminating may renegotiate a contract with the existing right holder.[30] For example, if a publisher has a license to make and sell reproductions of a photograph, the photographer or her appropriate heirs can give notice of termination and immediately thereafter renegotiate the contract. The renegotiated royalties do not, theoretically, take effect until the date the termination actually occurs, but if the license is lucrative, the publisher may well compromise on this point and pay more royalties in the interim to get a renewal of the grant.

It is important to remember that the right to terminate inheres in the person; it is less like property than like a privilege. It cannot be sold or given away. For example, if an author's widow dies, the termination right that she possessed dies with her, and the entire termination right belongs to the children or grandchildren, if any. However, once notice of termination is given and reversion of the copyright becomes vested in the people who had a right to terminate, we are talking not of a privilege but once again of a property right.

Unlike the right to terminate, this property right does not die with the owner; he can bequeath it in his will to anyone at all, and whoever receives the bequest can take part in any renegotiations or new grants. Presumably, also, the owner can sell or give away his right to receive income from his share of the copyright. But unless he owns the entire copyright, he cannot sell or give away during his life his right to take part in making a new grant, because the law makes very stringent requirements for new grants of terminated rights.

MECHANICS OF MAKING A NEW GRANT

A renegotiation, or a new grant, must be made in the following manner.[31]

1. It must be in writing. This requirement applies not only to transfers but also to nonexclusive licenses. (This is the only circumstance in which a nonexclusive license is required to be in writing.)

2. It must be signed by persons representing at least the same proportion of ownership in the right as was involved in the termination.

3. It must be signed by the same number of persons as signed the notice of termination.

These requirements concerning number and proportion are difficult to grasp. It may be helpful to take an example. Suppose that an author dies, survived by a wife, one daughter, and two grandsons born of a deceased son. Because termination of the original grant requires participation of over 50 percent of the termination right, in this case it will require 75 percent of the right—the widow's 50 percent, plus another 25 percent from either the living daughter or the deceased son as represented by his children. It will also require at least two signatures.

When the right vests in the author's family, upon the giving of notice of termination, it vests 50 percent in the widow, 25 percent in the daughter, and 12½ percent in each of the two grandsons. (Each of these people now owns a separate and distinct interest because the rights are vested.) Suppose the widow then dies, bequeathing her entire share of the right to one of the grandsons, so that he now owns 62½ percent of the right. The law provides that someone who inherits an interest in a right in this way "represents" the person from whom he received it, for purposes of signing a new grant. Thus the grandson represents his grandmother, and he may sign the new grant on behalf of his grandmother as well as on his own behalf, so that in effect there are two signatures on the document. This meets the "number" requirement because there were only two signatures on the notice of termination. However, despite the fact that he now owns over half the right, the grandson cannot single-handedly make a new grant, for the new grant must be agreed to by 75 percent of the ownership—that being the percentage of the ownership that agreed to the termination. Therefore, to make a new grant, this grandson must persuade either his brother or his aunt to join him. If he cannot, no new grant can be made.

Once a new grant or a renegotiation of an old grant has been made, it binds and benefits everyone who had a share of the right to make it, regardless of who actually signs the new grant or renegotiation.[32] In the previous example, if only the widow and the two grandsons join in making the new grant, the daughter is nonetheless treated as if she too had joined in. By "binds" I mean that when the new grant is made, she cannot make a grant of any kind on her own; on the other hand, she is entitled to her share of the proceeds. To take another example, if an author's husband and one of her two children terminate an old grant and then renegotiate it or make a new grant to someone else, the other child cannot go off on his own and arrange a separate sale, but on the other hand he is entitled to a 25 percent share of the profits that the rest of the family has negotiated.

4 Copyright Notice

Just as much as copyright is property, it is also a bundle of procedures, paperwork, and footwork. These should be followed scrupulously to protect a copyright to the fullest extent.

For purposes of the federal statute, you acquire copyright upon fixation of the work, and at any point before completed fixation you automatically have copyright in as much of the work as you have fixed. Until the United States joined the Berne Convention, a multilateral copyright treaty, on March 1, 1989, another important rite of passage was "publication." Under our pre-Berne law, once a work was published, you acquired federal copyright if you affixed proper notice of copyright to it, and forfeited all copyright if you did not.

This is no longer so. Notice is not required for works published after March 1, 1989. Works published before that date, however, will continue to be governed by the pre-Berne rules. And even though notice is no longer required, it is still advisable, because it deprives an infringer of the defense of innocence.[1] So in applying the rules that follow here it is critical to determine first whether the work in question was published during the period from January 1, 1978, to February 28, 1989, or earlier, or later. If later, then the rules governing copyright notice are advisory only; if during, then they are mandatory. If earlier, then even more stringent rules apply in some respects, and these are discussed in chapter 9.

PUBLICATION

The concept of publication has been crucial to copyright law from the beginning. It used to mark the boundary between common law copyright and federal copyright. Until we joined the Berne convention, it marked the moment when notice had to be affixed. Even now, it can be critical to determining eligibility for statutory damages and attorneys' fees, as discussed in chapter 8.

Publication is the act of offering copies to the public. There does not have to be an actual distribution.[2] Even if there is a distribution, it does not have to be a sale; giving copies away to the public is sufficient. The size of the public is irrelevant; handing out one or two copies can constitute publication.[3] And though performance or display of a work is not publication in and of itself, distributing copies to a group of persons who will themselves perform or display the work does count as publication, unless those persons are your employees or otherwise act under your control.[4]

The sale of one's painting, sculpture, or other unique work of visual art probably constitutes a publication in the eyes of the law, although there is some evidence that Congress did not intend this result.[5] But this is not a cause for great concern, because the rules of copyright notice do not require that a notice be placed on the original of an art work if no other copies are produced.

When is an architectural work "published"? The Copyright Office takes the position that publication occurs when the plans, drawings, photographs, or other pictorial representations of the work are published, but that construction of a building does not itself constitute publication. The latter statement may mean less than it appears to say. Upon construction of a building that is owned by someone other than the copyright owner—as is usually the case—a copy of the architectural work comes into the hands of someone other than the architect, and does so with the architect's permission. To say that this does not constitute publication would contradict the general rules of publication. We may hope for some clarification to this effect from the Copyright Office.

Performance and display of a work do not constitute publication. You can perform or display a work as often as you like, to as wide an audience as you like, and you will not be considered to have published it by doing so. (Both "performance" and "display" include broadcasting, film projection, and so on.)[6] Delivering a speech does not publish it.

Nor does circulation of copies within a limited group, for limited purposes, count as publication. However, the persons receiving those copies must understand that they have no right to perform or display them publicly or to make a further distribution outside the group.[7] Nor is the filing of copies or phonorecords with a court or other public authority a publication.[8]

Submission of a manuscript to a publisher is a classic example of such "limited publication," as it is called, for which copyright notice is not required. In the academic community there is also a custom of circulating so-called preprints (manuscript copies of forthcoming journal articles) among colleagues for comment and discussion. This too would be a limited publication in most cases. But if you are making what you intend as a limited publication under circumstances where your intent will not be absolutely clear to your audience, you would be well advised to place on the copy either a regular copyright notice or a legend to this effect: "This copy is circulated for comment only and may not be used or distributed in any other manner."

WHEN SHOULD NOTICE BE USED?

In the case of copies from which a work can be "perceived visually," copyright notice should be placed on all copies publicly distributed, whether in the United States or elsewhere. It is not necessary that visual perception be possible with the naked eye; it is enough that the copy distributed can be perceived visually with the aid of a machine or device, such as a movie projector. Remember that musical works are regarded as being visually perceived when they are written in musical notation, and the same applies to notation of choreography.

Sound recordings are works that by definition cannot be perceived visually. They are not distributed in the form of "copies" but in the form of "phonorecords." The term "phonorecord" is a hybrid word adopted by the new law. It includes records, tapes, player-piano rolls, and any other method now known or discovered in the future for fixing sounds, but it does not include the soundtracks of audiovisual works.[9] Every phonorecord that is distributed to the public should bear notice of copyright with respect to the sound recording that it embodies. However, no notice of copyright in the underlying music or other work need be affixed to the phonorecord.

A new and interesting question, which no court has yet faced, concerns the computer programs that embody so-called computer music. These programs are written to drive the synthesizers that both imitate (or embellish) sounds of more traditional instruments and create entirely new sounds of their own. By the time they enter the synthesizers (which are computers connected to sound-producing mechanisms), they are in disk, tape, or other object code form. Is such a tape or disk a phonorecord of a sound recording or a copy of a musical work? Like any more conventional phonorecord its primary function is to cause a machine to produce sound. On the other hand the program begins life as a series of written notations, which can be likened to ordinary musical notation, and hence constitutes a "copy." Under current doctrine an object code version of a source code program is a copy of it, not a derivative work. Thus, by an equally logical train of thought, we can conclude that the disk or tape is a copy of the musical work, not a phonorecord.

For now, this conundrum is merely intriguing. But the day is probably not far off when there will be a market for computer music among a large segment of the public who can afford to own synthesizers, and floppy disks of computer music will occupy a corner of every music store. How should the source codes be registered—as musical works or as sound recordings? Will it be possible to acquire a compulsory license (see chapter 7) to make other floppy disks of the same music? If so, what will be the scope of the license? Should the floppy disks bear copyright notice as copies or as phonorecords? (For the moment you'd be wise to use both.) It seems that fewer problems will arise if we consider the disk to be a copy of the underlying musical notation, but I would hesitate to predict that this will in fact be the rule.

NOTICE FOR CONTRIBUTIONS TO A COLLECTIVE WORK

A question frequently asked is, What notice should go on a magazine article, or a poem in an anthology, or any other contribution to a collective work? All contributions to a collective work are covered by a general notice affixed to the collective work as a whole, except for advertisements, which should bear separate notice.[10] However, under the pre-Berne rules, if the contributor retained copyright, omission of separate notice might be treated as if notice had been given in the wrong name.[11] It was and still is a good idea to require, if you can, that your contribution to a collective work have its own copyright notice.

FORMALITIES OF COPYRIGHT NOTICE

Notice comprises three things:

1. In the case of visually perceived works, the familiar symbol © or, if you prefer, the word *Copyright* or its accepted abbreviation, *Copr.* (In foreign countries, use ©; *Copyright*

and *Copr.* do not have international validity.) In the case of sound recordings published in phonorecords, the only symbol to use is ℗; © is of no effect. In the case of mask works there are three options: the words *Mask Work,* the symbol *M*, or the symbol Ⓜ.[12]

2. The year of first publication. This date is not necessary where a visual work is reproduced in or on greeting cards, postcards, stationery, jewelry, dolls, toys, or "useful articles" (articles having an intrinsic utilitarian function).[13] A good example of this useful-article exception is the reproduction of a painting on a place mat; in such a case the date when the painting itself was first published would not need to be included in the copyright notice. The date is also optional for mask works.

Bear in mind that the year of first publication of a work may not necessarily be the year in which you first need to affix copyright notice. For example, a musical work is considered to be "published" by the distribution of phonorecords or movie soundtracks embodying it, even though those phonorecords and soundtracks do not need to bear notice as to the musical work. Thus if a piece of music came out on a record in 1994 but not in written form until 1996, 1994 is the proper year to put in the notice.

3. The name of the owner of copyright. This may be abbreviated if the name remains recognizable. If the owner has a generally known trademark, abbreviation, or other symbol, that symbol may be used instead. This term "owner of copyright" is different from the term "copyright owner" (who may be merely the owner of the exclusive publication right). The owner of copyright is the author or anyone to whom the author has transferred the entire copyright or the bulk of copyright.[14] In the case of a sound recording, notice must be in the name of the owner of the copyright in the recording; the

name of the owner of copyright in the musical composition should not be used and may lead to substantial confusion.

There is an additional requirement in the case of works that consist preponderantly of works of the U.S. Government—for example, a collection of public documents edited by a private citizen, or a journal issue including articles by government scientists. Such works are supposed to include in the notice a statement identifying those parts of the work that are the author's and in which copyright is therefore claimed, or those parts that are the product of the U.S. Government and in which copyright is therefore not claimed.

The elements of notice need not appear all together, so long as they are all present on the copy and placed in such a way that a reasonable person would understand them to be parts of a whole.

The location of the notice as a whole is important, although the law's requirements have not, since 1978, been so strict as formerly. In the case of sound recordings, notice must be placed on the surface of the phonorecord, or on the label, or on the container in which the phonorecord is retailed. Its placement must be calculated to give "reasonable notice" to the public. In the case of visually perceived works, the only requirement is that placement be calculated to give reasonable notice to the public. Notice has to be fixed to the copy or phonorecord; the law will not be satisfied by, say, tying to a sculpture a tag with copyright notice written on it, unless no alternative is feasible. The regulations of the Copyright Office, giving examples of acceptable placement of notice, are reproduced in appendix A.

The principle that notice be "reasonable" has led to some judicial loosening of the rules. For example, it has been held that as long as notice appears on one of a group of items that are sold together, it will cover all those items. Thus it was sufficient to place notice on the cardboard box in which a toy puppy was sold, and not on the puppy itself, because the box was intended to be kept as a "kennel" for the puppy.[15]

As additional protection, it is advisable to place in your notice the statement "All Rights Reserved," to ensure protection in certain Latin American countries that do not recognize *Copyright, Copr.,* or © as proper notice of a claim of rights.

INCOMPLETE OR OMITTED NOTICE

If any one of the three principal components of proper notice—name, date, and the symbol, word, or abbreviation for copyright—is omitted, the work will be treated as if notice were omitted entirely.[16] Where the work consists preponderantly of U.S. Government works, and the notice does not say so, the work will be treated as if notice were omitted entirely.[17]

Omission of notice, under the *ancien régime,* destroyed copyright, casting the work into the public domain. For works that are wholly or partly of foreign origin, this harsh rule has recently been nullified (see the discussion in chapter 9). For U.S. works, it continues in effect for works published before March of 1989, with one important qualification: if the work was first published after 1977 and before March of 1989, forfeiture would be avoided if:

- the omission was in violation of an express understanding between the copyright owner and whoever was responsible for publication, or
- the notice was omitted from only a relatively small number of copies that were distributed to the public, or
- the application for registration, complete with fee and the necessary number of copies (see chapter 5), was filed before the date of the publication from which the notice was omitted, or
- the complete application for registration was filed within five years after first publication, and a "reasonable effort" was

made to add notice to all copies distributed to the public within the United States after the omission was discovered.

This so-called "cure" procedure remains applicable to works published before Berne accession. In fact, if a work was published without notice before Berne, the obligation to affix notice to copies distributed after discovery of the omission continues for the life of the copyright. By contrast, at least in the view of one court, if a work was published with proper notice before Berne, post-Berne copies need not bear notice.[18]

A few comments on these exceptions to forfeiture are in order. No one knows what a "relatively small number of copies" was or is. Twenty thousand copies of a book with a printing of 100,000 is the same percentage as one bronze casting out of a limited edition of five, yet the latter would have been acceptable and the former probably not. "Relatively," in other words, has only the vaguest of meanings. This is an instance where the law would look to what is fair and just in a particular situation.[19]

Difficult problems may yet arise in cases involving works of fine art. A painting does not need to bear copyright notice when the painter sells it; a unique canvas comes with the exception we are discussing here. But a lithograph in an edition of 200 is a different story. If the artist omitted notice from, say, 40 copies published in 1986, failed to register his copyright, and failed to make a reasonable effort to correct the omission, and if a purchaser of one of the 40 copies relies on the absence of notice and starts reproducing the work himself, the artist might be out of luck. If a court decides that 40 is a relatively large number of copies in an edition of 200, the work will have entered the public domain in 1991—and copyright, once lost, can never be regained.

What was or is a reasonable effort to correct an omission? Here is another question for ad hoc determination, and one on which the circuit courts have split doctrinally. In the First and Second Circuits one must have made an attempt to affix notice to copies not yet sold at retail, even if they were already in the hands of distributors or wholesalers. The other circuits that have ruled on this are more lenient.[20]

As to what constitutes "discovery" of the omission of notice, there is some dissension among the circuits, but the prevailing answer seems to be that an omission can be "discovered" as late as the time infringement occurs, so long as the original omission did not occur under circumstances where the copyright owner knew or had reason to know that failure to include notice would forfeit copyright and knowingly omitted it.[21]

What happens to a copyright owner who has failed to stipulate in a license agreement that the licensee will be responsible for proper notice? If the licensee's effort to correct notice is later found not to have been reasonable, the copyright owner, though practically powerless to correct the fault, may have lost his copyright. Can he sue the licensee? That remains to be seen.

The total effect of these rules has been to make it virtually impossible at any given moment to know whether a work published between January 1, 1978, and February 28, 1989, without proper copyright notice, is in the public domain or not. The matter is further complicated by the rule that forfeiture of copyright in a derivative work, such as a doll based on a cartoon, does not affect copyright in the original, as long as the forfeiture was not sanctioned by the copyright owner of the original.[22] This whole foggy state of affairs made it easier in the end for Congress to sweep away the notice requirement altogether.

DEFECTIVE NOTICE

What happens if a notice is facially correct, but information contained in the notice is erroneous? Under pre-Berne law the consequences of erroneous notice could be serious if the copies or phonorecords bearing defective notice were distributed with the copyright owner's permission. Defective notice on unauthorized copies or phonorecords—for example, albums distributed by a record pirate—or on copies or phonorecords distributed in violation of the terms of a contract did not affect the rights of the copyright owner at all.

The consequences of a mistake differed depending on the nature of the error. (I am referring to unwitting errors. Fraudulent misrepresentations in a copyright notice could, and still can, bring a fine of up to $2,500.)[23] Bear in mind that the following rules apply only to post-1977, pre-Berne publications.

MISTAKE IN NAME

If the person whose name appeared in the notice was not the real owner of copyright—for example, if a book bearing notice in the name of John Adams was actually the work of his wife Abigail, or if a publisher that had only the publication rights put its own name on the notice, or if a contribution to a collective work did not bear a separate copyright notice—the copyright notice retained some value; the public was put on notice that at least somebody claimed copyright in the work. What if someone in good faith purchased rights in the work from the person named in the notice and proceeded to exploit them? If the copies bearing erroneous notice were published before U.S. accession to Berne, the law states that the purchaser will be considered an innocent infringer if he "begins his undertaking" before the work has been registered in the correct name or before some other document has been recorded with the Copyright Office, signed by the person whose name appears in the notice but revealing the true owner of copyright.[24] This does not mean that the good-faith purchaser actually gets a right in the work; he does not. What he gets is a sort of limited privilege to exploit the right he believed he was buying.

Fairness requires such a result. If the law were otherwise, many unlucky purchasers would find themselves with no way to recoup their investment. Although this exemption by its very terms does not apply to post-Berne works, the principle of fairness within it could still be applied to post-Berne works.

Pre-Berne law provided that this limited privilege not exist until the purchaser "begins his undertaking." Clearly these words mean more than the mere act of purchasing the right, because at that stage the whole problem could be corrected simply by undoing the sale. Only an investment of time and resources in actually exploiting the right will tip the scales in the purchaser's favor. Will setting type be enough? Will hiring extra personnel be enough? As to that, no one knows, for this provision of the law has not been tested. Perhaps now it never will be.

And what is the extent of the limited privilege that the purchaser thus obtains? If, for example, he has sunk money into a big Broadway production in reliance on his bogus right, he will probably be permitted to exploit his bogus right at least until he has recovered his investment, perhaps even until he has made a reasonable profit. After that, does his privilege end? Again the law is silent.

From the perspective of the copyright owner whose rights are infringed, the situation is no less fraught with ambiguity. The law provides that he is entitled to receive the profits of the person who sold the bogus right. Suppose the seller has inadvertently sold the rights for a fraction of their true worth? Can the true owner sue anybody for the difference? Probably, but no one knows for certain.

MISTAKE IN DATE

If the date written in the notice was earlier than the true date of first publication, in the ordinary case there were no repercussions. But if the work was published anonymously or under a pseudonym or was a work made for hire, so that the copyright term would be computed with reference to the first date of publication, the term would be computed from the date given in the notice, and the copyright owner would lose a year or more of protection.

If the date given in the notice was later than the date of first publication by only a year, there were no repercussions. However, in the case of a work published anonymously or under a pseudonym or in the case of a work made for hire, the date given in the notice would be ignored and the copyright term computed using the correct date.

If the date in the notice was two or more years later than the actual date of first publication, then the pre-Berne statute treated the work as if the date had been omitted altogether.[25]

THE INNOCENT INFRINGER

In drafting the 1976 act, as Congress wrestled with the need to loosen notice requirements, it also wrestled with the plight of the unwitting infringer. Suppose somebody, seeing no copyright notice, decided the work was free to all? To protect this honest wretch proved to be, however, no simple task. In its final form the 1976 act exempted him from liability only if he was "misled" by the absence of notice. If he had reason to believe the work actually was copyrighted, was he under a duty to investigate? If a work that is obviously original lacks copyright notice, the first instinct of any moderately sophisticated person would be to suspect that this omission was an error. Could one who has such a suspicion still be "misled"?

Although this unauthorized user was, technically speaking, infringing the copyright, Congress decided to protect him from some of the penalties of infringement. For example, until it was actually brought to his notice that the work was registered with the Copyright Office, he could continue to publish without fear of liability. He might or might not be required to surrender his profits; that would rest with the discretion of the judge or jury hearing the case. He might or might not be required by the court to stop publication or, if permitted to continue, might or might not be required to pay royalties to the copyright owner. Under no circumstances would he be required to compensate the copyright owner for damages. Damages in this context would include lost sales and injury to an artist's reputation due to the circulation of poor copies of his work; they would also, presumably, include whatever harm might result from the fact that the copies or phonorecords distributed by the infringer bore, themselves, no copyright notice.

The innocent infringer is still with us. The elaborate notice rules I have described continue to apply where copies or phonorecords were published before the U.S. accession to Berne, even if the lawsuit is heard now. Post-Berne is another story. Vestigial references in the statute imply that there may still be an innocent-infringer defense, but who can invoke it and what protection it gives are not entirely clear.[26] One thing we can say for certain: it is as wise now as it was vital before to put proper notice on every published copy of a work.

NOTICE ON CONFIDENTIAL MATERIALS

One question often asked by people in business is, What sort of copyright notice does one place on materials that contain trade secrets—know-how, customer lists, business methods, and so on? It is not an easy question to answer. Now that the law regarding notice has changed, there seems less reason for concern on this point. But for those asserting trade-secret rights, a bare copyright notice has never seemed particularly helpful. It does not warn users against the actions that most worry the owner of the materials.

My suggestion is to place a legend to the following effect on copies distributed on a confidential basis:

The within material is an unpublished copyrighted work containing trade secret and other proprietary information of XYZ Corporation. This copy has been provided on the basis of strict confidentiality and on the express understanding that it may not be reproduced, or revealed to any person, in whole or in part, without express written permission from XYZ, which is the sole owner of copyright and all other rights therein.

5 Registration of a Copyright Claim

Registration does not affect the existence or validity of a copyright. It is and has been, however, important as a method of protecting one's rights under the copyright, for these reasons:

1. It could be of crucial importance if for any reason notice of copyright was omitted from copies of the work distributed to the public before March 1, 1989.

2. For works of U.S. origin, it is a prerequisite for bringing suit to enforce a copyright. The only exception is that if you have attempted to register in the proper manner, but the Copyright Office has rejected your application for any reason, you may still file suit for infringement, but you must give the Copyright Office notice of your suit.[1]

3. You cannot, in general, recover your attorneys' fees or so-called statutory damages for any infringement that commences before the "effective date" of registration. (The effective date of registration is the date on which the application, fee, and deposit were filed, regardless of when they were finally processed.) Registration, in other words, creates the right to receive these special compensations. In the case of a published work, there is a three-month grace period for registration: if you apply for registration within three months of first publication, you can collect attorneys' fees and statutory damages for any infringement that takes place after publication. However, there is no three-month grace period for unpublished works except works first fixed when broadcast.[2]

4. If you are the owner of copyright in a musical work, you are not entitled to royalties under a so-called compulsory license until your identity is a matter of record with the Copyright Office. In practical terms this makes registration a

prerequisite to receipt of those royalties. There is no three-month grace period here.

WHO MAY REGISTER

Anyone who owns or has an exclusive license for any of the rights comprised in the copyright of the work may register the work. It is the work that is being registered, not any of the subsidiary rights that make up the copyright. Registration is of the basic underlying claim in the original work.

WHO MUST REGISTER IN ORDER TO SUE?

If you are suing to enforce a moral right (see chapter 6), you need not register your work in order to sue. However, if you are suing to enforce a copyright, you must first register the copyright, unless the country of origin of the work is a foreign country that is party to the Berne Convention, the World Trade Organization Agreement, or one of a number of lesser copyright treaties. (In the discussion that follows I will refer to these countries, using the term in the statute, as "treaty parties.") The registration requirement still applies to U.S. works and to works from a few foreign countries. It also applies to mask works regardless of origin.[3]

Determining the "country of origin" is more complicated than the words might suggest. A work is exempt from registration if it passes one of three tests, which I shall call the author test, the country of publication test, and the location test.[4]

THE AUTHOR TEST

If at least one of the authors is a citizen of a treaty party or is domiciled in a treaty party, or has his or her "habitual residence" there, the registration requirement is waived. In the case of a published work, this test is applied as of the date of first publication. In the case of an unpublished work, this test appears to be applied as of the date the suit is brought, although that is unfortunately less than entirely clear. (The alternative would be to apply the test as of the date of creation of the work.) A special rule applies to audiovisual works: if the work is an audiovisual work, any corporation, limited partnership, or other "legal entity" that is the author is considered to be a "national" of a treaty party only if it has its headquarters there, regardless of where it is officially incorporated.[5]

THE COUNTRY OF PUBLICATION TEST

Even if it fails the author test, a work will avoid the registration requirement if it was first published in a treaty party. However, if the work is first published simultaneously in a treaty party and in the United States—for example, simultaneously in Canada and in the United States—the work will be treated as published abroad, and thus exempt from registration, only if the foreign country's law grants it a shorter term of protection than does U.S. law. For example, in some Berne countries photographs, sound recordings, works of industrial art, computer software, and mask works are protected for much shorter periods than in the United States. These works, if published simultaneously in those countries and in the United States, will be exempt from registration. Publication is "simultaneous" in two countries if no more than thirty days elapse between the two publication dates. Note that simultaneous first publication in a foreign *non*-treaty party does not affect the outcome of this test.

THE LOCATION TEST

A pictorial, graphic, or sculptural work, regardless of whether it is published and regardless of its author's nationality, will be exempt from registration if it is "incorporated" in a building or structure located in a treaty party. This exemption obviously applies to murals, friezes, and ornamental works that are embedded in the fabric of buildings. It may or may not also include architectural plans (remember that such plans are considered to be pictorial or graphic works) if the plans have been embodied in buildings; the answer depends on what "incorporated" means, and no one knows.

Oddly, there is no such provision for architectural works (remember that an architectural work is separate and distinct from the pictorial work that exists in the blueprints), even though one would have thought such works ideal for a test based on location. Thus, in considering whether an architectural work is a U.S. work or a treaty party work, one must determine whether it has been published. I have discussed in chapter 1 the ambiguities surrounding that question.

Overall, though at the cost of no small intricacy, these rules achieve the goal of encouraging registration for works of U.S. origin. If you ask "Why?" or "So what?" you would not be alone. And yet the Library of Congress depends in large measure on the registration system for the thoroughness of its collections. Moreover, in a country as large as the United States, with such a vast and diverse output of copyrightable works—larger and more diverse than in any other country in the world—it is a benefit to have as complete a public record as possible.

HOW IS REGISTRATION ACCOMPLISHED?

An application for registration has three components: the registration form, the filing fee, and deposit of copies of the work.

THE FORM

The registration form used will vary depending on the type of work being registered. For a nondramatic literary work other than a periodical or serial work, use form TX; for a periodical or serial work, use form SE; for a dramatic work or any other work of the performing arts (including music, dance, and film, among others), use form PA, unless you also own copyright in the sound recording of the work and are simultaneously registering your sound recording copyright, in which case you should use form SR; for a work of the visual arts (not including film or other audiovisual works), or an architectural work, use form VA; for a sound recording, use form SR. (If both the sound recording copyright and the underlying musical copyright are owned by the same person, one form SR may be used to register both. This would be a case, for example, with a composer who records a performance of his own work.) For a computer program or database use form TX, unless the audiovisual displays are the predominant part of the work, as they might be in a video game: in such a case use form PA. If the work consists of elements in more than one medium, use form PA if there is *any* audiovisual component, and if not, use form SR if there is *any* sound recording component; use form TX only if the work contains only text. Finally, ignore all of the above if you are registering a work that has been restored to copyright on account of GATT (see chapter 9); for such works use form GATT, or GATT/GRP for group registration.

All forms are available through the following sources:

• by mail, from:
Information and Publications Section
Copyright Office
Library of Congress
101 Independence Ave. S.E.
Washington, DC 20559;
• by phone at (202) 707-9100; or
• by e-mail from the Copyright Office's website, www.loc.gov/copyright.

It is also possible to register via e-mail, if you have a deposit account at the Copyright Office for payment of the registration fee. (Deposit accounts are a good idea if you register works frequently, but not otherwise.) For information on the details, go to the Copyright Office website and click on the topic CORDS.

The various forms do not vary much in content, but each requests information that is especially important to the type of work it covers. All of the registration forms require certain basic information:[6]

1. The name and address of the copyright claimant. An owner of any subsidiary right under the copyright is not a "copyright claimant"; that term is used only for the author or for someone who has acquired the basic, underlying claim from the author by sale, gift, or inheritance.

2. The name of the author(s), unless the work is published anonymously or under a pseudonym, and a brief description of each author's contribution to the work. This description can be as simple as "entire text" or "photographic illustrations" or "entire source code."

3. The nationality or domicile of the author(s), even if the work is published anonymously or under a pseudonym.

4. If one or more of the authors is dead, the dates of their deaths.

5. If the copyright claimant is someone other than the author(s), a brief statement of how the claimant came by the copyright (for example: "written transfer of copyright").

6. If the work is a compilation, a statement identifying the preexisting work or works that it incorporates; if it is a derivative work, a statement identifying the work or works on which it is based. These statements should also identify in a general way what material is original with the claimant, because that is all that is covered by the claimant's copyright. They can be as simple as "substantially revised and updated text" or "new modules added."

7. A statement that the work was made for hire, if it was so.

8. The title of the work and, if in its finished state it had any other titles by which it might be identified, those other titles as well. This is particularly important if the work has

been published before under a different title, a not infrequent occurrence in the case of books that were first published outside the country. The word *identified* refers to identification by the public; you need not include titles by which the work has been known only to the author or private viewers. In general if the work you are registering contains material that appeared in a different form under a different title, you would be well advised to make note of this fact when registering.

9. The year in which "creation of the work was completed"—that is, the year in which it was fixed in its final form, disregarding minor editorial changes. Remember that different versions of the work, if they differ substantially, are considered to be separate and distinct works; you should mention previous versions of this type not under this heading but in the space where you are asked if the work is a derivative work.

10. If the work has been published, the date of its first publication and the nation in which that first publication took place. Note that there is some uncertainty as to whether an online database should be regarded as "published." The Copyright Office has pointedly declined to take a position on this issue and will accept the copyright owner's assertion that the database is or is not a published work.

In any of these categories do not omit any information that may bear on the validity of the copyright claim. If you do so unintentionally, you may suffer much in lost time and money. If you do so intentionally, you run the risk of being fined up to $2,500, and if you have committed a fraud upon the Copyright Office you may find judges decidedly unsympathetic when you seek protection of your copyright in court.[7]

To illustrate how a registration form should be filled out, I have included a sample completed form TX as appendix B.

THE FEE

The application form must be accompanied by a fee. See appendix F for the amount of this fee.

DEPOSIT

The application must be accompanied by deposit of either one or two copies of the work or, in special cases, some other kind of material that will identify the work you are registering.

The rules governing deposit are quite complicated. First of all, although deposit is always made with the Copyright Office, it is intended not only for the purpose of registration but also for the archival purposes of the Library of Congress.[8] A single deposit can satisfy both of these requirements, but for it to do so, it must be made at the same time that the registration application is filed or be accompanied by a letter asking the Copyright Office to hold it until the registration application is filed.[9] If deposit is not made under one of these two circumstances, the Copyright Office will forward it to the Library of Congress, and you will have to make a separate deposit when you register your copyright.

Deposit with the Library of Congress can be required even if you have no desire or intention to register your copyright. If the Librarian of Congress decides that the Library should have a copy or copies of your work, the Register of Copyrights will send you a written demand for deposit. You have three months to comply; if you do not, you will be liable for a fine of $250 and for any expenses incurred by the Library of Congress in acquiring copies of your work. If your failure to comply is willful or repeated, you may also be liable for an additional fine of $2,500.[10]

The following rules govern deposit with the Library of Congress:[11]

1. Only published works will be held by the Library. Unpublished works may have to be deposited for registration purposes, but not for purposes of the Library of Congress

unless by some special arrangement between the author and the Library.

2. The following types of published works are exempt from deposit with the Library:

• Scientific or technical diagrams and models. Architectural plans, blueprints, and models are covered by this exemption.

• Greeting cards, picture postcards, and stationery.

• Lectures, sermons, speeches, and addresses unless they are published in an anthology or collection. Anthologies and collections are not exempt from deposit, even if all the contents are the work of one person.

• Literary, dramatic, and musical works published only in the form of phonorecords. In other words, if a sound recording is made of a piece of music, for example, but the music itself is never published in print form, the fact that the sound recording is published in the form of phonorecords does not subject the underlying musical work to the deposit requirement.

• Sculptural works.

• Works embodied only in useful articles or in jewelry, dolls, toys, games, or plaques. For example, if a graphic design is published only by being printed on textiles, it is exempt from deposit with the Library of Congress. Maps and globes are not defined as useful articles and do not come within this exemption.

• Advertising material, including labels.

• Tests and answer material for tests, if published separately from other literary works.

• Works that were first published as contributions to collective works. The collective works themselves are not exempt, only the individual contributions.

• Musical or other works that are published only in movie soundtrack form. This exemption is very similar to that concerning literary, dramatic, or musical works published only in phonorecord form. It means that if a musical work, for example, is not published except in a movie soundtrack, no separate deposit requirement applies to it.

- Television programs whose only publication has been by virtue of a license granted to a nonprofit organization, permitting the organization to make videotapes of it.
- Automated databases that are available in the United States only in online form.

3. For published works that are not covered by one of these exemptions, the general rule is that you must deposit two copies of the "best edition." (The current standards for determining what is the "best edition" are reprinted in appendix C.) However, there are certain kinds of works for which a single copy of the best edition will suffice, and if the work was first published only outside the United States, either one copy of the best edition or one copy of the work as first published will suffice:

- Two-dimensional visual works, so long as no more than four copies of the work have been published, or, if more than four copies have been, the publication has been in the form of a limited edition of no more than 300, of which every copy is numbered. If your work qualifies for this special one-copy arrangement, you can also satisfy the deposit requirements by depositing photographs or "other identifying material" instead.
- Motion pictures but not other audiovisual works. Also with regard to motion pictures it is possible to enter into a "Motion Picture Agreement" with the Library, permitting you to ask for immediate return of your deposit copy on the stipulation that the Library may demand it back at any time in the following two years.
- Globes, relief maps, and other three-dimensional cartographic works.
- Musical works published only by rental, lease, or lending but not by sale.

• Multimedia kits. Multimedia for these purposes means anything involving two or more of the following types of material: printed matter, which might for example be a book (even so humble a book as a user manual), a chart, a poster, or sheet music; audiovisual material; sound recordings; and machine-readable material. Multimedia kits of this type are not to be confused with the new generation of multimedia works that are embodied entirely in CD-ROM. However, a CD-ROM might be part of a multimedia kit if accompanied by a book.

4. Works published in the form of holograms are covered by special rules. In addition to two copies, you must deposit two sets of precise instructions for displaying the image and two sets of photographs or other material that will identify the image.

5. If you are depositing copies of a phonorecord, you must deposit with it any label or package on or in which it is usually sold.

6. In some cases you may make group registration of multiple issues of a periodical. The following rules apply:

• If the periodical is published weekly, quarterly, or somewhere in between, you must supply the Library of Congress with two complimentary subscriptions, mailed to arrive at more or less the same time as your ordinary subscribers receive theirs. These subscriptions should be mailed to:

Group Periodicals Registration
Library of Congress
Washington, DC 20540.

In addition, when you apply for registration of the group of issues, you must also deposit one copy of the best edition of each issue with the Copyright Office.

• If the periodical is a daily newspaper, you must deposit your group of issues—a calendar month's worth—in the form of positive 35 millimeter silver halide microfilm that reproduces all final editions published in the designated month. This microfilm may include editions other than the final edition, so long as all editions are released in the same metropolitan area. The other rules concerning group registrations are discussed later in this chapter.

7. The Register of Copyrights, in conjunction with the Library of Congress, can grant special absolution from the deposit requirement if you can give persuasive reasons why your work should be exempted. If you wish for such treatment, you must submit your request (and your reasons) in writing to the Chief of the Acquisitions and Processing Division of the Copyright Office. Any request must be signed by either the owner of the underlying copyright or the owner of the publication right. Thus, for example, the owner of only the performance right in a work right cannot apply on his own to have the work exempted from any deposit requirements.

8. If you would like a receipt for your deposit, you can obtain one for a fee. See appendix F for the amount of the fee.

The rules governing deposit for registration purposes are slightly different. For one thing there are no exemptions; and deposit may be a prerequisite for registration. There are differences in the deposit requirements between one type of work and another, and some of these differences are similar to those in the Library of Congress context, but you should be careful not to confuse deposit for registration with deposit for the Library.

The rules for registration deposit are as follows:[12]

1. Only one copy is required to register an unpublished work.

2. As with the Library of Congress deposit, the basic rule for published works is that you must submit two copies of the best edition. However, one copy of the best edition—or, at your option, simply one copy of the work as first published, if it was first published only outside the United States—will suffice for these types of published works:

- Two-dimensional visual works, as long as no more than four copies have been published or, if more than four have been published, as long as publication has been in the form of an edition limited to 300 or fewer, all copies being numbered. Any visual work qualifying for this one-copy arrangement can also be deposited in the form of photographs or other identifying material.
- Motion pictures but not other audiovisual works.
- Globes, relief maps, and other three-dimensional cartographic works.
- Scientific or technical diagrams. Architectural plans and blueprints come under this exception.
- Greeting cards, picture postcards, and stationery.
- Lectures, sermons, and similar material published individually and not as part of a collective work.
- Contributions to a collective work. The deposit for registration of a contribution to a collective work should be of a copy of the collective work as a whole.
- Musical works that have been published in notational form only, or in sound recording form only, but not in both.
- Musical works that have been published both in copies and in phonorecords, if the notational copies have been published only by rental, lease, or lending and not by outright sale.
- Any sculptural work that has been published only in the form of jewelry cast in base metal and measuring no more than four inches in any dimension.
- Literary and dramatic works published not in print but only as embodied in phonorecords or motion pictures.
- Choreographic works and pantomimes that have been published only as embodied in motion pictures.
- Two-dimensional games.
- Decals, and fabric patches or emblems.
- Calendars.
- Needlework and instructions for needlework.

- Craft kits.
- Works reproduced on three-dimensional containers such as boxes, cases, and cartons, if the object can be readily opened out, unfolded, slit at the corners, or in some other way made adaptable for flat storage, and if the copy, when thus flattened, does not exceed 96 inches in any dimension. (If these criteria are not met, you will have to deposit identifying material instead. See point 4.)
- Multimedia kits or any part thereof. If part of the kit is an audiovisual work or is sold in machine-readable form, you must deposit the same kind of identifying matter that you would deposit if that were the only element in your work. (See points 4 and 5.)
- Advertising materials, including labels, other than pictorial advertisements for motion pictures. If an advertisement was published in a magazine or other periodical, it is sufficient to deposit just the page of the periodical on which it appeared, not the entire periodical. If a print or label is physically inseparable from a three-dimensional object—for example, if it is stamped on the base of the object—different rules apply. (See point 4.)
- Tests and answer material for tests, if published separately from other literary works.
- Designs that are published only by being printed on textiles, wallpaper, wrapping paper, and similar merchandise. If the design is repeated on the material, the swatch submitted for deposit must show at least one repetition. However, if the only way that the design is published is by the incorporation of the textiles (or what have you) in dresses, furniture, or other three-dimensional articles, different rules apply. (See point 4.)
- Works first published abroad. In such a case the one copy deposited should be a copy of that first foreign edition, not a copy of the best edition.

3. You can make deposit in the form of identifying material rather than in the form of a copy or copies for certain kinds of works:

- Unpublished two-dimensional visual works.
- Published two-dimensional visual works, as long as no more than four copies have been published or, if more than four, as long as publication has been in the form of an edition limited to 300 or fewer, all copies being numbered.
- Unpublished motion pictures (but not other kinds of audiovisual works).[13]
- Unpublished works fixed only in motion picture soundtracks.
- Works that are published only in the form of motion picture soundtracks.

4. For certain kinds of works, the only proper deposit for registration purposes is in the form of "identifying material":

- Sculptural works, models, and maquettes.
- Computer programs and databases (see appendix D for a fuller discussion).
- Works available only online. For such works, you have two options for deposit materials. The first is to submit both a computer disk, clearly labeled with the title and author, containing the entire work, and a printout, audiocassette, or videotape, depending on the type of work, containing representative portions of the material being registered. The identifying material should include the title and author, and the copyright notice if any that appears online. The second option for registration of such works is to send a printout, cassette, or videotape of the whole work—again, showing title, author, and copyright notice. If the work is short (e.g., five pages of text or artwork, or three minutes of music, sounds, or audiovisual material), the second option is the appropriate one to take, because the Copyright Office will not accept "representative portions" of a work of that size.

• Websites. The Copyright Office has not yet decided what constitutes proper deposit material for websites, so you should handle this on an ad hoc basis. Call the Examining Division at (202) 707-8250 and ask for Jeff Coe.
• Works that are published, or that if unpublished are fixed, only in a machine-readable format, *other than* computer programs, databases, and websites. (Note, though, that this special rule does not apply to works published or fixed in CD-ROM format. CD-ROM-format works are instead treated like normal works because the Library of Congress is keen to build up its deposit collection of CD-ROMs.) For these special machine-readable works, identifying material is more complicated than for most. If the underlying work is pictorial or graphic, then you must follow the usual rules for identifying material. If the work is audiovisual, the deposit must consist of either a videotape or a series of photographs and drawings of "representative portions" of the work, plus in all cases a separate synopsis of the work. If the work is musical, include musical notation or a phonorecord of the entire work. If the work is a sound recording, include a phonorecord that can be played on an ordinary device (i.e., not on a computer or synthesizer). If the work is literary, include a transcription of the first and last 25 pages (or equivalent units) and at least five pages that are "indicative" of the remainder.
• Literary works containing both visually perceptible and machine-readable material. (Again, CD-ROM material is not covered by this special rule.) For the machine-readable portion, include a transcription of the first and last 25 pages (or equivalent units) and at least five pages that are indicative of the remainder.
• Unpublished visual works that are fixed only in useful articles, or in jewelry, toys, dolls, or games.
• Published visual works, if they are published only in useful articles or in jewelry, toys, dolls, games, or containers that

cannot be flattened (see point 2 above). This category includes visual works that are published only by virtue of the fact that the textile or other material on which they are printed is used in making a three-dimensional article. For example, if a design is printed on fabric used to upholster chairs and the only manner by which the design is published is the sale of chairs upholstered in that material, then deposit must be made in the form of identifying material. Neither this category nor the previous one includes visual works embodied in useful articles that are part of a multimedia educational or instructional kit.

• Works for which the copy deposited would be larger than eight feet in length, width, or height.

• Advertising material that is physically inseparable from a three-dimensional article. For example, if the design of a label is stamped into the base of a lamp, to register the label design don't send in a lamp; deposit identifying material.

5. There is a special additional requirement for motion pictures, whether published or unpublished. If you deposit in the form of a copy or copies, you must also submit a synopsis or some other description of the contents of the motion picture.

6. There are also special benefits given to motion pictures. First, the Library of Congress is given thirty days from the effective date of registration (the date on which registration, deposit, and fee are received) to decide whether it wishes to keep the copy or copies that have been deposited for registration. If it does not make a decision within thirty days or if it decides it does not want the motion picture for its archives, the copy or copies will be returned to the applicant. Second, as an alternative to this you can enter into a Motion Picture Agreement such as I have described. Third, the Copyright Office will accept motion picture soundtracks as deposits for purposes of registering simultaneously all works contained in them, including music.

7. In the case of unpublished architectural works, the deposit will vary depending on whether the work has actually been constructed. For unconstructed works, the deposit should consist of one copy of an architectural drawing or blueprint in visually perceptible form showing the overall form of the building and any interior arrangements of spaces and/or design elements in which you claim copyright. If the building has been constructed, you must also enclose photographic identifying material that "clearly discloses the architectural works being registered"; photographs should show several exterior and interior views. In either case, your deposit should disclose the names of the architect(s) and draftsperson(s) and the building site or, in the case of an unconstructed building, the intended building site. The form of the drawing or blueprint should be one of these, in descending order of preference:

- Original format, or best-quality form of reproduction, including offset or silk screen printing;
- Xerographic or photographic copies on good-quality paper;
- Positive photostat or photodirect positive;
- Blue line copies (diazo or ozalid process).

8. There is a special additional requirement for holograms. For each copy submitted, you must also submit precise instructions for displaying the image and some kind of material clearly showing the image.

9. The Register of Copyrights can permit you to deposit one copy instead of two, or to deposit an incomplete copy or copies, if you can present a convincing reason why you should receive special treatment. A request for special treatment must be signed by the applicant. (This signature rule is less strict than that for the Library of Congress deposit.) To make such a request, write to the Chief of the Examining Division of the Copyright Office. This is a different person from the person to whom you submit such requests in the Library of Congress

context. You can combine the two requests; if you do so, the Chief of the Examining Division is the person to address, and the application must be signed either by the owner of the underlying copyright or by the owner of the publication right.

The identifying material that can be used to satisfy the deposit requirement (except for works in machine-readable form) is a photograph, transparency, drawing, photocopy, or any other two-dimensional reproduction or rendering of the work. For example, a photograph of a limited-edition woodcut or a drawing of a sculptural work will suffice. There are a few special rules.[14]

• Material reproducing two-dimensional visual works must reproduce the actual colors of the work. This is not true of material reproducing sculpture or other three-dimensional works.

• If you submit more than two pieces of material for any one work, all must be the same size.

• Transparencies must be 35 mm and must normally be mounted in cardboard, plastic, or similar materials. All other types of material must be not less than 3 x 3 in. and not more than 9 x 12 in.; the preferred maximum size is 8 x 10 in.

• Except in the case of transparencies, the image must be at least life-size, except that it can be less than life-size if it is at least four inches in any one dimension.

• At least one piece of identifying material must indicate the title of the work and the exact measurement of at least one of the true dimensions of the work.

• These rules do not apply to unpublished motion pictures or to works that are fixed or published only in the form of a motion picture soundtrack. For unpublished motion pictures, identifying material is composed of a description of the movie, together with either a phonorecord of some kind, reproducing the entire soundtrack, or a set of visual reproductions of single frames—at least one frame from each ten minutes of footage. The description may be a synopsis, a continuity, or anything of that sort, but it must include the title and also the episode title, if it is an episode; the nature and general content; the date of first fixation; the date of first transmission; if the work was fixed simultaneously with transmission, a statement to that effect; the running time; and the credits appearing on the work.

• Because copyright notice is no longer legally required, deposit materials no longer need to show notice. However, if you are prudent enough to use notice anyway, the identifying material you deposit should show where the notice is placed.

GROUP REGISTRATION, THE FORMAL WAY

Because of the filing fee, it would in many cases be a burden to the author to have to register separately every work he has created. Fortunately an exemption from the rigors of registration has been given to individual authors (but not joint authors) who contribute to periodicals.[15] If you are an individual author you may now register on a single form (form GR/CP), for a single fee, all works published in periodicals (including newspapers) in a given twelve-month period, provided that:

1. Each of the works, on the occasion of its first publication, bore a separate copyright notice (separate, that is, from the general copyright notice on the periodical), and each notice identified you as author in the same manner (for example, not by name in one issue and by pseudonym in another).

2. You attach one copy of each periodical (or, in the case of a newspaper, one copy of the relevant section of each newspaper) to your application.

3. You identify each work on your application form and state the name and date of the periodical issue in which it first appeared. (Slightly different rules apply if the registration

is for renewal of copyright in contributions to periodicals published before January 1, 1978.)

Group registration such as this requires filing two forms: form VA, PA, or TX, depending on the type of work that your contributions happen to be, *and* form GR/CP. The VA, PA, or TX will contain all information except the titles of the works and the statistics of their publication; these facts will be put on the GR/CP.

Group registration is also available for multiple issues of periodicals. There are rules for periodicals published weekly or less frequently, and different rules for daily newspapers.[16] For weekly or less frequent periodicals, group registration is available if the following conditions are met:

• The group of issues presented for registration must all have been published within a three-month period, and all within a single calendar year. The purpose of this rule, like some of the others that follow, is to ensure that each question on the registration form (e.g., "year of publication") can be answered at one stroke for all issues.

• Each issue must have been a work made for hire. The rule that all issues must be made for hire does unfortunately disadvantage those entrepreneurs who publish newsletters that are entirely their own handiwork, unless they have incorporated and are thus working "for hire" for their own corporate alter egos.

• Each issue must have been actually created—i.e., assembled and arranged—within one year preceding the filing of the registration application.

• Each issue must be essentially a new collective work, not a revision or adaptation of a preexisting work. Thus, if an Italian architecture journal is being merely translated for sale in the United States, group registration is not available to it, although it might be available to the Italian original.

• The author(s) and copyright claimant(s) must be the same for all issues. Thus, if a magazine is sold by one publisher to another, the issues submitted as a group cannot straddle the change of ownership.

• The claimant must write a letter confirming that the Library of Congress has been sent two complimentary subscriptions of the periodical during the three-month period. This letter should be addressed to:

Office of the General Counsel
Copyright Office
Library of Congress, Dept. 17
Washington, DC 20540

but may be included with the other registration materials.

The form to use is SE/Group. Although the basis for the registration is the authorship of the issues as collective works, the registration form may also recite that the applicant owns copyright in specified contents of those issues. The fee charged is per issue being registered.

For daily newspapers, the rules are as follows:

• The group of issues must all have been published within a given calendar month.

• The application must be filed within three months after the publication date of the last issue in the group.

• The registration may include early editions as well as final editions of each issue, so long as all editions were published on the same day in a given metropolitan area served by the newspaper.

The form to use is form G/DN. The fee charged is per group of issues.

Group registration is also available for unpublished works of visual art, such as photographs, which may be submitted as a collection if the copyright claimant(s) for each element in each piece are the same and all elements are the work, at least in part, of the same author. The collection as a whole must bear a title (e.g., "Scenes of San Francisco") and will be included in the Copyright Office records only under that title.

GROUP REGISTRATION THE INFORMAL WAY

Apart from the regulations, many people carry out their own ad hoc group registrations by bundling things together and registering them on a single form. Courts have upheld this practice, at least for works of visual art, where the works are "related." For example, a jewelry designer's single registration of twelve different but thematically related pendants was held valid for each pendant included in the registration.[17]

CAN YOU REGISTER MORE THAN ONCE?

It is possible under certain circumstances that you may wish to make a second registration of a work. In fact, in the case of a work that you first registered when it was still unpublished, you will be well advised to register again when you publish it if you have changed the title. You will also want to make a second registration if the first registration was not made in the name of the true copyright claimant, or if the original registration was for some other reason unauthorized or legally invalid—for example, if it was made by someone not entitled to make it. However, these are the only circumstances in which the same version of a work may be registered more than once. For correction of nonfatal errors, there is a separate procedure, described below.

APPEALS OF DENIAL OF REGISTRATION

Although the Copyright Office rejects no more than about 5 percent of the claims that are submitted to it, its rejection can sometimes appear arbitrary, and the procedure for contesting rejection has in the past been even more arbitrary. The Office has now established a greatly improved procedure.

If you are denied registration of a work, the first appeal of the denial should, as before, be sent to the Examining Division that rejected the application. One new bureaucratism is that the appeal should be inside an envelope clearly marked FIRST APPEAL/EXAMINING DIVISION.

If this appeal fails, the refusal may be appealed to a newly formed Board of Appeals, consisting of the Register of Copyrights, the General Counsel of the Copyright Office, and the Chief of the Examining Division. Appeal to this Board should be sent to:

Copyright GC/I&R
P.O. Box 70400
Southwest Station
Washington, DC 20024.

Appeal from a denial by this Board is the final administrative action, and thus may be taken to federal court under general principles of administrative law. The fees for appeals are set out in appendix F.

CORRECTING AN ERRONEOUS OR INCOMPLETE REGISTRATION

After you have registered, you may wish to correct certain information contained in your registration or to supply additional information. This may be done by filing form CA, the application for supplementary registration, along with the appropriate fee (see appendix F). No additional deposit need be made. Supplementary registration does not change the legal validity of the original registration. Because of this, supplementary registration may not be used for adding to a list of works covered by a previously filed group registration. It may not be used to record transfers of copyright ownership. Nor is it an appropriate way to notify the Copyright Office of changes in the content of your work. If the content has changed so much as to constitute a new version, you should make a new registration, and if it has not, your old registration remains valid. Nor is it the right procedure to use if the original registration was made in the name of someone who was not the proper copyright claimant; in such a case a new registration must be made. Minor errors in the name of the copyright claimant, however, can and should be corrected by supplementary registration. Also, use form CA to bring to the Copyright Office's attention any prior registrations of materials incorporated in a registered work.

An application for supplementary registration may be made by anyone who at the time of filing would be eligible to make the underlying registration.

REPRODUCTION OF WORKS FOR THE BLIND AND HANDICAPPED

Space 8 on form TX (for nondramatic literary works) deals with reproduction of your work for the use of blind or physically handicapped persons. Completing this part of the form is purely voluntary. By completing it you give the Library of Congress a special nonexclusive license to reproduce your work for the benefit of the blind and the handicapped. This reproduction may be in braille, in phonorecords that are specially designed for use by the blind and the handicapped, or in both media; the choice is up to you.

The terms of this nonexclusive license are as follows:[18]

1. It can be granted only for works that have already been published.

2. It can be granted only by a person who owns the exclusive publication right or the exclusive sound recording right, as the case may be.

3. The Library of Congress assumes the burden of ensuring that every copy or phonorecord carries proper copyright notice.

4. The license, being nonexclusive, does not prevent you, as the owner of the publication or sound recording right, from making other nonexclusive licenses of your right. You

can even make an exclusive license or an absolute sale of your right subsequent to this, but whoever takes that exclusive license takes it subject to the special Library of Congress license.

5. The license will last for the duration of the copyright, unless it is terminated before that.

6. Termination can be made at any time, unlike termination of other nonexclusive licenses. You must give the Library of Congress at least 90 days' notice. To terminate, send a signed statement to the Library of Congress's Division for the Blind and Physically Handicapped. Once termination goes into effect, the Library cannot make any more copies or phonorecords, but it can continue to use the ones it has already made.

7. Someone who purchases an exclusive publication or sound recording right subject to this license can terminate the license in the same way.

8. After termination the license can be given again by filing a supplementary registration form (form CA).

CERTIFICATE OF REGISTRATION

When the Register of Copyrights approves your application for registration or for supplementary registration, the Copyright Office will issue you a certificate of registration or a certificate of supplementary registration. The certificate has no separate legal significance, but it is useful to have it in your possession in case the official record of your registration is misplaced by the Copyright Office. Moreover, in subsequent transfers and other contracts involving the copyright, it will prove convenient to refer to the certificate because it contains, or should contain, the exact description of the copyright. It will also inform you of the registration number, to which you should refer when making or terminating transfers of copyright. (The registration number will be changed if a supplementary registration is made.) Additional copies of the certificate can be obtained from the Copyright Office for a fee (see appendix F).

SPECIAL HANDLING

The registration process can take months. If you need to register on an expedited basis, the Copyright Office will give your application "special handling" upon payment of an additional fee (see appendix F). A request for special handling should be accompanied by the form designed for that purpose, or by a letter explaining why you have an "urgent need for special handling." On the form or letter you must certify that your explanation of urgent need is correct to the best of your knowledge. A request for special handling should be sent to the following exact address and no other:

Library of Congress
Box 100
Washington, DC 20540.

6 Rights in Copyrighted Works

One of the many respects in which copyright resembles property in land is divisibility. If you own a parcel of land, you can sell mineral rights to A, water rights to B, and a right of way to C, and still be considered the owner of the underlying property. Copyright too can be exploited in many different ways. It comprises five basic rights, which, along with certain limitations and exceptions, are set forth in the statute.

THE RIGHT TO COPY

The right to copy is the right to reproduce the work in copies or phonorecords. With regard to sound recordings, this right is limited in several ways. First, anyone else is free to make a recording that blatantly imitates yours; only if he actually lifts sounds from your recording is he infringing. This rule shows practical wisdom. Two renditions of a symphony are bound to sound alike; it would stifle artistic competition to require performers to differentiate themselves in unproductive ways. Second, it is permissible to copy sound recordings in the context of educational programs distributed by or through public broadcasting entities, provided that the resulting copies are not distributed commercially to the general public. Third, certain limited classes of other broadcasters and transmitters may make phonorecords for their own internal use.[1]

The statute also limits to some degree the exclusivity of the right to copy computer programs. It provides that anyone who is an "owner" of a copy of a computer program may make an object code copy of it, so as to be able to use it in a computer. Such a copy may not, however, be transferred unless the original copy is also transferred and unless the owner is also transferring whatever rights he may have in the program. The owner is also permitted to make copies for archival purposes, so long as the archival copies are destroyed if continued possession of the program "should cease to be rightful."[2]

Curiously, the statute does not in so many words require destruction of the object code version when possession of the program ceases to be rightful, but one can only presume that this was an oversight and that any cessation of rights in the program would cover all copies made, as well as copies originally received.

It is not clear why these provisions were added to the statute at all. It is hard to believe that the concept of fair use, which I discuss in chapter 8, would not permit anyone in rightful possession of a program to take whatever steps might be necessary to make full use of it. Even more obscure, and more troubling, is the limitation of these statutory rights to the "owner" of a copy of a program and the apparent exclusion of a lessee. Did Congress intend to say, by negative implication, that loading a program into a computer would not be permissible for a lessee without specific authorization? One assumes not, though the legislative history is ambiguous. As originally proposed by CONTU, this provision of the statute spoke of "possessors," not owners. Somehow, somewhere, the word was changed, and there is no public record as to why.

In 1998, this section of the statute was amended to state that the "owner or lessee" of a program may copy it, or permit it to be copied, for purposes of diagnosis and system repair, provided the copy is erased when the work is finished. The express use of "lessee" here should not necessarily be construed as shedding any light on Congress's reason in earlier legislation for mentioning only "owners."

THE RIGHT TO CREATE DERIVATIVE WORKS

The general concept of "derivative works" has already been discussed. As with the right to copy, this right has also been limited by statute where computer programs are concerned. The "owner" of a copy of a program is entitled to adapt it to his own needs, but may not transfer the adaptation except with the consent of the copyright owner in the original. Again it seems unnecessary to have provided this in the statute, since the concept of fair use is surely broad enough to protect this kind of activity. Also, the limitation of the statute to "owners" ought not to be read as implicitly depriving lessees of a similar right. However, software licenses usually impose specific contractual restrictions on licensees or lessees.

In the case of sound recordings, the only derivative work that is covered by copyright is a rearrangement of the *actual sounds* of the recording.

It is possible to make a derivative work of a derivative work, but, as I have mentioned, anyone doing this should take great care to obtain all necessary permissions. If, for example, a company wishes to make dolls based on a movie character derived from a novel, it must buy the right to do so not only from the person who owns the movie rights but also from the novelist.

The most important restrictions on the right to make derivative works affect architectural works embodied in constructed buildings. The copyright owner cannot prevent anyone from making photographs, postcards, drawings, and other "pictorial representations" of a constructed building if the building is located in or "ordinarily visible from" a public place. Furthermore, a recent (questionable) case has extended this rule to artistic material embedded in an architectural work, even if that material is conceptually separable from the building.[3] Some wags have suggested that since the air is public space, and all buildings can be photographed from the air, all buildings are free to be photographed from any angle. This is almost certainly not correct, but it does raise an interesting (and unanswered) question of whether aerial photography of otherwise private buildings is a copyright violation. Lawyers could spend many a happy hour debating the question.

Pictorial representations of publicly visible buildings may be reproduced, distributed, and displayed without liability to the copyright owner. However, the statute says nothing about performance. Thus the movie industry will need the same sorts of licenses from architects as it has routinely sought from visual artists and composers of music.

The same new statute that creates this exemption for pictorial representations also provides that the owner of a building may alter or destroy the building without infringing the copyright owner's derivative work right. This exemption is (one hopes) redundant; no one had ever before suggested that to destroy a work is to make a derivative work based upon it, and the suggestion seems ludicrous. I put it down to an excess of caution, or to paranoia on the part of the real estate lobby.

THE RIGHT TO DISTRIBUTE COPIES OR PHONORECORDS TO THE PUBLIC

This is the right to publish and needs no elaboration. It should be noted, though, that once you part with a particular copy of a work you lose control over its further distribution. The buyer can sell it, rent it, throw it away, or whatever he pleases. The only exceptions to this "first sale" doctrine are for computer software and recordings of musical works.[4] Attempts to enact an exception to the first sale doctrine for videos have so far failed.

The distribution right owner also has the right to prevent importation into this country of unauthorized copies, or even of authorized copies if such copies were made outside the United States.[5]

With respect to computer software, no one may rent, lease, or even lend it to anyone else without permission of the copyright owner.[6] Only certain nonprofit institutions are immune from this new restriction, and then only in part. A nonprofit library may rent, lease, or lend software to any person for "nonprofit purposes" if the loan copy bears a warning of copyright. (See appendix E for the proper text of this warning.) A nonprofit educational institution may rent, lease, or lend software for nonprofit purposes without the need of any warning notice. Just what the phrase "nonprofit purposes" includes or excludes is nowhere made clear. From one point of view, *any* revenue generation by a nonprofit institution is for nonprofit purposes. Congress evidently intended, however, that some business enterprises by nonprofit institutions would be viewed as "commercial" and not pass muster, though where the line should be drawn is left ambiguous. Curiously, Congress thought it necessary to specify that any rental, lease, or loan by a nonprofit educational institution to its faculty, staff, or students, or to another nonprofit educational institution, is deemed to be for a nonprofit purpose. I respectfully suggest that this attempt at clarification, while no doubt well-intentioned, in fact confuses the issue. In some minds it may well leave a nagging doubt: if Congress thought that something so obvious needed to be spelled out, what other uses that seem just as obviously nonprofit may be suspect? My own view is that what prompted Congress to this unnecessary clarification was probably an excess of caution, not some hidden meaning of "nonprofit." But that is as much light as I can shed on the matter.

Another unanswered question is what liability, if any, a library has if it lends in good faith for a purpose that turns out to be commercial. A strict reading of the statute would make the library liable, but it is hard to picture any court imposing more than a nominal liability in such a case.

While these rules cover most types of programs, they do not cover all. Programs that are embedded in machines or products, and that cannot be copied during ordinary operation, are still subject to the first sale doctrine and may be rented out (as so embedded) without liability. Common examples of this are your pocket calculator, or the diagnostic software in your office photocopy machine. Secondly, video games are still covered by the first sale doctrine insofar as they are rented, leased, or lent for use in video game machines, rather than in general-purpose computers that could be used to copy the programs.

With respect to musical works, no one may rent, lease, or lend phonorecords of such works without the permission of those who own copyright in both the music and the sound recording. As with computer software, nonprofit libraries and educational institutions may rent, lease, or lend phonorecords so long as they do so for nonprofit purposes. There is no requirement that any copyright warning be placed on phonorecords before they go out the door.

THE RIGHT TO PERFORM THE WORK PUBLICLY

"Publicly" in this case means outside the normal circle of family and social acquaintances. "Perform" includes both live performance and indirect performance by means of electronic broadcasting and similar processes. In the case of a movie or other audiovisual work, to perform the work means to show it by means of a projector or other device.

Until recently, the right to control performance was denied to the owner of copyright in a sound recording. Only the author of the underlying work would receive royalties from, for example, the playing of a Top 40 record on the radio; the record company would receive nothing.[7] To put it another way, if you have written a song and a singer has made a compact disc of it, you are the person who controls the playing of the CD in public; the singer has no voice in the matter. She cannot prevent the performance of her recording and receives no royalties from it. Of course you can sell the performance right to the singer if you wish, but the two rights are separate.

What, then, of a videotape, which in theory seems indistinguishable from a sound recording? Alas, there is no logical consistency here. If you permit someone to videotape a performance of your song, the video producer will control public performance of the videotape, as such, although you will continue to control performance of the music. (Anyone who wants to perform the video will thus need permission from both of you.) There is no logical reason for applying this principle to audiovisual derivative works and not to sound recordings. The causes of the inconsistency are more powerful than logic, though; they have their roots in history. The rule is like certain rules of grammar that you can only memorize and should not struggle to understand.

Like many other copyright industries, the music recording industry fears that its livelihood is being threatened by the emergence of digital distribution technology. The digital revolution will enable people who receive digital transmissions of their favorite recordings to make endless, undegraded copies of what they receive. To prevent this, the industry lobbied hard in the mid-1990s for the right to control digital transmission of their sound recordings.

There were powerful lobbies opposing restrictions, and all the music recording industry got in the end was an exclusive right to control digital transmission by means of interactive services (where the customer sends in an online order for the transmission), most kinds of subscription services, and certain other such arrangements; the performance right does not cover traditional radio or TV broadcasting. Furthermore, the right to control digital transmissions is subject to two compulsory license schemes. (See chapter 7.)

The long and complex negotiations that produced this compromise led to one rather peculiar, and unprecedented, addition to the statute. This addition provides that "no interactive service shall be granted an exclusive license [of the digital performance right in a sound recording] for a period in excess of 12 months."[8] If the interactive service is a small one, with fewer than 1,000 sound recordings in its repertoire, the maximum period is extended to twenty-four months. The purpose of this restriction on licensing freedom was, apparently, to prevent the recording industry from gaining dominance over public performance of music by forcing digital performance to pass through tollbooths it could control.

Separately from the recording industry, music performers have been lobbying Congress to obtain the right to be paid for performance of their recordings. A treaty, whose adoption was pending at press time for this edition, urges but does not require all signatories to enact performers' rights.

How would performers in fact be paid? One answer would be to set up a clearinghouse that would handle the licensing of performers' rights on a nationwide basis, as BMI and ASCAP do for music copyright, and be able to grant "blanket licenses" covering a performer's entire oeuvre. This would of course mean that, in addition to paying music copyright holders, the owners of bars, discotheques, radio stations, and the like would have to pay another fee to performers.

Simple as this sounds in theory, in practice it faces major political hurdles. User industry groups have become rebellious of late against the copyright system, and music copyright owners worry that Congress will protect these groups from additional financial burden by forcing the copyright owners to share their existing revenue stream with performers, rather than creating a new revenue stream for performers. But such a solution also has its problems, because the two systems do not neatly overlap. Indeed, there is a vast amount of public domain music that would suddenly begin to generate revenue for performers but not composers. The Boston Symphony Orchestra would be able to demand performance royalties whenever its recordings are played on public radio, even if the composers—Beethoven et al.—have no concurrent right. Assuming the orchestra receives the same fee when its recording of an Aaron Copland work still under copyright is broadcast, should that fee *reduce* the fee that Copland's estate gets? That hardly seems fair. Nor can we overlook the logistical problems inherent in trying to administer a system that attempts to combine performers' rights with composers' rights.

Given these difficulties, it is hard to say whether Congress will ever see its way clear to adopt this part of the treaty and the necessary enabling legislation.

SPECIAL EXCEPTIONS TO THE PERFORMANCE RIGHT

The law permits certain types of performances in spite of copyright. These exceptions are elaborately defined.[9]

EXCEPTIONS APPLICABLE TO ALL WORKS

An exception is created for performances by nonprofit educational institutions in the course of face-to-face teaching activities. A performance in a Berlitz classroom, for example, would infringe the copyright because Berlitz schools are commercial, not nonprofit. Moreover, the exception does not apply to performance of audiovisual works if the person performing the work knows, or has reason to know, that the copy being used is an unlawful copy. Thus, for example, a teacher cannot show a film that she suspects was pirated.

Another exception covers the cable systems used by hotels and apartment houses, which connect all of the rooms or apartments to a common antenna. Cable systems used by governmental bodies or nonprofit institutions are also exempted, so long as they are not used for any sort of commercial advantage, charge no more than enough to meet expenses, and are available either to anyone who wants to hook into the system or only to private viewers or listeners.[10]

A third exception to the performance right covers the use of radio and television reception in bars, restaurants, shops, and other public places. It exempts all performances occurring in such places by means of a "single receiving apparatus of a kind commonly used in private homes," provided there is no direct charge to patrons for watching or listening to the performance. As public appetite for large TV sets grows, the definition of what is "commonly used" will also grow, presumably.

EXCEPTIONS APPLICABLE TO NONDRAMATIC, NONVISUAL WORKS

In a 1998 amendment to the statute, Congress substantially altered the relationship between music copyright owners and the owners of restaurants, hotels, and other establishments. To understand what has happened, it is important to know the history of music licensing.

Decades ago, music publishers, composers, and other copyright owners organized themselves into so-called "performing rights societies"—ASCAP, BMI, and SESAC. Of these, SESAC is the smallest, being primarily European in membership. ASCAP and BMI each represent the owners of well over a million musical works. These societies have the right, on a nonexclusive basis, to license the entire repertoire of their members. They offer what they call "blanket licenses": licenses that entitle a licensee to use all the music in the society's repertoire for a fixed fee. They license the premises where music is performed, not the performers, on the theory that premises are easier to monitor than itinerant musicians. The fee varies depending on the type and size of establishment, whether live or recorded fixed music is used, and so on. Due to antitrust considerations, the fees charged by the societies have long been subject to the supervision of the federal court in New York.

The premises owners had been complaining that they were being gouged by the performing rights societies. After long and bitter lobbying and negotiation, Congress decided to cut back the reach of music copyright—at least as regards public performance on the premises of small business. The result, to my mind, unconscionably impinges on copyright, and it may be a violation of the Berne Convention into the bargain. Be that as it may, here are the terms:

The new exemption for performance of music by means of radio and television reception covers:

- any food service or drinking establishment with less than 3,750 square feet of floor space (other than parking space);
- any other establishment—e.g., a shop, a car wash, a bus station—if its total area excluding parking is less than 2,000 square feet;
- any establishment of any kind that uses no more than six loudspeakers, of which no more than four are located in any one room or adjoining outdoor space. If the speakers are connected to "audiovisual devices" (TV sets, video monitors, etc.), there may not be more than four of these and no more than one in any room, and none of them may be bigger than 55 inches.

Any proprietor of an establishment who defends against an infringement claim on the basis that his equipment or his premises fall below one of these thresholds should be careful in doing so. If the court finds that this claim of exemption was not reasonable, he will be liable (in addition to other damages) for a special penalty of twice the fee that he would have paid during the previous three years to ASCAP, BMI, or SESAC for the right to use the music in question.[11]

As an alternative, the proprietor could bring an action seeking a ruling that the fees charged him for blanket licenses are too high. For a discussion of this new right of action, see chapter 7.

Other exceptions are created by law for performances of nondramatic literary or musical works. The first is for educational broadcasts. It covers broadcasts whether on the air or by cable, so long as they are a regular part of the educational program of a nonprofit educational institution or a governmental body. A broadcast must be made primarily for reception in classrooms or "similar places normally devoted to instruction" (which, for handicapped persons, may mean their own homes) or on governmental premises. Interestingly, the school or governmental body making any such broadcast is free to make up to thirty copies of the program, so long as all except one archival copy are destroyed within seven years.[12] Just what can be done with the copies is unclear, but it seems fair to say that any educational use within the institution or agency would be all right.

A performance of such a work not for commercial profit is also outside the scope of copyright. However, for a performance to fit under this exception, there must be no admission charge—or the profits must go to charity—and no compensation may be paid to any performer, producer, or promoter. Both of these conditions must be met: a charity concert will be a copyright infringement if the performer receives any payment beyond reimbursement of expenses.

The privilege given to charitable benefit performances has one other important qualification. It is still possible for the owner of the exclusive performance right in a work to prevent such a performance, if he gives written notice of objection to the promoters or other persons responsible at least a week in advance.[13] The notice must comply with two rules, relating to content and to timing.

First, it must be signed by the copyright owner or by the performance right owner, or by someone empowered to act on behalf of one of them, and the signature must be dated and accompanied by the name, address, and telephone number of the signer, printed legibly or typed. The notice must include this information:

1. Reference to the statutory authority on which you rely. The statute should be cited. It is 17 U.S.C. §110(4).

2. The date and place of the performance that you object to or, if you do not know this information exactly, as much information as you do know about it, as well as your source, unless your source is confidential.

3. The reasons for your objection.

4. Clear identification, by title and at least one author, of the work you do not want performed or, if you prefer, a blanket identification of a group of works that have something in common, which can be as general as being written by the same author or published by the same publisher. If you choose the blanket-notice route, you must give the name, address, and telephone number of at least two persons from whom the other party can obtain a more specific identification of the works. Also, if your notice does not identify the copyright owner or owners of all the works, you must offer to provide that information, including names and last known addresses.

5. A statement that the persons will be free to go ahead with the performance if no admission charge is made and if no profit inures to the performers or the promoters, but that otherwise those persons may be liable for copyright infringement.

The second rule is that the notice must be received at least a week before the performance. You can instead give brief notice by telegram or "other similar form of communication," if you get a signed letter with all the above information to the proper party before the performance. The phrase "or other similar form of communication" has not been updated in the Copyright Office regulations. Given that telegrams barely exist any more, it might be reasonable to assume that a fax or e-mail would qualify, but so far no court has actually said so.

Exceptions for performances of nondramatic literary or musical works have also been made where the performance takes place as part of a service of religious worship or at a function organized and promoted by a nonprofit veterans' organization or fraternal organization. The latter exception applies only if the general public is not invited to the performance and if the organization uses any proceeds (after paying reasonable production costs) exclusively for charitable purposes. It is designed, in short, to permit the local VFW or Elks or what-have-you to hold a fund raiser for their members without paying royalties. It does not, by the way, extend to college fraternities or sororities unless the performance is held to raise money for charitable purposes that are specified in advance.

OTHER SPECIAL EXCEPTIONS

In addition to the above, the law has carved out some more specialized exceptions. A dramatic musical work (such as an opera or a ballet) may be performed in a religious service. A nondramatic musical work may be performed in a store for purposes of advertising sheet music, phonorecords, or the electronic devices used for performing such works. (Implicitly, the movie on the monitor at your local video store may be an infringement—but who is likely to sue?) And a nondramatic literary work may be broadcast to blind, deaf, or other handicapped persons by a governmental body, a public broadcasting station, a cable system, or a radio subcarrier. The governmental body or public broadcaster can make up to ten copies of the program and keep them on hand for this purpose or lend them to similar organizations for the same purpose.[14]

The only exception created for performances of dramatic literary works, such as plays, is in the case of performances for the benefit of people who cannot read normally. Such a performance may not be made for profit, may be made only once by any one group of performers or under the aegis of any one organization, and may be made only of works that were first published at least ten years previously.

Lastly, if a governmental or nonprofit body sponsors an agricultural or horticultural fair, it will not be liable for unauthorized performance of music at that fair unless it arranges for or is in charge of the performance.

THE RIGHT TO DISPLAY THE WORK PUBLICLY

Display, like performance, includes broadcasting and other mechanical forms of communication. Where audiovisual works are concerned, display should not be confused with performance: you perform a film by playing it in the usual way; you display a film by projecting isolated frames.

The display right is a significant change from prior law and is of great importance to artists working in the visual arts. Someone who buys a painting has the right to place the work on exhibit in a museum or to display it to the public in any other way, so long as the public are physically present at the place of display. But the buyer has no right, unless he specifically buys the right from the artist, to broadcast an image of the painting or permit anyone else to broadcast it. Moreover, this limited right to display a painting is given only to buyers; people who rent, borrow, or lease works of art have no right to display them in any way outside the circle of their friends and guests.

When it created the display right, Congress was thinking of works of visual art. However, the most important (that is, economically important) displays now occur in the computer field. When a central database such as Dialog permits a subscriber to bring data onto a remote terminal screen, it is "displaying" the contents of the database, although one could also argue that it is "distributing" an evanescent copy of the database. Some databases of course contain visual works such as scientific drawings—and, who knows, perhaps when the technology of screen picture resolution becomes good enough someone will put the contents of all the world's museums at our fingertips. If so, the ownership of display rights in paintings and other works of art will become economically significant.

Like the performance right, the right of a copyright holder to control display of a work does not extend to display in the course of face-to-face nonprofit or governmental teaching.[15] (However, as with performance, this does not give a teacher the right to display a copy of an audiovisual work if he knows or has reason to believe that the copy was unlawfully made.) Nor does the right to control display extend to display by a hotel proprietor or someone of that sort if all she uses to display the work is an ordinary television set and if she charges nothing to the public for the privilege of seeing the display.

Exceptions are also made for display in a service of religious worship[16] and display, in an advertisement or a news report, of a useful work—for example, a pillowcase or a place mat—that lawfully incorporates a work of visual art.[17] Thus if a painter licenses a wildlife painting to a maker of plastic place mats, the maker can advertise the place mats without infringing the painter's display right.

MORAL RIGHTS IN VISUAL WORKS

In many European countries, and especially in France, the law has long protected artists even beyond the sale of their works, by what are known as the *droit de suite* and *droit moral*. *Droit de suite is* the right to share in the profits of future sales of a work; when a work is sold by one collector to another, the artist gets a portion of the profit made by the seller. *Droit moral* ("moral right") is the right to control alterations of the work and to prevent its destruction, sometimes referred as the "right of integrity," and the right to be acknowledged as its author if one chooses (or when appropriate to disclaim authorship), sometimes referred to as the "right of paternity."

The Berne Convention requires all its signatories to give some measure of recognition to the moral right. At the time of U.S. accession to Berne it was argued, by those who did not wish to rock the boat, that U.S. laws prohibiting false designation of origin of goods in commerce already, in effect, protected the rights of integrity and paternity. This may have been wishful thinking.

In any event, the United States has now enacted a very limited moral right for certain works of visual art.[18] By this it is generally assumed that we have fulfilled whatever duty we had to our Berne partners. Tightly circumscribed as the statute is, I think it unlikely that it will be expanded at any time in the foreseeable future.

SCOPE OF WORKS PROTECTED

The statute is narrow in two ways. First, it covers a fairly limited range of art objects. The types of works protected are:

• A painting, drawing, print, sculpture, or art photograph of which there is only one copy. In most instances this one copy will be the original created by the artist. In the case of a photograph, the artist's signature must be affixed for the work to receive moral right protection.

• A painting, drawing, print, sculpture, or art photograph that is part of a limited edition of no more than 200 copies consecutively numbered and signed by the artist; in the case of a sculpture, the artist's identifying mark may be used instead of a signature.

A number of things need to be said about these definitions.

First, the statute appears to be inflexible on the subject of numbering and signing. Any print in a limited edition that is not both signed and numbered will be beyond the reach of moral rights. That may seem needlessly draconian, but it is the inescapable meaning. Although the statute could well be read to exclude the entire edition if the artist's signature is accidentally left off one copy, this result is probably too draconian and one suspects that courts will struggle to avoid it.

What of the widespread custom of selling so-called "artist's proofs" of prints? Artists will be well advised to drop the practice, unless the proofs plus all numbered copies total 200 or fewer. The proofs will in any case be unprotected because they are not numbered; the greater damage is that by increasing the size of the edition they may render the entire edition ineligible for moral rights.

The term "print" was almost certainly intended by Congress to be broader than the art world's use of that term. I think it is safe to assume that it includes lithographs, monotypes, and any other work in which an image is applied to paper (or similar medium) from another surface. Likewise, omitting collages from the list of protected works was almost certainly the unintended result of terminological ignorance, and I would assume that a court will supply the missing link when it must. (Until that happy day, your lawyer should call your collage a painting, drawing, print, or sculpture.) On the other hand, the list does deliberately omit works of equivalent merit: pottery (except those pieces that can be construed as "sculpture" or whose decoration can be construed as "paintings"), textiles, calligraphic works, and many "craft" items, to name the most obvious examples.

The most troublesome provision concerns photographs. I have used the phrase "art photograph" above in place of the statutory phrase "photographic image produced for exhibition purposes only" because I *think* that the former, more conventional term is what the drafters of the statute intended. A literal reading of the statute would disqualify all pictures from a news photographer's roll of film even if never published. It would disqualify things, such as portraits, that are never intended for exhibition—assuming we interpret "exhibition" in the usual way. It is hard to believe that the drafters of the statute intended such results. More likely, their intent was to exclude two types of photographs: those that are actually used for advertising and other "commercial" purposes, as that term is popularly understood; and those that, while they may come out of the darkroom in limited numbers, are destined for large-scale reproduction in the news media. Note that in this respect photographs are severely disfavored relative to other works, for a painting may be created for reproduction on something as common as place mats and still receive moral right protection, while the original of a Pulitzer Prize–winning photograph receives none. Here we see the heavy hand of the newspaper and magazine lobby in the shaping of this statute.

In addition to what is excluded by omission, there is a long list of things that Congress specifically excluded from the list of protected works. These are:

- posters
- maps and globes
- charts
- models, diagrams, and technical drawings
- "applied art" (defined as artistic ornamentation incorporated in utilitarian objects)[19]
- motion pictures and other audiovisual works

- books, magazines, newspapers, and periodicals (a curious exclusion, since none of these could ever qualify as a painting, print, etc. anyway)
- databases, electronic information services, electronic publications, and "similar" publications (ditto my comment immediately above)
- merchandising items and advertising, promotional, descriptive, covering, or packaging materials and containers
- any portion of any of the above
- works made for hire, even though they might otherwise qualify for protection
- works not subject to copyright protection—such as, for example, utilitarian works in which design elements are not "physically or conceptually separable."

The phrase "any portion" has odd ramifications. Suppose that an artist issued an illustrated book in a limited edition of 200 copies, signed and numbered: she would not have any moral right in any print in the book. Unfair, but inescapable. Or suppose an artist produces a work consisting of projected images with soundtrack: he has no moral right in any of the images. Would it matter if the images had earlier been exhibited separately? Probably not. Could moral rights be reclaimed if the artist subsequently broke up the work and sold each slide as a separate, self-contained work? It seems they should. Finally, if the work is broken up and sold by the purchaser rather than the artist, would moral rights attach to the components as separately owned? Probably not, for the logical focus of the statute should be the form of the work as sold by the artist.

RIGHT OF ATTRIBUTION

The other respect in which the U.S. moral rights statute is narrow is in the scope of protection it gives. The two rights granted artists are the right of attribution and the right of integrity.

The first of these rights has both a positive and a negative application. In the positive mode, it enables the artist to "claim authorship" of his work. What does this mean? Unquestionably it entitles an artist to prevent removal of his or her name from a work, and to insist on receiving credit whenever the work is displayed. It does not, however, go much beyond this, since it extends only to the particular objects made by the artist and not to the underlying work, the copyrightable image. Thus, the moral right does not entitle an artist who has sold her copyright to object when the copyright owner sells copies or derivative works without attribution. There may, perhaps, be some remedy under laws that forbid false designation of origin, but not under the copyright statute.

The negative side of the right of attribution is the artist's right to prevent having his or her name attached to works he or she did not create, and to insist on removal of his or her name from a work of visual art that has been distorted, mutilated, or otherwise modified in a manner that would be "prejudicial to his or her honor or reputation." However, since the statute prevents misattribution only on "works of visual art," it only half protects the people it ought to help. The moral right will prevent, for example, sale of a fake Andrew Wyeth original; it will not prevent fraudulent sale of a mass-produced poster of a fake Andrew Wyeth. It will entitle Andrew Wyeth to remove his name from a defaced canvas, but not from 100,000 copies of a painting altered without his approval by someone who owns the derivative work right in the painting. Again, other laws may well fill the void, but they are laws lacking the unusual benefits given to actions under the Copyright Act.

RIGHT OF INTEGRITY

An artist has the right to prevent any distortion, mutilation, or other modification of a work of visual art, if the modification is intentional and if it would be prejudicial to the artist's honor or reputation. The requirement of intent is critical; it means that no one will be liable for mistakes, or negligence, or Things That Happen. The accidental nail through the canvas, the mover's bad packing that breaks the nose off your sculpture, the burst pipe that water-stains a painting: these are not actionable. An open question, though, is whether reckless or willful disregard will be construed as intent. One can imagine circumstances where it ought to be. The statute does say that grossly negligent conservation, and grossly negligent exposure to harmful light or similar damaging influences, will violate the artist's right.[20]

The question of what is prejudicial to an artist's honor or reputation sounds complicated in theory but probably is not in practice. When someone has deliberately distorted or mutilated a work of art, no court is going to need much encouragement to find the result prejudicial. The whole moral rights statute is premised on the right of the artist to safeguard his reputation. Who can judge better than the artist whether her unique vision has been compromised? What court is going to say, "We like the altered painting better than the original; you should be grateful for the improvement"?

Prejudice to honor or reputation seems to imply public exposure of the modified piece, but here too I suspect the courts will apply the law liberally. A work that may happen to be kept in private hands now may easily be sold or hung in a museum tomorrow, and there is no good reason to postpone enforcement of the artist's right until that day.

The moral right to prevent modification conflicts to some degree with the right to make derivative works. In essence, where a work of visual art is concerned the artist can prevent modification of his or her own original, but control over modified copies lies with whoever owns the derivative work right.

Strange as it may at first seem, the right to prevent modification of a work does not include the right to prevent destruction of the work altogether. Someone seems to have decided that destruction of a work is somehow less prejudicial to an artist's reputation than its preservation in altered form. One might well question such reasoning. In any event, there is a separate right to protect destruction, but it protects only works of "recognized stature." This unhappy phrase is nowhere defined. In the only case to date that has had cause to interpret it, the judge observed that a plaintiff need not demonstrate that the work is "equal in stature to that created by artists such as Picasso, Chagall, or Giacometti." Rather, the artist must show that the work is "viewed as meritorious" by "art experts, other members of the artistic community, or ... some cross section of society."[21]

For this category of recognized works, the law prohibits not only intentional destruction but also destruction that is "grossly negligent." In other words, the owner of a work of visual art may be liable for destruction of a work if he acts with gross negligence in its storage, handling, or conservation. The line between gross and ordinary negligence will be for the courts to draw on a case-by-case basis.

These rights against modification and destruction are subject to special limitations where buildings are concerned.[22] If the owner of a building wishes to remove a work of visual art (such as a mural) that is "incorporated in" or "part of" the building,[23] and if there is a chance that the work can be removed without suffering modification or destruction, the owner must make a diligent, good faith effort to notify the artist of the intended removal. If such effort fails, there will be no liability to the artist. If the effort to notify succeeds, then the owner must give the artist 90 days to remove the work or pay for its removal. If the artist removes the work or pays for its removal then the artist gets back the title to the work.

What will constitute a good faith effort to notify is somewhat ad hoc, but the Copyright Office has established a Visual Arts Registry for artists whose works are "incorporated in or made part of" buildings, and if the owner attempts notice by registered mail to the address shown in that registry then he will have satisfied his statutory obligation. The owner would be well advised to file a statement of his efforts at compliance in the Visual Arts Registry.[24]

Any statement by the artist for filing in the Registry should be titled "Registry of Visual Arts Incorporated in a Building—Artist's Statement." It should identify the artist by name, address, age, and (if publicly listed) telephone number. It should identify the work by title, dimensions, physical description, and copyright registration number if known. The Copyright Office recommends but does not require further identification in the form of 8 x 10 inch photographs. Finally, the Artist's Statement should identify the building by name, address, and (if known) the owner's name, and preferably should include 8 x 10 photographs of the building and of the location of the artist's work in the building.

A statement of compliance by an owner should be entitled "Registry of Visual Arts Incorporated in a Building—Building Owner's Statement." It should identify the owner of the building and give the name of a person who represents the owner and a telephone number if publicly listed. It should identify the work and the building in the same manner as if it were an artist's statement, except that the copyright registration number is unnecessary. It should include copies of any contract between the artist and the owner (or the owner's predecessor in title) regarding the rights of attribution and integrity. Finally, it should state the measures that the owner has taken to notify the artist of the removal or pending removal of the work, and should include photocopies of any relevant correspondence or other documents.

The recording fee for these statements is the same as for other copyright documents. These statements may be updated as needed. Updates should in any case identify the artist, work, building, and building owner.

All this paperwork is a boon for culture, and at the cost of mere nuisance to the building owner, in cases where the owner is tired of the work and wishes to replace it with a nice clock or fountain. But what if the owner loves the work and wants to remove it to another location—perhaps even a better location? Here, it seems to me, the notion that title should revert to an artist who pays for removal of the work seems open to constitutional challenge. If the owner wants to remove the work so as to incorporate it in another building, by what right should the artist get it back for (perhaps) a fraction of its worth? I suggest that this right should survive challenge only where the owner of the building has no intent to keep the work.

What of the situation where removal cannot be achieved without modification or destruction of the work? In such a case, the owner will not be liable if the artist has signed a written acknowledgment that the installation of the work may subject the work, in the event of removal, to modification or destruction. Buyers of buildings beware: failure by the original owner to obtain such an acknowledgment creates a potential for legal liability on your part to the artist.

EFFECTIVE DATE OF THE LAW

The moral right statute became effective on June 1, 1991. Any work that an artist still owned on that date is covered, as is of course any work created afterward. What counts here is not whether the artist still owned copyright in an existing work on that date, but whether he still owned legal title to the physical object. In no case does the moral right reach back to punish modification or destruction that occurred before June 1, 1991.

WHO CAN EXERCISE THE RIGHT?

The artist's moral right cannot be transferred. It can be waived, but only by an instrument signed by the artist. Furthermore, any waiver must specify the potentially damaging uses of the work that are permitted, and any modification or destruction that results from a use not specified will still impose liability.

If the work concerned is a joint work, any of the joint authors may enforce or waive the moral right, and a waiver signed by one is binding against all. The statute has thus created the irrational and unfair possibility that an artist who does not want his own name used on a work can permit the owner to remove his coauthors' names as well, or can permit the mutilation or destruction of a work to which he has contributed only fractionally. Furthermore, since all this is specifically sanctioned by the statute, there seems little scope for a suit by an injured coauthor against the artist who did these things, other than for a share of any compensation received for the waiver.[25] Thus we have the anomalous result that coauthors may be less protected against their collaborators under the new moral rights laws than they were before its enactment. One may hope that Congress will rectify this in the future.[26]

DURATION OF MORAL RIGHTS

Works of visual art created before June 1, 1991, but which remained the property of their creators on that date, are protected by moral rights for as long as their copyrights last. Works created on or after June 1, 1991, are protected only for the lives of their creators. Why works created before the moral right was even enacted should be given longer protection than new works is a mystery I cannot explain. And since the statute specifically says that moral rights cannot be transferred, what happens to them after the artist's death is an even greater mystery.[27]

As with copyright, where joint authors are concerned the measuring life is the life of the last author to die. Also as with copyright, all terms run to the end of the calendar year in which they would otherwise expire.

REMEDIES FOR INFRINGEMENT

Anyone whose moral right has been or will be infringed can sue for damages or the profits of the infringer derived from the infringement, or for statutory damages in lieu of damages and profits, and for injunctive relief, all in the same degree as if the infringement were of the copyright itself. These various remedies are discussed more fully in chapter 8. However, there is no criminal prosecution available for infringement of moral rights.

In contrast to copyright suits, registration is not a prerequisite for suit on moral rights or for eligibility for statutory damages or attorneys' fees.

STATE LAW MORAL RIGHTS

Before Congress enacted the moral rights legislation I have just described, a number of states passed somewhat similar statutes. These laws are now null and void insofar as they give to the same types of works any right that is "equivalent" to any of the federal moral rights. "Equivalent" should probably be interpreted broadly; any state law creating a right of attribution, or preventing modification or destruction of a work, will probably be void as applied to federally protected works even though it may differ in minor respects from the federal scheme.

However, state law can still apply to infringements that predate June 1, 1991, or that occur after the death of the artist. (Yes, this is what the federal law says, even though the federal law can itself apply to some works beyond the artist's death.)

Regrettably, the various state laws are neither uniform nor, on the whole, much better thought out than the federal. For example, Connecticut prohibits intentional alteration or defacement of a work of fine art, and gives an artist the right to claim (but, curiously, not to disclaim) authorship. Maine, New Jersey, New York, and Rhode Island give a full right of attribution and also prohibit the display or publication of a work with attribution to the artist if the work has been "altered, defaced, mutilated, or modified" without the artist's approval, but they do not prohibit the defacement itself. California and Massachusetts give the artist a cause of action for unauthorized modification or destruction; Louisiana and Pennsylvania go so far as to declare that negligent conservation and grossly negligent maintenance are actionable by the artist. This crazy patchwork of laws makes for a most unsatisfactory situation.[28]

MORAL RIGHTS FOR PERFORMERS?

A treaty that was pending at press time of this edition would require the United States to create moral rights for aural performers. In essence, performers must have the right, at least during their lifetimes, to be identified when their performances are used "except where omission is dictated by the manner of use of the performance" (whatever that means), and to prevent any distortion, mutilation, or other modification of their performances that would be prejudicial to their reputations. Curiously, the treaty does not expressly provide that performers can prevent improper attribution to them of recordings they have not made, but one should expect such a provision to be added in the legislative process. Legislators will also have to grapple with issues such as: (1) Can an orchestra's conductor grant waivers of moral rights on behalf of the entire orchestra? (2) What happens when half of a band objects to a particular modification and the other half approves? (3) Does the second violinist have to be identified by name on every album, or is it enough to say "Boston Symphony Orchestra"? And most importantly: (4) Does the moral right in a sound recording trump the derivative work right, or vice versa, if the owners of the two rights are at odds? Our present moral rights law avoids this problem by being limited to the specific art objects that an artist creates; the artist may object to alteration of these but not to the creation of derivative works that may distort the image. No such fudge is available for sound recordings.

For some reason, the treaty specifically includes dancers among the performers whose rights it seeks to protect. It is hard to imagine any value in the sound of a dancer's feet hitting the floor. Does the treaty language mean that a dancer who collaborates in a musical performance has a protectable right in that performance even though he or she has not contributed to the aural portion of the performance?

Compliance with this treaty would leave us with an odd mix of moral rights. We have at present—at the federal level—an extremely limited moral right for certain works of fine art. Will the addition of a performer's moral right create pressure to widen the scope of our moral rights legislation? Perhaps, but powerful lobbies remain ranged against it.

THE *DROIT DE SUITE*

The moral right is a highly personal right that aims to protect the artist's honor and reputation, and to preserve our common cultural heritage. The *droit de suite* is often mentioned in the same breath with it, but is really a very different creature.

The *droit de suite* is the right of an artist to be paid a royalty on profits made from resale of his or her work. It has been enacted in France and a few other countries; in the United States only California has such a statute.[29] Some claim that its primary effect there has been to drive the art market out of California, but reliable data are not available. I would not, personally, rate very high the chances of passage of a national *droit de suite* rule in this country. Too many powerful interests oppose it, and the art market here is too lucrative. Is it an accident that the headline-grabbing sales of French paintings occur not in France but in England and America, both of which have no *droit de suite* on their books? England may soon be compelled by the European Community to adopt a *droit de suite*; that will provide an interesting lab test of the economic consequences.

MASK WORKS

In the area of rights as in other areas, semiconductor chip masks are subject to special limitations. The copyright owner of a mask has the exclusive right to reproduce the work by optical, electronic, or other means, and to distribute chips in which the mask work is embodied. The other rights generally afforded copyright owners are denied. Like most other copyright owners, the owner of a mask work loses control of the distribution of chips once they are sold.

The Compulsory Licenses

Implicit in the ownership of property is the privilege of determining who reaps the profits of it and what those profits will be. This is true of copyright no less than of other kinds of property. But in recent decades our laws have tended to make exceptions to this privilege; in the case of copyright these are the so-called compulsory licenses.

The Phonorecord Licenses

The most venerable of the compulsory licenses affects the right to make and distribute phonorecords of nondramatic musical compositions. In essence, once phonorecords of a piece of music have been distributed to the public in the United States (and remember that a movie soundtrack is not a phonorecord), any other person may make another sound recording of the work and distribute phonorecords of the recording.[1] Moreover, and more important, the artist who records the work under a compulsory license may arrange the music, though not the accompanying words, to suit his own style or interpretation, if he does not change the basic melody or what the statute calls, with admirable complacency, the "fundamental character" of the work. What "fundamental character" means, no one knows, and no one has shown any eagerness to find out in court.

To obtain a license of this type—commonly called a "mechanical license"—one must serve notice by registered or certified mail on whoever owns the underlying copyright in the musical work. If there are two or more owners, only one needs to be served.[2] If the records of the Copyright Office do not identify the copyright owner or do not give an address, or if the last known address yields no results, notice may be served instead on the Copyright Office, accompanied by a $12 fee. If the person seeking the compulsory license does not serve notice one way or another before distributing any phonorecords or within thirty days after he makes his first phonorecord, he cannot obtain a compulsory license, and his phonorecords will be copyright infringements.

At the top the notice should bear the caption, "Notice of Intention to Obtain a Compulsory License for Making and Distributing Phonorecords." It should state the title of the work and the names of the author or authors, so far as they are known. It should contain the following information about the person or entity seeking the license:[3]

1. The full legal name. All trade names and stage names used in the record business should also be listed, even if they are not going to be used in connection with this particular work. For example, if Bridget Mahoney, known to the world as Wanda Waverly, intends to take out the license, she should list both her names.

2. The full and complete business address used in the record business. A post office box number or similar address is not sufficient unless there is no street address.

3. A statement of the type of business organization used in connection with the record business—for example, individual proprietorship, partnership, corporation, or charitable foundation. Publicly traded companies must identify themselves as such; other corporations must list their directors and officers and the names of every stockholder owning 25 percent of more of their stock. (The true beneficial owner is what is wanted here; if the stock is held by a trustee for someone else's benefit, the beneficiary's name must be given.) Every noncorporate organization must list the names of every true owner (beneficial owner) of 25 percent or more of the enterprise, and if any of these is itself an organization, it has to be identified

in the same way as for actual licensees. Suppose that a private individual forms a joint venture with a corporation to make records. The joint venture is the licensee, but the corporation's officers, directors, and so forth must still be listed.

4. The accounting year. For example, if a company seeking the license keeps its books and pays its taxes on a June 30 fiscal year, that must be stated.

5. Every type of phonorecord that the licensee will publish, such as cassette or compact disc.

6. The intended date of publication.

7. The name of the principal recording artist or group that is or will be involved.

8. The catalogue number or numbers that published phonorecords will bear.

The notice has to be signed, and the name of the person signing has to be legibly printed.

If you are the copyright owner in the musical work, you will not receive any royalties under the compulsory license until the copyright has been registered and any other documents necessary to identify you have been recorded. However, these filings are not onerous, and they are all you need to do to receive a compulsory license royalty.

The amount of the royalty to be paid on each phonorecord distributed under a compulsory license stood in 1998 at either $0.071 for each separate work on the phonorecord or $0.0135 per minute of playing time for each separate work, whichever might be larger. Effective January 1, 2000, and every two years thereafter, these rates ratchet upward to keep pace (very roughly) with inflation. In 2000, for example, the rates are raised to $0.0755 per work and $0.0145 per minute of playing time. Royalties must be paid every month, on or before the twentieth day of the month. Once a year every person making phonorecords under a compulsory license must send to the copyright owner an accounting statement showing his calculations of how many phonorecords he has distributed and any other relevant information. Failure to pay royalties on a monthly basis and to file accounts when they are due can result in loss of the license.

It is important to remember that royalties are to be paid to the copyright owner. This is the person who owns the sound recording right in the musical work, for that is the right that is being sublicensed to others. In almost all cases this will be the composer or someone who has obtained the basic copyright from the composer.

There are several qualifications to the compulsory license:

1. It may be obtained only if the primary purpose of producing phonorecords under it is to distribute them to the public for private use. Phonorecords made primarily for broadcasting or for background music systems cannot be made under a compulsory license. These must be expressly authorized by the copyright owner. However, sale of a phonorecord to a broadcaster, if the phonorecord is available to the general public, would not invalidate the compulsory license.

2. It may be obtained only if phonorecords have already been distributed with the permission of the owner of the underlying copyright in the music. In other words, the music copyright owner has the right to control the first release of a phonorecord, and only after that does the compulsory license kick in. The distribution of a bootlegged phonorecord, being an infringement, does not give rise to a compulsory license in anyone else.

3. The compulsory license does not permit a subsequent producer simply to duplicate a recording made by someone else.

4. Every sound recording made under a compulsory license is copyrightable as a derivative work. But an arrangement of the music, made to suit the style or interpretation of a particular performer, will not be deemed a derivative work

and cannot be copyrighted except with the express consent of the music copyright owner.

5. The compulsory license may be lost if royalties are not paid on time and if the required monthly and yearly statements of account are not sent to the copyright owner on time. In the case of such a default, the copyright owner may give written notice to the licensee, and if the matter is not remedied within thirty days, the license will terminate. If the license terminates, continuing to make or distribute phonorecords will be regarded as infringement of the copyright.

I should add that most performers do not go through the complexities of obtaining a compulsory license but instead deal directly with the copyright owner or with the Harry Fox Agency, Inc., a large phonorecord license clearinghouse located in New York City. "Harry Fox licenses," as they are called, are sometimes cheaper than the statutory license and are generally considered safer for someone who wishes to adapt music to his or her own style.

DIGITAL TRANSMISSION

As noted in chapter 6, the newly created right of sound recording copyright owners to control digital transmission of their works is subject to two compulsory licenses. One of these applies to performances by subscription transmitters, who are eligible so long as they offer fixed programming rather than custom programming or programming on demand, and so long as they do not exceed certain ceilings on the amount of material used. This favored class of digital transmitters includes the new breed of "webcasters," who transmit music on the Internet. It does not include persons who use music as background for other commercial transactions.[4]

The other compulsory license permits digital transmitters to, in effect, distribute phonorecords over the Internet by allowing customers to download and store the sound recordings they play.[5] This is a welcome recognition by Congress that digital transmission can be either a performance or a distribution, depending on what happens at the user end. Any digital transmitter that allows its customers to download and store sound recordings should abide by the terms of this license, even if the work is simultaneously being performed for real-time listening. This particular compulsory license is basically a digital variant of the old "mechanical license" for making phonorecords. As of early 1999, the rates for such a license were the same as for ordinary mechanical licenses.

THE JUKEBOX LICENSE

Under the 1909 Copyright Act, performance of a nondramatic musical work by means of a jukebox was not considered an infringement of the performing right in the work unless the place where the jukebox was located charged an admission fee. The 1976 Act ended this unconscionable state of affairs, creating instead a compulsory license.[6]

Because the Berne Convention does not permit compulsory licenses for jukeboxes, the 1988 revision of the law recast the compulsory license royalty as a sort of floor to which royalties will sink unless music copyright owners and jukebox owners can negotiate an alternative. Because negotiations have superseded the compulsory license and because these are the business of only a handful of industry groups on either side, I will not discuss the matter further here.

THE CABLE BROADCASTING LICENSE

The third of the compulsory licenses involves performance or display of works by cable television and cable radio. The creation of this compulsory license did not take away from copyright owners anything they had before. On the contrary it was a long-awaited recognition of their rights. The Supreme Court had held in 1968 that cable transmissions were not "performances" and therefore not infringements of copyright;[7] the 1976 Act rectified this anomaly and provided a new source of revenue for copyright owners in musical works, films, and other broadcast material.

The 1976 Act clarified the law governing cable television and radio in many ways and drew clear lines among cable transmissions that need not obtain a license, those that can acquire a compulsory license, and those that cannot obtain a compulsory license and are, by definition, infringements (unless specifically authorized).[8] Regrettably, more recent legislation has put this rational copyright scheme on a collision course with federal communications law, as I will discuss briefly after first describing how the compulsory license works.

A cable transmission is an infringement of the performance or display right in a work if any change is made in the program containing the work, or if any change is made in the advertisements that immediately precede or follow the program or are interspersed in the program. The reason such alterations constitute infringement is that a cable system that indulges in them is really playing the role of broadcaster, not simply of transmitter, and also is interfering with the justifiable expectations of advertisers. This rule is not absolute; alteration of advertisements is permitted for the purposes of advertising market research, if the research company doing the alteration has obtained the agreement of the advertiser, the broadcaster, and the cable system itself. Also there are certain circumstances under which the Federal Communications Commission permits or even requires alterations of the content of the signals. These exceptions, however, are of minor importance.

Cable transmission will also infringe copyright if it is not "simultaneous," that is, if it is recorded and then transmitted at a later time. The only exception is in the case of cable transmissions made in Alaska, Hawaii, or any U.S. possession or protectorate, and this exception is available only if the videotape copy made by the cable system is performed only once and is not changed in any way, and only if the cable system takes steps to ensure that no duplicate is made of its videotape. (The owner or other officers of the cable system must file a public affidavit that those steps have been taken.)

Cable transmission will also infringe copyright if it is not made available to the general public. Unless required by the FCC, any transmission that is made to a limited group, such as a group of pay-television customers, will infringe copyright unless authorized by the owner of the performance or display right. By this rule Muzak and similar systems are infringers if they transmit without specific authorization.

Those are the circumstances under which a cable transmission runs the risk of being regarded as an infringer. Unless one of these violations occurs, cable transmission of a *network-made* program is not regarded as an infringement, and no license of any kind is required for it.

The compulsory license fee is levied only on the transmission of *nonnetwork* programs. Although this seems discriminatory, it reflects the view of Congress that broadcasters are already well paid for the markets they intend to reach. Network broadcasting revenues and the royalties that networks pay to copyright owners are structured to reflect the existence of cable transmission, and it is also true that cable extends into very few areas that are not served by one or another affiliate of each major network. Congress decided under these circumstances to leave network broadcasting where it found it. Even within the area of cabling of nonnetwork programs, Congress has made a further limitation according to the same logic: the cable system need pay royalties only for transmission outside the area served by the broadcaster of the program.

The computation of royalties to be paid by cable systems is extraordinarily complicated. Payment of the royalties, like payment of jukebox royalties, is made to the Copyright

Office. If you have reason to believe that a work in which you own the performance or display right is being transmitted by a cable system, you must file a claim to that effect during July of any given year. Partly because the computation of royalties is so complicated, the establishment of a claim to part of them will not be easy. If you believe that you are entitled to royalties, you will be well advised to hire a lawyer to present your claim.

How will you know whether you have a valid claim? Every cable system is required to file a special statement with the Copyright Office twice a year, listing all the broadcasting stations whose broadcasts it has transmitted during the previous six months. This at least will alert you to the possibility that the particular program in which you have an interest has been cabled. Beyond this you are left more or less to your own devices.

Who is entitled to present the claim? The answer to this question depends on who owns the broadcast performance right in the work or the broadcast display right. If an author has written a play, for example, and sold or licensed to someone an exclusive right to perform that play by means of broadcasting media, the performer is the person who has the right to present a claim, not the author.

In the realm of visual works, the same rule applies. If you, the artist, have given a television station an exclusive right to display your work by means of broadcasting, the station has the copyright that counts. On the other hand, if you have given the station only a nonexclusive license, you are the one who should present a claim.

These rules determine who can present a claim for compulsory license royalties. The rules as to who can sue for infringement are different and more open-ended. If an author has sold or licensed his performance or display rights in return for royalties, he can sue the infringer himself, because the infringement affects his income interest. A broadcaster, even one who has only a nonexclusive license, can sue. Furthermore if the cable system has altered the content of a cabled program, the statute gives every broadcaster in the area where the cable system operates the right to sue, regardless of whether the broadcaster has any interest whatsoever in the particular copyright being infringed.[9]

In the case of a lawsuit, notice must be given to all persons whose interests in the copyright might be affected. This is indeed the general rule for all copyright suits.

As I have mentioned, there now appears to be a conflict between copyright and communications law. The problem lies in a new rule that gives local broadcasters the choice of either requiring cable systems to carry their signals or requiring them to get retransmission consent on a case-by-case basis. There is concern that in some markets broadcasters could use the retransmission consent requirement to vitiate the compulsory license.[10] How this will actually play out remains to be seen. Corrective legislation may be necessary.

THE PUBLIC BROADCASTING LICENSE

This license is for the benefit of PBS, National Public Radio, and other noncommercial broadcasters. It is a fairly narrow license, permitting only the performance of published nondramatic musical works and the display of published works of art.[11] It also permits a public broadcasting station or network to tape a show where the performance or display occurs and reuse the tape. It is not, however, a license to dramatize a musical work or to make any other kind of derivative work; nor does it extend to display of any compilation of works of art.

The license will supersede any privately negotiated license not recorded with the Copyright Office within thirty days of execution. Most affected industry groups have negotiated licenses with the public broadcasting entities.

Every public broadcaster is required to keep cue sheets and other records concerning its uses under the license, and you as a copyright owner have the right to see them. You are not obliged to take any affirmative steps; the broadcaster will forward your royalties to you. However, if you do not register your copyrights, the broadcaster may not know where to find you and after three years will not be obliged to pay you.[12]

THE SATELLITE TRANSMISSION LICENSE

The past decade or two have seen a proliferation of satellite dishes in people's yards. Where cable cannot economically reach, these dishes provide television viewers their only link to the airwaves.

To ensure dish owners access to national programming, in 1988 Congress enacted a new compulsory license. In fact, the license helps these viewers only indirectly: the direct beneficiaries are companies that retransmit television signals by satellite.[13]

The license is complicated, and to parse it thoroughly here would be inconsiderate to the reader. The salient points are these:

- For a satellite company retransmitting broadcasts of "superstations," the license applies not only to transmissions directly to home satellite dishes but also to transmissions to intermediary carriers such as local cable companies that capture the signal and deliver it to households.
- For a satellite company that wishes to retransmit network broadcasts, the license applies only where viewers cannot receive network broadcasts directly and do not subscribe to cable.
- As with royalties for the compulsory cable television license, royalties from the satellite license are held in escrow by the Copyright Office and divided up by the Copyright Royalty Tribunal.

• The fees were initially fixed by statute until the end of 1992. Since then, fees have been established by negotiations.
• The license is due to expire at the end of 1999. Thus it may be viewed as an experiment, the results of which (political as well as economic) Congress will be assessing during the final year.

The license cannot be interpreted as giving any kind of encouragement to unauthorized decoding of encrypted satellite broadcasts. In fact, in the same act of Congress the penalties for unauthorized decoding are raised, and the penalties for selling decoding devices are raised by an order of magnitude.

THE DIGITAL AUDIO TAPE LICENSE

One of the most heated copyright controversies of recent years has been the dispute over digital audio tape ("DAT") technology. The cause of the discord is that DAT technology permits a consumer to make a tape copy of any digital sound record. Because the recording being copied is in digital form, the copy will be perfect, without the degradation that inevitably occurs in making a conventional analog copy. Understandably, the U.S. recording industry at first viewed the advent of consumer versions of this technology with dread.

Just as politicians speak of the "lessons of Vietnam," the recording industry spoke of the "lessons of the Betamax [home video recording] battle," in which home VCR technology had become widespread by the time a lawsuit to stop it came to fruition. The movie industry lost the public relations battle over VCR technology long before it lost its case in court. The lesson: stop any copying technology before it can establish itself as a public "entitlement."

The recording industry had sufficient lobbying muscle to stop the invasion of DAT recorders at the water's edge, so to speak, and it did so. But the electronics manufacturing industry was not without powerful friends, and in the end a legislative compromise was worked out that amounts to something unprecedented in this country: a compulsory license of the right to sell technology that will enable consumers to make copies of copyrighted works.[14]

Manufacturers of digital audio recording equipment and blank recording media (tapes, disks, etc.) are required to give notice to the Copyright Office of each new technology they introduce into the marketplace, and to pay a royalty on sales into the Copyright Office. The royalties thus collected are to be distributed to affected copyright owners, using the same rough justice as already applies to cable royalties and the like. Most important from the consumer's point of view is that though the consumer is now expressly permitted to copy both analog and digital sound recordings for private, noncommercial use, all digital audio recorders must contain a device that will prevent them from copying *copies* of digital recordings. In practical terms, consumers are free to copy digital recordings off the air (at such time as digital broadcasts become reality) and to copy digital recordings sold by the recording industry, but not to copy second-generation copies. And from the tapes and recorders they buy, a tithe will go to the copyright owners whose products they are presumed to be copying.

From the point of view of the music industry, this is a major victory, with one possibly bittersweet aspect: for the first time, performers of sound recordings are given a vested financial interest in the revenues from those recordings. Not only the lead performers but also the back-up vocalists and musicians are entitled to shares to the kitty formed from the DAT compulsory license fund.

COURT-IMPOSED LICENSES

Courts often become involved in interpreting licensing agreements, when disputes arise between the parties over questions such as what technologies were meant to be covered. Rarely, though, do courts attempt to second-guess the pricing of a contract; judges have no training for that sort of thing. Notable exceptions have arisen in cases involving governmental regulation of licenses. In the copyright arena, the most significant of these have been the cases involving the performing rights societies ASCAP and BMI. These societies were sued by the U.S. Department of Justice on antitrust grounds over the validity of the "blanket licenses" they offered to restaurants, hotels, and other public users of music. (I discuss these in more detail in chapter 6.) The government withdrew its claims in return for the societies' agreeing to certain fee structures. Those fee structures are revised periodically, always subject to ongoing oversight by the federal district court located in New York City.

Congress has now expanded the role of the courts in overseeing blanket license fees. As of late 1998, the proprietors of bars, restaurants, and other places where music is performed have the right to challenge the fairness of the societies' fees not in general, but as applied to their particular establishments.[15] Thus, the owner of the Sidetrack Tap in Lake Wobegon, Minnesota, may sue claiming that to charge him, say, $650 a year for the right to use BMI's repertoire is unfair because, although he offers live music in a bar that seats 100 people, he actually has live music on the premises only on Christmas Eve. Jurisdiction over such cases no longer lies exclusively in the Southern District of New York; ten other courts around the country are empowered to hear them.

This new type of proceeding hands proprietors a gun with one bullet. That is to say, a proprietor can sue each performing rights society only once. Furthermore, even if the bullet hits the target, it helps no one but the plaintiff: Congress has also provided that the outcome in any given case cannot be used as precedent in any other. This lack of precedential value creates a risk of voluminous and inconsistent litigation, especially from region to region. (One may assume that within any of the eleven designated courts there will be a fair degree of consistency.) It appears that the prevailing party in any such action is eligible to recover its attorney's fees, but one cannot say for certain.

The idea that courts are qualified to determine the fairness of licensing fees may strike you as odd. If so, it may worry you that Congress seems to have developed a taste for this sort of thing. Only a few years earlier, Congress passed GATT-implementing legislation that empowers courts to set reasonable royalty rates for ongoing use of specific "existing derivative works" based on specific restored copyrights. (See chapter 9 for a detailed discussion of this.) At the time this was a highly unusual, if not unprecedented, mandate. Time will tell whether it will prove a model for solving problems of this sort, or an example of what not to do.

8 Infringement and Fair Use

If copyright is like property in land, infringement is like moving onto someone's land without permission, chopping down trees, mining coal, and stealing water from the well. But unlike boundaries in land, the boundaries of a copyright are never clearly defined and frequently are not known until the end of a lawsuit. I can give, then, only general guidelines for determining those boundaries ahead of time.

Some cases are relatively easy. If an artist claims that someone has performed or displayed his work or made and sold copies of it without his permission, he has raised a simple question of fact. Either the defendant did these vile deeds or he did not. The difficult infringement cases are those in which the artist claims that someone else's creation is so like his or her own that it infringes the underlying copyright in his or her work. The legal phrase for non-verbatim copying is "substantial similarity"—a phrase so obviously subjective that one can only pity judges, who must try to apply it predictably.

In the early days of copyright law, the only theft for which the law took retribution was theft of the exact words of a writing. However, as the literary marketplace grew and new forms of literature emerged, and as the public began to pay more attention to the artist and the demands of the artistic ego, this literalism became untenable.[1] In the past few decades it is doubtful if even five infringement suits out of one hundred have charged the defendant with actually using the plaintiff's language, word for word. Suits now are more likely to allege theft of plot, theft of characters, theft of musical theme, and so on. Necessarily in such cases the courts make judgments that are at least partly intuitive.

HOW DOES A COURT FIND INFRINGEMENT?

The following are some of the factors that a court will consider when someone claims copyright infringement:

Did the defendant see or otherwise have knowledge of the plaintiff's work? If not, the defendant will not be regarded as an infringer. This is the effect of the doctrine of subjective originality, which I have discussed above. Knowledge of a prior work, however, does not have to be conscious; the plaintiff will win if he can prove that the defendant must have been exposed to the work, even though the defendant may honestly have forgotten the event entirely.

Is the plaintiff's work original? This question is closely similar to the previous one, only we are asking now whether the plaintiff himself has a valid copyright on which to sue. If the elements he claims are infringed are things that in fact he took from someone else's work, whether knowingly or not, his copyright claim in those elements is invalid.

Is the copied material expression that can be protected, or is it only the author's ideas, or historical fact, or the like? Like the first two questions, this is a threshold test that, if determined adversely to the plaintiff, will be fatal to his case. As discussed in chapter 1, this analysis can become quite complicated, especially as regards computer programs, in which courts must try to determine what elements are dictated by considerations of efficiency and the like.

When the suit charges theft of a story line in a novel or movie, courts will look at how closely the defendant's details track the plaintiff's. Are the details unusual, or are they the sort that anyone would be likely to choose who set out to write a variation on the same old theme? One famous copyright judge has suggested that upon any work "a great number of patterns of increasing generality will fit equally well" and that at some level of generality copying must be excused.[2] The same judge once observed that no one ever has reliably defined, or ever will be able to define, the boundary between idea and expression.

A related question is, *Is the similarity between the works dictated by their subject matter?* Remember that where there are only a limited number of ways of expressing an idea, the "merger" doctrine denies copyright to any of them.

Details can be misleading, and to avoid this danger courts will frequently step back some distance and ask, *What is the intent of the two works?* If characters, for example, or sequences of musical notes seem similar in certain particulars but are, taken as a whole, quite different from each other, the court will be less likely to find infringement.

In considering infringement claims, courts will generally shy away from the type of close textual analysis used in doctoral dissertations; they will look at the two works from the standpoint of an ordinary observer.[3] This does not mean that they will ignore plagiarism merely because the offending work contains some original matter. A thief is liable for what he has stolen, even if he has possessions of his own; a plagiarist is liable for what he has copied, whether or not he has added to it material of his own invention.[4]

The "ordinary observer" test is certainly appropriate for most works. It is probably not appropriate for highly technical works such as computer programs, and, as I predicted in an earlier edition of this book, courts are coming increasingly to rely on expert opinions in such fields.[5] Less persuasively, courts have also held that works addressed to a juvenile audience should be judged by how children, not adults, would perceive them.[6] Perhaps this is valid, but I am skeptical that we can reliably determine how children perceive "substantial similarity." Furthermore, we should be wary of fragmenting the audience test, for we then run the risk of having a different standard for every sort of work, and thus becoming dependent on surveys and "experts" to tell us whether infringement has occurred.[7]

INFRINGEMENT IN THE VISUAL ARTS

Where works of visual art are concerned, certain special problems exist. So many piracies that offend our moral sense are not, strictly speaking, infringements. For example, imitation of style, though frequently egregious and irritating, and possibly a violation of other laws,[8] is not infringement unless concrete elements of previous works are plagiarized. The many famous fakes that have been painted in this century, to the extent that they imitate style—brushwork, use of light, type of subject, and so on—and do not actually replicate elements of pictures by the real artist, are not copyright infringements. The fakers may be sued on other grounds—for example, for palming off their works as those of someone else. This is an ordinary action at common law and has nothing to do with copyright.

In the area of visual arts, the problem of subject matter becomes particularly acute. The physical world is of course in the public domain. Any number of artists can paint a face, a harbor, or a street without infringing each other's copyrights. As Justice Oliver Wendell Holmes said, "Others are free to copy the original. They are not free to copy the copy."[9] Does this mean that anyone is free to photograph Yosemite from the same angles as Ansel Adams did, without liability to Adams's estate? Perhaps so, but surely one is not free to copy the special effects Adams achieved through his use of special filters, lenses, and development techniques.

Difficulties multiply when we talk of arranged subjects. In a well-known case involving a posed photograph of Oscar Wilde, it was held that a photographer's copyright covers any arrangement he makes of natural objects to compose his shot.[10] Should the rule foreclose another photographer from shooting the same subject with different filters and special effects? Or in the realm of painting, should an artist who paints a still life of an identical composition but in a radically different style be considered an infringer? My personal belief is that he should not. What would such a rule have done to the great visual dialogues among the impressionists, or between Picasso and Braque? Perhaps fortunately, no case on point has yet arisen.

It is generally agreed that when two works are being compared, all material that is unprotected by copyright should be excluded from the analysis; one should not give the plaintiff any subconscious credit for material he doesn't own.[11] This is fairly easy to do where literary works are concerned, because we perceive such works one word at a time. Where visual works are involved, though, the task is much harder; we tend to perceive such works as totalities. More than one court has gone seriously astray by overlooking this problem, and the proper procedure for judging infringement in visual works remains one of the most perplexing questions in all of copyright law.

SUING THE INFRINGER

An infringer is anyone who violates any of the rights created by law. Suppose you have written a story that someone in Hollywood adapts into a screenplay without your permission. You may sue not only that scriptwriter but also the studio, the film distributors, and the movie theater where the movie is shown ("performed"). If the infringer is a corporation, you may sue not only the corporation but also the individuals in it who had the authority to prevent the infringement and who profited from it. Such persons are called vicarious infringers.[12]

A copyright infringement suit must be brought in federal court within three years of the time that the infringement took place. Because the law regards each separate copy, distribution, performance, and so on as a separate infringement, if an infringing book was published in 1995 and you bring suit in 2001, you can receive damages only for copies made or distributed from 1998 on.[13]

As is discussed in detail in chapter 5, for most works of U.S. origin it is necessary to register a copyright in order to sue upon it. And for all works, regardless of origin, registration must be made within three months of first publication, or in the case of unpublished works must precede the infringement, for statutory damages and legal fees to be recoverable. The possibility of an attorneys' fee award is often a key element in both parties' assessment of a case, and prompt registration is for this reason highly advisable.

Only a person who owns the particular right that has been infringed, or who owns that right jointly with others, or who is entitled to royalties from that right, can sue.[14] Suppose that a playwright has sold stage performance rights in his play to a Broadway producer for $200,000 and has licensed United Artists to make a movie version (a derivative work) in return for a royalty of 2 percent of profits. Suppose that another film studio has made an unauthorized film based on the play. Who can sue? United Artists can, because it owns the movie rights, and the author can, because he receives royalties from the movie rights. However, the Broadway producer cannot bring suit even though he may stand to lose box office revenues, because he has no ownership interest in the particular right that has been infringed.

For another example, suppose that a singer sets up a trust for the benefit of her child and transfers to it the right to exploit her sound recordings. In such a case either the trustee or the child can bring suit, because the trustee is the legal owner of the copyright and the child is entitled to the profits.

To return to the example of the play, the fact that the Broadway producer cannot bring suit does not necessarily mean that he will never get into court. Quite the contrary. If his interest is likely to be affected by the outcome of the suit, the law requires that he be given notice of it, and he will then be able, at the court's discretion, to join in the fray. The law requires that notice be given to every person whose interest in the work may be affected, and the court may even require that persons whose claims could not possibly be affected also receive notice. All of these people can join in the lawsuit, if the court permits.[15]

Monetary recovery in an infringement suit may take the form of actual damages and, to the extent that they exceed the plaintiff's lost profits, the profits that the infringer has made.[16] Actual damages can include lost profits, compensation for injury to reputation, and compensation for loss of business opportunity (difficult to prove, but valuable if you can prove it).

If at any time during the lawsuit it appears that you will not be able to prove actual damages or the infringer's profits, or if the amount you can prove seems small relative to the expense of proof or the moral turpitude of the defendant, you should consider electing to receive statutory damages. Statutory damages are in the discretion of the court—or of the jury, in jury cases—and are often set at a goodly sum to punish the wrongdoer. They cannot be less than $200—and that minimum figure will be applied only if the infringer can prove that he had no reason to believe that he was committing an infringement. If he cannot prove this, damages will be not less than $500 and not more than $20,000, unless you in turn can prove that the infringer committed the infringement willfully, in which case you may be awarded as much as $100,000. (For mask works the maximum is $250,000.) These figures are for all infringements of any one work, by each infringer or group of jointly liable infringers.[17]

In addition to damages and profits you may, in the court's discretion, be reimbursed by the infringer for your court costs and also for your attorney's fees. On the other hand, if you lose your lawsuit and the court decides that in fairness the defendant should be made whole, you may be required to pay the other side's costs and attorneys' fees.[18]

Whether or not you receive damages, you may receive injunctive relief, which is to say that the infringer will be prohibited from any further acts of infringement. Such an injunction is good only against the defendant you have brought to court and anyone acting in concert with him, although it may serve as a warning to others.

Courts have shown a willingness to issue broad injunctions to protect copyrights. In one recent case, the court enjoined distribution and performance of a movie in which one of the sets was modeled on a copyrighted drawing.[19] The defendant did not even attempt a fair use defense; its major plea was that the remedy of injunction was out of proportion to the injury, especially given that plaintiff had not sued until after the movie was already in release. The court was not impressed. It enjoined all distribution of the movie, even though the set appeared in at most five minutes of the movie's two-hour run time. This remedy strikes me as excessive, but anyone contemplating deliberate use of copyrighted material, however small, at least in a commercial context, must take heed.

THE SOVEREIGN IMMUNITY PROBLEM

As of this writing, one rather large group of possible infringers may be exempt from all of the above remedies, and that group consists of the fifty states. In April of 1998 the Fifth Circuit Court of Appeals held that Congress, in 1990 legislation that explicitly made states subject to copyright infringement suits, had exceeded its authority; the states, said the Fifth Circuit, are immune from such suits under the Eleventh Amendment to the Constitution. Two months later the Federal Circuit Court of Appeals came to a directly opposite conclusion with respect to patents. Since the patent and copyright laws both derive from the same clause of the Constitution, the Federal Circuit's reasoning would apply to copyrights as well. Indeed, the Federal Circuit made clear that it disagreed with the Fifth Circuit's logic. The Fifth Circuit is reexamining its position. If it does not change its opinion, the Supreme Court will have to step in to sort out the confusion.[20]

The risk to copyright owners if the Fifth Circuit's rule prevails is enormous. State colleges and universities are heavy users of copyrighted scholarly materials; if such institutions are free to photocopy at will, a large source of revenue to publishers will be cut off. State governments have become heavy users of software; would they pay for multiple copies if the governor could buy one and have it passed around the state house? Theoretically, there may be state tort claim laws that would permit suits to recover lost revenues from such activities, but procedures of this type are cumbersome and slow. Also, sovereign immunity does not apply to injunctive actions, so even in the worst case it will still be possible for a copyright owner to seek an injunction against anticipated infringement by a state. Such actions are costly, however, especially if (as may be the case) the court has no power to compel the state to pay attorneys' fees to the winning copyright owner.

CRIMINAL INFRINGEMENT

A willful infringer can be prosecuted by the federal government and, if convicted, can be fined or sent to jail or both. Criminal prosecutions are rare, but when they occur the stakes are high: fines up to $250,000, or up to $500,000 for organizations, with up to five years in jail for a first offense and up to ten years in jail for a second offense. Typically, prosecutions under this statute are aimed at record pirates, video pirates, smugglers of counterfeited goods, and the like. But no one engaged in "Robin Hood" software piracy should assume that he is out of the government's sights. In fact, the criminal copyright provisions were recently amended to characterize as criminal any willful reproduction or distribution (including by electronic means), during any 180-day period, of a copy or copies having a total retail value of more than $1,000, *whether or not the infringer acted with any motive of financial gain.* This amendment, contained in the No Electronic Theft Act of 1997, was overtly aimed at people who distribute unauthorized copies of software over the Internet, sometimes for free and sometimes in barter for other pirated software.[21]

FAIR USE

In infringement suits the two great principles of copyright law almost invariably clash: on one hand the need to protect the financial interests of creators, to make it worth their while to create; on the other hand the need to make each person's addition to the sum of human art and knowledge available for the use of all. From this second principle has evolved the concept of "fair use" of copyrighted material. Fair use, as its name makes no attempt to conceal, is not a fixed navigational point; in any given case much will depend on the judge or jury's instincts.

Underlying the concept of fair use is the problem of economic competition. In English law what we call "fair use" is called "fair dealing"; while that term is inadequate in certain ways, it also captures something important. A use is most likely to be considered permissible if the resulting work does not poach on the commercial value of the original. In this context the quality or nature of the use becomes of primary concern. The Supreme Court has stated that "transformative" uses are more likely to be fair than mere duplicative uses; I will discuss this point further in a moment.

The statute adopts four criteria, developed by courts over the last 150 years, by which a use should be judged fair or unfair:

1. The purpose and character of the use, including whether such use is of a commercial nature or is for nonprofit educational purposes.

2. The nature of the copyrighted work.

3. The amount and substantiality of the portion used in relation to the copyrighted work as a whole.

4. The effect of the use on the potential market for or value of the copyrighted work.[22]

The statute says that these factors are not necessarily exclusive, but the courts have not in twenty years strayed from them.

Scholarly quotation is one of the most ancient forms of fair use. The law's interest in propagating knowledge requires that critics, news reporters, and similar persons be allowed to quote from works without paying for the privilege. In one interesting case the writer of a book on how to win at Pac-Man was permitted to use Pac-Man drawings for instructional purposes in the text but not for promotional purposes on the cover.[23] As this case suggests, at some point a quotation will cease to be merely a functioning part of the critical text and begin to stand by itself—to be, in short, a copy. As a general rule a critic or reporter should not quote at any one point more than two or three paragraphs of a book or journal article, a stanza or two of a poem, or a solitary chart or graph from a technical treatise.

Is it fair use for a scholar to quote someone else's work in support of his own thesis rather than for purposes of criticism? The custom in the publishing industry is to request permission wherever possible in such cases, and this is certainly an honorable approach. However, it is simply not necessary so long as credit is given to the author and the quotation is kept to a minimum.[24] In my view, the publishing industry has become needlessly punctilious in seeking permission to quote short passages. Worthy publishing projects have languished or died as a result. Short quotations are the lifeblood of scholarship and should be presumed lawful except in unusual circumstances.

By the same token, too frequent quotations from any one work or related body of work will not be fair use. For example, a biographer of Stravinsky was found to have infringed by excessive reliance on copyrighted statements of the composer to express certain themes. He claimed he used his subject's "radiant, startlingly expressive phrases to make a richer, better portrait of Stravinsky and to make better reading than a drab paraphrase reduced to bare facts." The court was not impressed.[25]

What of the common practice of quoting short passages from poems or other works as epigrams? To my eye, such uses rarely if ever rise to the level of infringement. Leaving aside those few cases where the quotation might be seen as insulting the author (such as quoting religious poetry in an obscene novel), the quotation is more likely to benefit, through increased public exposure, than to harm. More importantly, such uses are, it seems to me, part of the continuum without which our culture would be atomized, as indeed many fear it is becoming already. Allusion is integral to the evolution of literature—indeed of every art form—and copyright should never choke it off. But of course, at some point the use of epigrams for thematic richness may shade into mere repetition of one's favorite quotations, at which point it becomes clearly impermissible.

The principle of moderation applies equally well to the use of visual works. However, I have been asked so often to define "moderation," to give guidelines on this topic, that in an effort to respond I will state here what seem to me appropriate rules of thumb, always with the caveat that fair use is an ad hoc matter and can never be reduced to formulae.

First, it seems to me that graphic works that convey factual information are more susceptible to fair use than artistic works. It is important, though, to distinguish between charts and graphs that simply convey data in spatial format, and those that are embellished by artistic elements. Good examples of the latter are the graphs found in the popular press, but any average computer-literate person can, with computer graphics, create a chart or graph that not only conveys information but conveys it in a pictorially interesting way. Those pictorial elements should rarely be used without permission unless the purpose of using them is a scholarly critique of the original.

Before the issue of fair use is even reached, of course, there is a threshold question of whether the spatial arrangement of data is protectable by copyright. As I have discussed earlier in this book, the U.S. Supreme Court has held that the "white pages" of a telephone book lack the necessary creativity, in terms of selection and arrangement of data, to be eligible for copyright. This suggests that some charts, graphs, and tables may be too elemental in their organization to be eligible for copyright.

Be that as it may, where a chart, graph, or table is being reproduced in a critical study of the work from which it is taken, no permission is necessary. For example, an economist seeking to rebut the work of another economist may reproduce a graph from the other's work and then criticize it as misleading, inadequate, etc. It need hardly be added that the reproduction must be entirely accurate. Similarly, it seems to me no sin to reproduce a simple chart, graph, or table (but probably not more than two or three, well spread out) from a given work for any other scholarly purpose: in effect, to "quote" it to buttress an argument of the writer, in the same way that a short passage of text would be quoted. In all of these cases, proper credit to the original is essential.

Different considerations apply to artistic works, photographs, and architectural works. In my view, there is no need for a license to reproduce small portions of such a work, to the extent that you need to do so in order to reinforce or illuminate a critical discussion of the work. For example, if it would assist your discussion of a painter's brushwork to reproduce a portion of one or more of his paintings, that should be acceptable even without permission of the copyright owner. Nor do I see a problem with reproducing the entirety of a work, albeit on a significantly reduced scale, to the extent necessary to reinforce or illuminate a critical discussion of the work, but for works originally in color the reproduction should be in black and white except in very unusual cases. Furthermore, what is permissible for critical discussion should be equally permissible for political discussion, in those unhappy cases (such as the Mapplethorpe photography dispute) where a visual work is also a political issue.

Where architectural drawings and other utilitarian design works are concerned, entire images, even in reduced scale, should be used sparingly. On the other hand, use without permission is more acceptable where the reproduction eliminates detail that is not germane to the author's critical analysis.

In any case, the images you seek to reproduce under fair use should always be subordinate to your text, rather than your text serving as an accompaniment to the images. An image is subordinate to the text if it directly serves the scholarly purpose of critical analysis of the image itself—or, perhaps, of the artist's technique or style in general—and is directly related to a specific portion of the text. The obvious example at the other end of the spectrum is the coffee table art book, in which text is strictly secondary; we buy such books for the pictures, not the words.

In contrast to these fair uses, I suggest that you will almost always need permission to reproduce an entire image in full color, to reproduce an entire image in full scale, or to reproduce a full or partial image for any purpose that is not subordinate to the text. Use of an image on the cover of a book or journal without permission is usually a bad idea, except where the image is part of the subject matter of the critical analysis of the book and its use on the cover continues, so to speak, the dialogue of the text. I suggest that permission will almost always be required where the artist is *not* the subject you are writing about. This would apply even to something as basic as a news photograph, and would probably not be affected by how much or how little of the image you propose to use.

These rules have discussed copying. Fair use also applies to performance and display, but its scope in those areas of use is harder to define and few cases give us any guidance. Outside the classroom it is difficult to imagine any public performance of a dramatic or musical work, or any public display of a visual work, that would be fair use. Performance of small portions, however, would generally be acceptable for purposes of criticism, a common example being the movie reviews on the evening news. Also, news coverage will sometimes perform bits of music or display public art almost inadvertently; think of political conventions, for example, with their brass bands and pop stars. Such news coverage is certainly fair use.[26]

The foregoing comments apply to fair use of published materials; courts have shown less lenience toward quotation of unpublished materials. In a case involving President Gerald Ford's memoirs, the U.S. Supreme Court found it unfair for *The Nation* to "scoop" *Time* magazine by quoting small excerpts from Ford's memoirs before they were published by *Time*, which had purchased from Ford's publisher the right to be the first magazine to publish excerpts. The Court noted that the use made by *The Nation*, though small, was qualitatively significant, and damaging to Ford's publisher since *Time* backed out of its contract as a result. But the Supreme Court also went out of its way to express a special solicitude for unpublished material in general.[27]

Following this lead, the Second Circuit found infringement where an "unofficial" biographer of J. D. Salinger quoted from Salinger's unpublished letters. The court's opinion made much of the fact that the letters were unpublished, even though Salinger's letters were already on deposit in libraries, having been donated by the recipients. The defendant had been using quotations more to spice up his prose than to make scholarly points, and so the nature of the use was less than compelling as a defense.

By contrast, in a case involving an unauthorized (and quite critical) biography of L. Ron Hubbard, the founder of Scientology, the author quoted unpublished materials not to "enliven or improve" his book but to "prove a critical point, or to demonstrate a flaw in the subject's character." Yet here too the Second Circuit found the use unfair, notwithstanding strong evidence that the quotations were necessary to prove deceit and venality on the part of Hubbard.[28]

Many in the copyright bar, in Congress, and on the court itself believed that the Second Circuit had at this point gone overboard in its zeal to protect unpublished works. A broad application of the Hubbard ruling could stifle scholarly use of unpublished materials, even where they are used as source materials and not as mere embellishments to a scholar's prose. Reacting to this danger, Congress amended the law to make clear that use of an unpublished work, while it will be scrutinized perhaps more closely than use of published material, must still be scrutinized according to the time-honored principles of fair use.[29] I should note, though, that the Berne Convention can be read to prohibit application of the fair use doctrine to quotations from unpublished works.[30] To date none of our Berne partners has tried to make an issue of this, but some mischief may yet come of it.

Another time-honored fair use, but one even less clearly defined, is parody or burlesque. Court after court has wrestled with the question of how much a parodist can appropriate from the original work. To draw too tight a boundary will foreclose the possibility of effective parody, but on the other hand parody cannot be an excuse for a free ride.

One case that in its time caused tremendous controversy is that of *Loew's, Inc. v. Columbia Broadcasting System,* in which Jack Benny was sued for his parody of the movie *Gas Light.*[31] The melodramatic mood in *Gas Light* is so splendidly created that it virtually cries out to be parodied. Jack Benny was not one to pass up such an invitation, and his television parody, entitled *Auto Light,* is a grand example of burlesque. The court, however, found Benny's parody to be infringement because the outline of the plot, the characters, the setting, and some dialogue were copied from the original. Well, you may ask, how can someone burlesque a work without copying these things? Who would even know the object of the satire, or be instructed by it, were these things omitted?

Posterity has not taken a kindly view of the decision of this case. Nonetheless we must recognize that the judge had to grapple with a difficult problem, for, as he remarked in another case, "The defense, 'I only burlesqued,'...is not per se a defense."[32]

The Supreme Court has recently brought a remarkable degree of clarity to the troubled area of parody fair use. The case before it involved two unlikely adversaries: the copyright owner of Roy Orbison's famous 1960s song "Oh Pretty

Woman," and the rap group called 2 Live Crew, whose song "Pretty Woman" sought, at least in part, to parody the Orbison original.[33]

Justice Souter, writing for the Court, distinguished between parody, which is a particular species of criticism, and satire, which may use a work as a vehicle for criticism that is not directed at the work itself. For example, the troupe known as Capitol Steps is famous for its songs lambasting politicians, set to well-known tunes from Broadway musicals and the like. Such use is satire, not parody, and as Justice Souter observed, is not inherently a justifiable taking of the original work. Parody is inherently justified so long as it does not take more of the original than is appropriate to its purposes of criticism.

The Court took the occasion of this case to quash two mischievous doctrines that had grown out of overzealous application by lower courts of certain earlier Supreme Court cases. First, said the Court, commercial use (a term that certainly includes parody such as 2 Live Crew's) is not presumptively unfair, at least where the use is "transformative" as opposed to simply verbatim duplication for commercial purposes. "Transformative" use, as the term implies, is use that builds upon prior material, transforming it into something new, and is generally accepted as the preferred form of fair use. Of course, any derivative work is "transformative," which makes this phrase less than optimal. What the Supreme Court really means by "transformative" is that the original becomes involved in dialectic with the user's own expression.

The Supreme Court's second corrective action was to decree that the fourth factor—harm to the value or market of the work—is not a consideration overriding all others; its importance will vary depending on the other factors. The opinion shows great sensitivity, in fact, to the interrelated nature of the four fair use factors, which some other courts had tended to treat as being watertight compartments, separate from each other.

The Court also had interesting things to say about how to assess a work's impact on the value or market of the copied work. Where a later work is alleged to preempt a market for an earlier work, that market must be one that the copyright owner of the original work either has entered or might reasonably be expected to enter. Parody is categorically neither of these; no one is going to license others to parody his own work. However, although the distinction drawn by the Court seems unassailable in the context of parody, it may be more difficult to apply in other markets, where it cannot be so clearly said that the copyright owner would or would not be disposed to attempt to exploit his work.

As it happened, the Court remanded the case to the courts below to determine if 2 Live Crew's song had inflicted any market damage on Roy Orbison's song. Because "Pretty Woman" was not purely a parody of "Oh Pretty Woman," the Court thought it legitimate to inquire whether "Pretty Woman" had damaged the potential market for rap versions of the original. What the courts below are supposed to do if they find market harm is anybody's guess, and the Court's analysis of this point is the one weakness of its decision. What if the judge or Appeals Court were to find serious market harm to "Oh Pretty Woman," other than whatever harm the parody might cause simply by being an effective parody? The statute does not expressly permit a Solomonic decision, in which the parody could continue subject to a royalty of some kind. But one suspects that courts will be tempted to craft such decisions, with or without the Supreme Court's blessing.

In the visual arts, parody cases are quite rare, though why this should be is not self-evident. One recent case of interest involved the portrait photographer Annie Liebovitz and the *Naked Gun* movie series.[34] The defendant had copied, in part, Liebovitz's famous *Vanity Fair* nude cover photograph of Demi Moore, eight months pregnant. Defendants had posed a different model so as to replicate the overall impression of the plaintiff's photograph, but had superimposed on it the smirking face of actor Leslie Nielsen, and placed underneath the photo the legend "Due This March." All this was to promote the forthcoming movie *Naked Gun 33⅓: The Final Insult.* The defendant argued that the poster was simply taking a free ride on her photograph for commercial, albeit perhaps satiric, purposes. The court, however, found the use to be a parody of Liebovitz's work, notwithstanding its obvious commercial motivation. The court said:

Like all parodies, it relies for its comic effect on the contrast between the original—a serious portrayal of a beautiful woman taking great pride in the majesty of her pregnant body—and the new work—a ridiculous image of a smirking, foolish-looking pregnant man. It thus fits squarely within the definition of parody as a "literary or artistic work that imitates the characteristic style of an author or a work for comic effect or ridicule."...Because the humorous nature of the Nielsen ad depended on the unique qualities of the Moore photograph and its instant recognizability, it demonstrates the necessary "joinder of reference and ridicule" to qualify as a parody.

The court went on to find that it was unlikely there could be any market substitution of the defendant's work for the plaintiff's, given its transformative and parodic character, and that in any event Liebovitz had failed to present evidence of any injury to her own ability to sell or license her photograph.

This finding on the fourth fair use factor, which the Second Circuit upheld, is questionable. One cannot help wondering if the court, having found that the parody element outweighed the commercial element, then ignored the possibility that the Nielsen ad had damaged Liebovitz's market for *nonparodic* advertising use of her photograph. Would any movie producer want to make use of her photo now that its *advertising* value has already been exploited? If not, then the court may have dismissed Liebovitz's claim too quickly. In any event, the court placed the burden of showing harm on the plaintiff, whereas the Supreme Court had said the burden should be on the defendant to disprove harm.

The question of market harm and the concept of "transformative use" may tend to obscure one of the other defenses that can be raised for some kinds of copying, namely, the right of free speech. Where lies the boundary between copyright and freedom of speech, both of which derive from the Constitution? One's first answer is to say that although a citizen may be free to speak, he is not entitled to speak his mind in the same words as his neighbor. He is free to speak the idea, if you will, but not the expression. However, when you consider that "expression" can mean an arrangement of ideas, this answer wears a bit thin. In the end, discussions on this subject are generally reduced to "Well, we know what we mean by free speech, even if we can't put it into words."

I once came close to having to put it into words. A publisher whom I represent had reprinted two speeches by the Reverend Sun Myung Moon in a book that was a study of Moon's organization and theology. The book, a collection of scholarly pieces by sociologists and students of religion, showed Moon in rather a bad light. Two satellite organizations of Moon's church—The Bicentennial God Bless America Committee and the International Cultural Foundation—sued the publisher, claiming infringement of copyright.

We had a number of technical defenses—prior publication without notice among them—and as our last line of defense, the First Amendment. I never learned the strength of any of them, though, because both plaintiffs settled out of court.

I have often wondered what would have happened had I raised the issue of the First Amendment. The precedents were not favorable. One that particularly worried me was a case involving a group of Catholic priests who went on tour with their own theologically corrected version of *Jesus Christ Superstar*.[35] Among their defenses to an infringement suit was that the original musical was sick and perverted, and that therefore they were within their First Amendment rights in defending the true faith. The court did not agree. Copying verbatim all but a small fraction of a two- or three-hour musical could not be justified in the name of freedom of speech and religion.

On the other hand there was the case of Abraham Zapruder's movies of President Kennedy's assassination. Zapruder, a Dallas dress manufacturer, had by sheerest chance been aiming his home movie camera at the President's car when the shooting occurred. He sold his film to *Time* magazine, which later brought suit when someone used various film frames in a book analyzing the assassination. The court in that case held that the use was in the public interest and therefore was a fair use.[36] This was not exactly a First Amendment case, but it came close.

Which precedent would have counted for more in the Moon case? I firmly believe that the speeches were of great public importance but, more tellingly, that excerpts or abstracts of them would not have been sufficient. Taken as a whole, the speeches were extraordinary jumbles of disconnected platitudes and logical absurdities, and the essence of what the book's readers deserved to know lay precisely in that.

Some recent cases suggest that this argument might well have won. In one, a police officer had written a "fable" that appeared in the Police Officers' Federation monthly newspaper.

A newspaper, in the context of reportage, reprinted the article in its entirety, along with commentary that criticized the "fable" as racist and inappropriate material for a Police Federation publication.[37] This was held to be fair use.

In a similar vein, another court exonerated a reporter who published quotations from a speech in editorials and distributed transcripts of the speech. It weighed heavily with the court that the copying and distribution were for the purpose of validating the reporter's analysis of the speech and its author.[38]

A third case pitted the Rev. Jerry Falwell against Larry Flynt, publisher of *Hustler* magazine. *Hustler* had printed an obscene attack (which was itself a parody, presumably unauthorized, of a Campari ad) on Falwell, accusing him (albeit tongue-in-cheek) of incest with his mother. Falwell photocopied the piece and sent it to all his followers to show what evil deeds *Hustler* was up to, and to raise money for his cause. The court found this to be fair use. Of all the characters in this farce Campari, which seems to have decided to ignore the whole thing, comes off best.[39]

Formulating rules in this area is risky, but these cases suggest, and it makes sense, that use of a copyrighted work is fair to the extent that the user could not otherwise convey or demonstrate his ideas in exercise of his freedom of speech. In this respect, the concept of a "dialectic" unifies these cases with the more traditional cases of parody and scholarly quotation.

My remarks thus far have focused on public use. But there is also much copying for private use. Private use has not been the subject of much litigation; we therefore know little about its legality. We know, for example, that an individual cannot go into a museum and photograph a work of art without permission of the copyright owners, even if he only intends the copy for his personal archives.[40] But what about photographing, for his own private enjoyment, a work of art that he has bought and rightfully owns? Many for a long time assumed that this would be acceptable, but without more reason than simply a sense of good sportsmanship. The famous Betamax case was a welcome confirmation.[41]

The case was brought by Universal Pictures and Walt Disney Productions to prevent Sony from marketing the Betamax videocassette player and recorder. To do so, they alleged that by selling these machines Sony was a co-infringer of copyright because it provided infringers with tools of piracy. This in itself was a rather far-fetched notion. Although it was true that the Betamax was used largely to tape programs off the air, it was also used to play the very videotape cassettes that the plaintiffs were selling. Moreover, although most television programming is under copyright, many old movies are not, and as time goes by, more and more material will enter the public domain. Moreover, as the Supreme Court pointed out on appeal, the copyright owners of a majority of television programming do not object to taping and may even be said to encourage it.

Nevertheless the District Court chose to make a ruling on the merits and to decide whether copying by the purchasers of Betamax machines constituted fair use or infringement. To bring this issue before the court, Universal and Disney had also sued William Griffiths, a private user of a Betamax machine. Griffiths was a client of the plaintiffs' law firm, was not represented by counsel, and the plaintiffs waived all monetary claims against him. These irregularities the court also chose to overlook, believing the underlying issue to be important and urgent.

The District Court held for the defendants, and on appeal the Supreme Court, overruling the Court of Appeals for the Ninth Circuit by a 5–4 vote, agreed. In part the decision relied on the fact that the copyright owners of television programs and movies are already compensated by advertising revenues and so are not necessarily harmed. As the District Court noted, Griffiths and other television watchers were not paying a fee for access to the broadcast. Indeed, since advertising revenues are the financial underpinnings of commercial television, "time-shifting" (that is, taping a show so as to be able to watch it at a more convenient time) would seem to benefit, rather than harm, the copyright owner. The Supreme Court found time-shifting to be a fair use and rejected the plaintiffs' argument that they should be able to deny the privilege to their viewers simply because it was, in "amount and substantiality," enormous.

It is hard to say what impact the Betamax case will have on the law in general. Certainly it gives no comfort to those who think everything they can get on the Internet ought to be free, for there is no "time-shifting" on the Internet. The Supreme Court wrote a careful and narrow opinion, emphasizing the peculiar facts of the case. For example, the court nimbly skirted the issue of "librarying" (that is, retaining copies for an indefinite period), which may more clearly harm copyright owners by cutting into rerun revenues. Thus the Supreme Court has not given a blanket endorsement to home copying. The one broad principle we can perhaps extract from the case might be this: For copying, even wholesale copying, in the confines of one's home to be an infringement, harm to the copyright owner must be clear.

Even if this is so, it seems clear that use of the copy must remain personal. No one who has made a copy for his personal use may distribute it to others. Moreover, even if a given individual's use might otherwise be considered personal, this would not necessarily hold true if his copying were part of a community pattern. For example, a company or college would be exposed to risk if it came to light that its members were photocopying works as part of a systematic program for avoiding purchase of the works from the copyright owner.

How does this rule apply to copying done for an individual for a fee? One specific exemption is unofficially given to calligraphers in the Congressional report on the 1976 Act. (One would not have thought the calligraphers' lobby was so powerful.) If a calligrapher copies a portion of a work, or even the entirety of a very short work such as a poem, for a single individual and does not make another copy of the same work for any other individual, he will not be considered an infringer.[42]

Congress also makes an exemption, although unofficially, for single copies or phonorecords made without charge for the use of blind persons.[43]

By implication, other copying for private customers is probably not fair use. However, we may never know for certain, because it is not likely to be worth anyone's time and money to sue to prevent it. Kinko's, a national photocopying chain, was successfully sued on its practice of preparing photocopied anthologies of printed works selected by professors and selling them to students.[44] But this was peculiarly blatant infringement, not at all like sporadic copying for private customers.

What about less directly commercial copying? Businesses and law firms, if they wish to comply with the law, will have to alter many of their traditional practices. For example, it was commonplace in the past for a company or firm to take out a single subscription to an expensive newsletter and circulate photocopies through the office. This is not a fair use. Indeed most business photocopying, because it is made for commercial advantage, is likely to be an infringement of copyright.[45] Cases have been brought by publishers against a number of major corporations to stop this and related practices. Most have been settled on terms very favorable to the publishers. The only defendant that has gone to the mat is Texaco, which argued strenuously that photocopying to assist in scientific research was for the public good and a fair use.

The trial court held against Texaco.[46] It found the use, although for scientific research, to be for commercial ends, and damaging to the publishers by depriving them of subscription revenues and photocopying fees.

On appeal, the Second Circuit somewhat criticized the breadth of that opinion. It stated that the court below had placed too much weight on Texaco's being a commercial, for-profit enterprise. The Appeals Court drew a distinction between direct commercial copying and copying, such as Texaco's, that yields at best an indirect commercial advantage. The latter is less disfavored than the former, it said, and some recognition should be made of the potential public good of Texaco's research. Nevertheless, the Second Circuit reached the same result as the lower court, placing considerable weight on the economic harm done to the publishers by depriving them of photocopying license fees.

After this decision it is clear, if it were not already, that any business that requires multiple copies of works on a regular basis should sign on with the Copyright Clearance Center in Salem, Massachusetts. The CCC offers companies an "Annual Authorization Service" granting permission for unlimited copying of a wide range of periodicals for a flat yearly fee, which is computed on the basis of the customer's own self-conducted audit. Indeed, the Texaco decision made a particular point of the availability of this service, as demonstrating that Texaco had damaged the publishers and had no excuse for its extensive photocopying.

Although the bitterest court battles over fair use have concerned commercial copying, the bitterest legislative battles have concerned nonprofit copying. And the two areas of greatest controversy, the areas where a clear need for public access conflicts with an equally clear need to prevent substantial economic loss to authors, are educational use and library photocopying.

EDUCATIONAL USE, OR, WHY JOHNNY CAN'T COPY

PHOTOCOPYING OF LITERARY WORKS AND WORKS OF ART

In working on the 1976 law, Congress attempted to establish a code of conduct for educational photocopying. Feelings ran so high on the matter, however, that Congress at last shied away. Instead it gave its unofficial approval, in its report on the statute, to a compromise worked out by the Ad Hoc Committee of Educational Institutions and Organizations on Copyright Law Revision; the Authors League of America, Inc.; and the Association of American Publishers, Inc. Those guidelines are as follows:[47]

I. *Single Copying for Teachers.*

A single copy may be made of any of the following by or for a teacher at his or her individual request for his or her scholarly research or use in teaching or preparation to teach a class:

A. A chapter from a book;

B. An article from a periodical or newspaper;

C. A short story, short essay, or short work;

D. A chart, graph, diagram, drawing, cartoon, or picture from a book, periodical, or newspaper.

II. *Multiple Copies for Classroom Use.*

Multiple copies (not to exceed in any event more than one copy per pupil in a course) may be made by or for the teacher giving the course for classroom use or discussion, provided that

A. The copying meets the tests of brevity and spontaneity as defined below, and

B. Meets the cumulative effect test as defined below, and

C. Each copy includes a notice of copyright.

Definitions

Brevity

i. Poetry: (a) A complete poem if less than 250 words and if printed on not more than two pages or, (b) from a longer poem, an excerpt of not more than 250 words.

ii. Prose: (a) Either a complete article, story, or essay of less than 2,500 words or (b) an excerpt from any prose work of not more than 1,000 words or 10 percent of the work, whichever is less, but in any event a minimum of 500 words.

[Each of the numerical limits stated in "i" and "ii" above may be expanded to permit the completion of an unfinished line of a poem or an unfinished prose paragraph.]

iii. Illustration: One chart, graph, diagram, drawing, cartoon, or picture per book or per periodical issue.

iv. "Special" works: Certain works in poetry, prose, or in poetic prose which often combine language with illustrations and which are intended sometimes for children and at other times for a more general audience fall short of 2,500 words in their entirety. Paragraph "ii" above notwithstanding, such "special works" may not be reproduced in their entirety; however, an excerpt comprising not more than two of the published pages of such special work and containing not more than 10 percent of the words found in the text thereof may be reproduced.

Spontaneity

i. The copying is at the instance and inspiration of the individual teacher, and

ii. The inspiration and decision to use the work and the moment of its use for maximum teaching effectiveness are so close in time that it would be unreasonable to expect a timely reply to a request for permission.

Cumulative Effect

i. The copying of the material is for only one course in the school in which the copies are made.

ii. Not more than one short poem, article, story, essay, or two excerpts may be copied from the same author, nor more than three from the same collective work or periodical volume during one class term.

iii. There shall not be more than nine instances of such multiple copying for one course during one class term.

[The limitations stated in "ii" and "iii" above shall not apply to current news periodicals and newspapers and current news sections of other periodicals.]

III. *Prohibitions as to I and II Above.* Notwithstanding any of the above, the following shall be prohibited:

A. Copying shall not be used to create or to replace or substitute for anthologies, compilations, or collective works. Such replacement or substitution may occur whether copies of various works or excerpts therefrom are accumulated or reproduced and used separately.

B. There shall be no copying of or from works intended to be "consumable" in the course of study or of teaching. These include workbooks, exercises, standardized tests, and test booklets and answer sheets and like consumable material.

C. Copying shall not

a. Substitute for the purchase of books, publishers' reprints, or periodicals;

b. Be directed by higher authority; or

c. Be repeated with respect to the same item by the same teacher from term to term.

D. No charge shall be made to the student beyond the actual cost of the photocopying.

These guidelines are intended to be not a set of maximum standards but rather a set of minimum standards. If copying for classroom use stays within these guidelines, it will without question be considered fair use. It is conceivable that in a given case a substantial departure from the guidelines might also be considered fair use, by application of the four basic statutory criteria.

Where an anticipated use falls outside the boundaries drawn by the guidelines, it is advisable to seek permission of the copyright owner. One way of doing this is to write directly to whoever is named in the copyright notice on the work. There will of course be works for which no copyright owner is clearly designated. For example, the copyright may be given in the name of a publisher that has gone out of business, or you may be working from a reprinted excerpt that does not bear copyright notice. In any case, unless it is appropriate to write to the publisher, you should write to the Copyright Office to request information regarding the copyright owners. If the Copyright Office is unable to provide guidance, it is likely that reproducing the work would be considered reasonable under the circumstances.

In general, publishers and authors are fairly accommodating in granting permission for educational uses of their works. However, that permission must be explicit. One is not entitled to rely on silence.

"Spontaneity" is a difficult quality to prove or disprove. However, your credibility will decrease, and your liability will increase, if the photocopying that you authorize begins to assume a pattern or if photocopying is "spontaneously" authorized for works that ordinarily would be considered obvious parts of the curriculum.

The requirement that each copy reproduced for classroom use include a notice of copyright should be strictly complied with. Where you are taking an excerpt from a work in such a way that the copyright notice included in the work will not be reproduced, it is your responsibility to ensure that copyright notice in the proper form is put on each copy reproduced. This notice should be identical to that on the work itself. If you are reproducing a previously unpublished work—for example, a friend's manuscript—be certain to obtain his permission for publication. You should put on it proper notice or a legend such as I have suggested for limited publications: "This copy is for private circulation only and may not be used or distributed in any other manner." To be safer yet, you might require that each copy be returned to you at the end of the term.

The guidelines purport to cover single copying for a teacher's personal use. In my opinion they are probably too narrow in this respect. However, copying for personal use must be distinguished from copying in the course of business, and "business" includes teaching duties.

It is important to remember that these guidelines expressly forbid the making of anthologies composed of materials from periodicals and books, even though these may be sold to students at or below cost. They also forbid the copying of consumable items such as workbooks, standardized tests, and answer sheets. Although some flexibility may exist in other parts of the guidelines, it is doubtful that any court would sanction much deviation in either of these respects.

Finally, these guidelines do not apply to sheet music, which is governed by a different set of guidelines.

A group of concerned interest groups attempted to reach consensus on further sets of guidelines to cover digital copying of materials in an educational context. The negotiating group, which called itself CONFU (Commission on New Fair Uses of Copyrighted Works), issued proposed guidelines covering the creation of digital copies of images for educational use; the inclusion of protected works in educational multimedia projects; and distance learning, defined as "teaching through the use of telecommunications technologies to transmit and receive various materials through voice, video and data." In the end, none of these drafts was adopted, because the parties in one camp or another found them unacceptable. (It appears that the disgruntled were mostly in the educators' camp.) Only the draft on educational multimedia projects has any life left in it, and only in the sense that all sides agreed to wait and see whether, over the next two years or so, individual schools might adopt them and find them useful. I include these guidelines in appendix G, with the caveat that they may end up on the scrap heap.

My own view of these particular guidelines is that they are too restrictive. I am also concerned that for the first time the copyright owners' camp thought it necessary to address *student* use of material. I have always believed that student use of material for strictly educational projects of any kind is fair use, and well below any copyright owner's legitimate radar screen. (By "strictly educational" I mean to exclude things such as school plays, which may well have educational value but are also in part simple entertainment.) Finally, I am concerned that while the guidelines are set forth as a safe harbor, in several places they talk about what users "must" do, which runs counter to the spirit of a safe harbor. Are these guidelines, then, better than nothing? That remains to be seen. They do offer an interesting window onto technology's permeation of the classroom. They may serve as a useful starting point for a more permanent resolution. I would not urge any educator, though, to treat them as more than that.

Why did all the earnest, well-meaning, even strenuous efforts of CONFU come to grief? It is pure speculation on my part, but I suspect one of the reasons was that CONFU tried to grapple with fair use of *visual* materials. Whether analog or digital, visual works present special problems to fair use analysis. By their very nature they may, unlike musical and literary works, be perceived *in toto* all at once. Unlike literary works, they are not easily paraphrased, and it is almost impossible to discuss the "ideas" in them without reproducing the expression. Considering that no one has been able to agree on guidelines for such antiquated activities as making slides of paintings to illustrate lectures, it is little wonder that we are hopelessly at odds where newer, more powerful technology is concerned.

PHOTOCOPYING OF MUSIC FOR CLASSROOM USE

With respect to music in notational form, a compromise similar to that for literary works and works of art was made by the Music Publishers Association of the United States, Inc.; the National Music Publishers Association, Inc.; the Music Teachers National Association; the Music Educators National Conference; the National Association of Schools of Music; and the Ad Hoc Committee on Copyright Law Revision. The guidelines worked out by this group of organizations are as follows:[48]

A. Permissible Uses

1. Emergency copying to replace purchased copies which for any reason are not available for an imminent performance, provided purchased replacement copies shall be substituted in due course.
2. For academic purposes other than performance, single or multiple copies of excerpts of works may be made, provided that the excerpts do not comprise a part of the whole which would constitute a performable unit such as a section, movement, or aria, but in no case more than 10 percent of the whole work. The number of copies shall not exceed one copy per pupil.
3. Printed copies which have been purchased may be edited or simplified provided that the fundamental

character of the work is not distorted or the lyrics, if any, altered or lyrics added if none exist.

4. A single copy of recordings of performances by students may be made for evaluation or rehearsal purposes and may be retained by the educational institution or individual teacher.
5. A single [phonorecord] of a sound recording . . . of copyrighted music may be made from sound recordings owned by an educational institution or an individual teacher for the purpose of constructing aural exercises or examinations and may be retained by the educational institution or individual teacher . . . [This guideline deals only with copyright in the music itself and not with copyright in the sound recording; the recording industry was not involved in negotiating these guidelines. However, I believe that the identical standard would apply to the sound recording copyright as well.]

B. *Prohibitions*

1. Copying to create or replace or substitute for anthologies, compilations, or collective works.
2. Copying of or from works intended to be "consumable" in the course of study or of teaching such as workbooks, exercises, standardized tests, and answer sheets and like material.
3. Copying for the purpose of performance, except as in A(1) above.
4. Copying for the purpose of substituting for the purchase of music, except as in A(1) and A(2) above.
5. Copying without inclusion of the copyright notice which appears on the printed copy.

Like the other photocopying guidelines, these are intended to define not the outer limits of fair use but minimum standards within which use may safely be assumed to be fair.

Guideline A(3) should not be understood to prohibit editing a piece of music in one's personal scholarly pursuits or as a classroom exercise. However, no teacher should make substantial revisions of a piece of music and distribute copies of the edited version or cause it to be performed, in class or elsewhere.

With respect to guideline A(4), no copyright owner's permission need be sought to sell recordings of student performances if the works performed have been previously recorded for public sale by someone else. The compulsory license for phonorecords would apply here.

The prohibition against the making of anthologies and the requirement that proper copyright notice be placed on each copy made for classroom use apply to sheet music just as to other printed works.

OFF-AIR VIDEOTAPING FOR EDUCATIONAL USE

Guidelines have also been developed for off-air videotaping of television programs for use by nonprofit educational institutions.[49] These guidelines do not attempt to define fair use of commercial cable television programming such as Home Box Office, but they do apply to all free programming regardless of whether a particular viewer gets the signal by antenna or by cable service. The term "program" is broad and includes movies as well as works specifically prepared for television.

These guidelines like the others emphasize spontaneity and brevity—in this instance, not brevity of air time but brevity of retention. Programs of any length may be videotaped but may not be retained for more than forty-five days. At the end of that period they should be erased or destroyed. They should be made only at the request of, and used only by, individual teachers, and in the spirit of spontaneity should not be regularly recorded in anticipation of requests.

These guidelines forbid recording the same material off-air more than once for any one teacher, although, with seeming inconsistency, they permit making multiple copies of a recording to meet "the legitimate needs of teachers," provided that all copies are used and ultimately erased or destroyed pursuant to the guidelines.

Recordings may be used for teaching programs over any period of ten consecutive days within the forty-five-day retention period. During the rest of that forty-five-day period they should not be performed generally, although they may be viewed for pedagogical purposes by the faculty. In no event should a recording be altered in any way, or combined or merged with other recordings to make any sort of anthology or other compilation.

Although these guidelines speak of copying by educational institutions, there is no reason why they should not apply to copying by the teachers themselves, so long as the copies are made for instructional purposes. Furthermore, like all the fair use guidelines that have been developed, these represent a safe harbor, not the entire universe of fair use. For example, although CNN is commercial programming, I see no reason why someone at journalism school who is critiquing for her students the television coverage of the Gulf War should not have been able to tape CNN's news programs off the air and retain the tapes beyond the forty-five days. It cannot be too much stressed that fair use is a rule of reason and fairness, not a rigid set of rules.

COPYING OF COMPUTER PROGRAMS

None of the foregoing guidelines applies to copying of computer software. I am told that unauthorized copying of floppy disks is becoming a widespread practice in many schools. Any such copying is clearly beyond the bounds of fair use and should be avoided, unless of course the copies are strictly for archival purposes.

CLASSROOM PERFORMANCE OR DISPLAY

It is permissible for teachers and their students to perform or display any work in class so long as the class is held on campus or, if off campus, in classroom-type circumstances and classroom-type surroundings. However, you cannot show a motion picture or other audiovisual work or display individual images from such a work if you know or suspect that the copy you use was not lawfully made.

SPECIAL EXEMPTION: INSTITUTIONS FOR THE DEAF AND HEARING IMPAIRED

In the Conference Committee Report on the 1976 Copyright Act, Congress adopted the view of Congressman Robert Kastenmeier, one of its leading copyright authorities, that fair use covers certain uses of television programs by nonprofit educational institutions for the deaf and hearing impaired. Congressman Kastenmeier had said that such an institution can make an off-the-air copy of a television program, make a captioned version of it, perform that version within the confines of the institution, and lend it to similar institutions for similar use. This use will be fair use only if it is noncommercial in every respect and if its purpose is to contribute to the student's learning environment.[50]

LIBRARY COPYING

Among the issues of greatest concern in this area is that of copying for reserve use. Unfortunately Congress has not spoken on this matter. I believe that photocopying a chapter or similar small portion of a work for placement on reserve is a fair use, but this is no more than an informed guess.

The law does, however, specifically exempt from liability certain copying done in libraries.[51] (For convenience I use the word *library* to include archives.) The exemption is limited to circumstances in which the library making the copy owns the work as part of its own collection, only one copy is made, no charge is made for the copy beyond recovery of costs, and the copy made by the library bears the copyright notice that the work itself bears. Subject to these limitations it is permissible for a library to copy works under five circumstances:

1. If the work is unpublished and a copy is necessary for purposes of preservation and security. To qualify under this exemption, the copy must be in "facsimile form." The meaning of this phrase is extremely broad—it includes, for example, microfilm—but it does not include putting a work into machine-readable language for storage in an information system. What Congress had in mind when it made this distinction is unclear. A reasonable guess is that facsimile form is any form that stores the work in more or less its given appearance. Microfilm qualifies because it reproduces the printed page; a computer database will not qualify if it stores a work in text format. Might it qualify if it stored pages in bitmapped format? I cannot say.

2. If the work is unpublished and another library requests a copy for its own collection. Here, too, the copy must be in facsimile form.

3. If the work is published and the copy is needed to replace one that has been damaged, lost, or stolen, or is deteriorating. However, the library must first have made a reasonable effort to obtain an unused replacement at a fair price. The effort to find an unused replacement at a fair price would involve resorting to commonly known trade sources in the United States, to the publisher, and to any copyright owner other than the publisher (if the owner can be located at the address listed in any copyright registration that has been made of the work). It will also involve checking with any central photocopying service that is authorized to reproduce the work. Certain additional efforts beyond these may be regarded as reasonable in a particular case but will be unnecessary in most cases. A copy made under this exemption must be a facsimile copy.

4. If the work is in the last twenty years of its copyright, and the copy is needed for preservation, scholarship, or research. This exemption, uniquely, permits not only facsimile copying but also digital copying. It is not available if the work is in print (to use a soon-to-be-antiquated phrase) or otherwise generally obtainable from the copyright owner or its licensee. It is also not available if a copy can be obtained at a reasonable price. Note that this particular exemption does not speak of "reasonable efforts" to find a copy at a "fair price." The reason for this difference in language is obscure. In theory, it would create liability for the library if the copyright owner could prove that a copy was obtainable in some obscure place at a reasonable price, even if the library had been unable, after a reasonable effort, to find one. This seems absurd; one can only assume that in practice a reasonable search will exonerate the poor librarian. Finally, and most oddly, the statute denies the exception where the copyright owner provides notice that the work is commercially available or that a copy is available at a reasonable price. This makes no sense. If a copy is commercially available, then no notice is needed. If a copy is not commercially available, then a notice is not going to make it so, and a notice saying it is so amounts to fraud. I am truly at a loss to explain what Congress thought it was doing in enacting this language. Perhaps the Copyright Office, which has the duty of promulgating regulations for such notices, will be able to shed some light on the matter.

5. If the copy has been requested by a user of the library or by another library on behalf of one of its users. A copy made under this exemption must become the property of the user, and the library making the copy must have no reason to believe that it will be used for purposes other than private study, scholarship, or research. The exemption applies only if the library prominently displays a copyright warning

notice at the place where patrons order copies and on its order forms.[52] The form and placement of notice are prescribed by regulations, which are reproduced in appendix E. The exemption, moreover, is limited in subject matter; it does not apply to musical works, to pictorial or graphic works (except when used as illustrations of literary works), to sculptural works, or to motion pictures or other audiovisual works. Nor does it apply to any more than a small part of a work (meaning, in the case of a periodical or other collective work, one solitary contribution), unless a copy of the work cannot be obtained at a fair price after a reasonable effort of the type I have described above. Furthermore, this exemption does not apply if the library is systematically distributing photocopies of copyrighted material, except where copies are not obtainable in the market at a fair price.

What is "systematic" copying? With respect to user requests, copying is probably systematic if it is available to any user with no questions asked. Copying done on a case-by-case basis only, with a clear requirement that there be some special need for it, will probably be all right. With respect to interlibrary arrangements, copying is systematic if it is so great or continuous as to substitute, in practical effect, for a purchase or subscription. The National Commission on New Technological Uses for Copyrighted Works developed a set of specific guidelines to give flesh to this rather bare definition.[53] These guidelines, which have the unofficial blessing of Congress, may be summarized briefly:

- With respect to periodical issues less than five years old, one library may obtain from another no more than five copies of material from any given periodical—as opposed to any given issue of a periodical—in any given calendar year.
- With respect to material other than periodicals, one library may obtain from another no more than five copies of or from any given work in any one calendar year.

- No guidelines are given for periodical issues published more than five years before the date of the request.
- If the requesting library has on order or in its collection the item that it wants copied, but does not have the item in its possession at the time and cannot reasonably repossess it at the time, the copy made at its request will not count toward the maximum number of permissible copies. For example, if a library has a book out at the binder, it can request a copy from another library without using up any of its five-copy allowance.
- A library cannot satisfy a request unless it is accompanied by a representation from the requesting library that the request conforms with these guidelines, if these guidelines apply.
- Every library must keep on file for three years each request it makes to another library.

None of these library exemptions applies if a library has reason to believe that its copying is, or is part of, a concerted reproduction or distribution of multiple copies of the same material. A "related and concerted" reproduction can take place over a period of time and need not involve one single user, but can be with respect to a number of different users; it can also be found where a copy is requested by a group for the separate use of its various members.

None of the numerical restrictions on the library exemption applies to videotape copies of news programs. A library may tape news broadcasts off the air and lend them to scholars and researchers for research purposes. Presumably it may also lend to other libraries for the same purposes. However, the term "news programs" is fairly narrow. It does not apply to documentaries (except "documentary programs involving news reporting") or to magazine-format shows or other public-affairs broadcasts dealing with subjects of general interest.[54] For example, the special same-day reports prepared by the major networks on the downing of a Pan Am jet over Scotland were "news programs"; segments of "60 Minutes" devoted to discussion of terrorism are not.

None of these exemptions either restricts or expands the rights of fair use. It is conceivable that in some cases the library would be safe in going beyond the limitations described here if, in its considered judgment, the activity it contemplated was a fair use. On the other hand, the fact that a library may be exempt from liability in no way relieves an individual user who requests a copy from the library if the making of that copy would not be a fair use. In short these exemptions are for the benefit of the library and its personnel, not for persons making use of the library.

None of these exemptions overrules any contractual understanding a library may have with a copyright owner.

Finally, libraries are not liable for wrongful copying done on public machines if they have placed on the machines a warning against copyright infringement. (See appendix E.)[55]

REVERSE ENGINEERING

A particularly important question of copyright as applied to computer software is whether a competitor is entitled to copy a program solely for purposes of analysis, so as to be able to design a product that is better than or compatible with the original. In the software industry this is referred to as "reverse engineering." If the resulting product in any way copies the source code of the original, the obvious answer is a simple "no." But if the resulting product is noninfringing, what then?

The question has been hotly debated. The European Community allows reverse engineering, at least where the goal is to make the new product compatible with the old. Our own law started out on a much more ambivalent footing, but has recently shown a strong trend toward an even broader scope of fair use than Europe might permit. Two important Courts of Appeals have ruled that reverse engineering will be allowed as fair use to the extent that it is necessary to enable the second party to copy the unprotected elements—the ideas, etc.—of the first party's program.[56] This approach is eminently sound and in all likelihood will be adopted nationwide.

INFRINGEMENT (AND OTHER OFFENSES) ON THE INTERNET

The Internet has greatly increased the opportunities for distribution of copyrighted materials. It may ultimately change fundamentally how the copyright industries conduct their business, how they make their money, and how much money they make. It also, of course, has increased the opportunities for unauthorized distribution.

Some people, including breathless columnists for *Wired* magazine and the like, have hailed the era of the Internet as marking the end of copyright. Such announcements remind me of broadcasts from third world radio stations made by coup leaders before the government troops close in. Make no mistake about it, the government troops are closing in.

In late 1998, Congress enacted the most far-reaching copyright legislation of the last twenty years: a sweeping attempt to forestall cyberpiracy of every kind. Portentously named the Digital Millennium Copyright Act (DMCA), this legislation regulates in excruciating detail many of the activities that have posed the greatest threat to copyright owners. It protects the sanctity of copyright-related information placed on works by their copyright owners, and prohibits unauthorized decryption of encrypted works. It circumscribes the liability of online service providers, including those in academe as well as in commerce, but at the same time places new weapons in the hands of copyright owners policing infringement on the Internet. These are only its most prominent features.

The DMCA has an unusual history. It began in discussions among interested groups under the aegis of the Patent and Trademark Office, which was at the time seeking to exert influence over copyright issues beyond its normal purview. These discussions led to a "Green Paper" which I will discuss in a moment. From those discussions also grew an effort to develop an international treaty, under the aegis of the World Intellectual Property Organization (WIPO) in Geneva, Switzerland. The treaty negotiations ultimately bore fruit, although the fruit was much more modest than some had hoped. The treaty was brought back to the United States for ratification and implementation by statute. Attempts to get implementing legislation through Congress bogged down in an epic lobbying struggle, which in turn led to another year or two of intensive negotiations among interested parties. As will happen with such endeavors, the bill became the vehicle for a good many more agendas than it started out with, and the sheer gross weight of it slowed it down. But in the end it passed. Much of it is so complicated that no one but those who wrote it (and I'm not sure about them) can read it easily. In the discussion that follows I have endeavored to translate it into plain English, while sacrificing as few details as I could consistent with that goal.

First, though, a few comments on the Green Paper are in order.

In 1993 President Clinton appointed an Information Infrastructure Task Force to study the whole range of legal and other issues presented by the National Information Infrastructure (NII). Within that task force a Working Group on Intellectual Property Rights studied the copyright issues. Its preliminary draft report, while far from definitive, addressed a number of the interesting questions raised by the new digital technology. Because the preliminary report, styled a Green Paper, achieved so much attention among interested parties—and because it is so much more interesting than the watered-down White Paper that was ultimately released as the Task Force's formal statement on the issues—I will use the Green

Paper as a framework for some observations on some of the frequently asked questions concerning digital copyright.

When a work of visual art, performing art, or music is transmitted in digitized form, do we have a performance or display, or do we have a distribution?

The answer may have important implications. The owner of the distribution right may not be the same as the owner of the performance right, or the royalties owed may be different for the two rights. The question is even more important for sound recordings of musical works, since the owner of copyright in a sound recording, as discussed elsewhere in this book, has no performance right except for certain limited kinds of digital transmissions.

The Working Group proposed the idea that the transmission could be labeled a performance or a distribution depending on its "primary purpose." Such a test seems perilously and needlessly subjective. Whose "purpose" are we going to study, the sender's or the receiver's? If the receiver is authorized by the sender to make and retain a copy, and does so, then a distribution has occurred, regardless of the "primary purpose" and regardless of the time elapsed. (And if an unauthorized copy has been made, the reproduction right has been infringed.) In fairness the copyright owner should be paid for the reproduction, regardless of the fact that a performance or display also occurred and is being paid for. This should be a pricing and reporting issue, not a legal one. On the other hand, a transmission that the recipient can view, more or less simultaneously with the transmission, but is not allowed to retain, should be considered a performance or display even though the technology requires that the data be buffered, or stored in RAM, until the performance or display is complete. And of course one transmission can serve both purposes and exercise (or infringe) both rights.

The Working Group also asked another variant of the "performance (or display) vs. distribution" question: *When does unauthorized importation of a copy occur in the online context?*

This question is important because the copyright owner can prevent the unauthorized importation into this country of any copy of the work that was not lawfully made here and first sold by the copyright owner. One may argue that in fairness to the copyright owner, every transmission should be treated as an importation, since it enables the end user to obtain a copy, lawfully or otherwise. But if the transmission is clearly a performance designed to substitute for a broadcast-type performance, and the transmitter does not authorize downloading of the transmitted material, should this still be so? Traditional wireless television and radio broadcasts have never respected national boundaries, and copyright owners have been resigned to that for decades. Should a "performance" over the Internet be treated differently?

Should a copyright owner have the explicit right to prevent unauthorized transmission into the United States?

The Working Group proposed a statutory change to make clear that the copyright owner does have that right. Such a change seems unnecessary but harmless. The transmitter who acts without authorization is or is not infringing either the distribution or display right, depending on the factors already discussed.

Will the new online age require new definitions of fair use?

The Working Group did not say much on this point. It speculated, with considerable justification, that courts will be unfriendly to fair use claims in any context where an easy method of monitoring use and paying for copyright permission exists.

The greatest challenge in digital fair use cases will be to find the right analogy in our print past for events in the digital present and future. The Green Paper mentions one such challenge: how do we allow students to browse in a digital library as they have browsed in the hard-copy libraries of the past? From one perspective, there is little lost by allowing library users to browse through the library's digital holdings so long as they do not make unauthorized copies. Only the (comparatively) rare book of which a library would normally buy multiple circulation copies is disadvantaged by this. On the other hand, such an arrangement does infringe on the copyright owner's right of public display, and one can argue that a fee ought to be paid for the privilege of such display. The crux of the issue may be whether one views "browsing" as an inherent right, or simply as a compromise born of now-vanished technological constraints. The old library paradigm (runs the publishers' argument) arose out of the simple fact that limitations of space, and the expense of producing copies, drove scholars to share a centrally located physical copy. Where space is unbounded, and reproduction cheap, scholars will not willingly "share" a single dog-eared copy—nor is it conducive to research to require them to; they will seek their own individual copies, leading to multiple access that in a print world would require heavy purchases of duplicate copies. Should the publishers' claim here be rejected because the publisher is no worse off than it would have been had computers never been invented, or should the publisher reap the windfall (as the librarians see it) created by technology?

This is a fundamental and perplexing question. Framed as "Who reaps the windfall?," it has echoes in many other areas where technology has created new sources of wealth. Other questions like it will bubble to the surface the farther we move ahead into a digital world.

Also in the library context, the Green Paper opines that the special copying privileges given to libraries do not extend to digital copying unless the work to be copied is itself digital.

For example, a library may reproduce a work in "facsimile form" to replace a damaged or stolen copy if it determines "after a reasonable effort" that an unused replacement "cannot be obtained at a fair price." It is not as clear to me as it seemed to be to the Working Group that "facsimile form" excludes all digital reproduction of the work. Why should a more sophisticated, digitized bit-mapped image be treated differently from a photocopy? I think it no accident that we use the word "facsimile" for fax transmissions, and fax, though quintessentially a digital medium, is very close kin, technologically speaking, to photocopying.

It requires no fevered imagination to see other areas of fair use conflict. For example, will the rules that were created for educational photocopying be expanded to apply to electronic distribution over a schoolwide computer network? Will posting topical information on an electronic bulletin board be considered similar to "news," and hence favored in fair use terms, or will it be considered a common-or-garden distribution? (I discuss the issue of online service provider liability later in this chapter.)

Problems abound in the area of derivative works. When someone takes a digital image and "morphs" it to look like something altogether different, has an infringement occurred? Should we say yes because of the initial taking, or should we say yes or no based only on the finished product? It may be that the finished product in no way competes with the original. Holding it next to the original, we might not even call it a derivative work unless we know its ancestry, for nothing of the original can be recognized in it. And yet, the second artist has undeniably made use of the first artist's work.

The leading case on "intermediate copying" held the defendant liable. In that case, the defendant was an animation studio and was found in possession of unauthorized copies of Disney movies. It claimed that these were for study purposes only, and that it should be judged by its final product, which it claimed would be noninfringing. The court rejected the defense.[57]

This was an easier case for the plaintiff, though, than the cases that the digital age will present. Defendant had been caught *in medias res*, and the court was not required to believe its protestations of good intent. Had it come out with its noninfringing product before being sued, one wonders if the result would have been the same. In the context of digital morphing, where one artist's information is used as a sort of raw material, the speed with which the information can be manipulated makes it less likely that one will ever "get the goods" on an unauthorized user. And we need to be aware that leaning too hard on defendants in this whole nascent field of arts and letters may quash the creation of useful or important works. In fact, cases in the computer software field have allowed reverse engineering, including the making of copies where necessary to get at the unprotected components of a computer program.[58]

This is not an area where we can expect a frictionless electronic licensing scheme to operate. We cannot presume that artists will necessarily grant morphing licenses willingly to all comers, or that a one-size-fits-all payment schedule will be fair or appropriate. We will not be able to avoid making value judgments.

This problem already exists, for images can already be bit-mapped and morphed. But the Internet will magnify it greatly.

Nor is this problem necessarily limited to images, although images present its most interesting examples. What about databases? Downloading can be monitored and paid for, but not the user's end product. If that end product is not recognizably derived from the original database, is there an infringement? Will we ever know? Should we care?

Another interesting question involves so-called framing. A website can, through hypertext links, enable a user to view the text content of another website, but with its native advertisements, etc., stripped off. What you see on the screen is the linked text framed inside the initial home page's advertisements, etc. The owner of the linked text will complain that the "framer" is creating an unauthorized derivative work. Maybe so, maybe not. There are cases in the analog world that resemble this, but their outcomes are frankly less than coherent.[59]

In all of these controversies the risks are, on one hand, that a rush to cram novel methods of communication into inherited pigeonholes may stunt the growth of information technology and deprive us of the full functionality of the Internet; on the other hand, that the magic of it all will clothe old-fashioned theft in clever disguises.

In addition to discussing these broader issues, the Green Paper addressed the need to maintain the integrity of so-called "copyright management information." This was the least controversial part of the Green Paper, and it is the one part that ultimately came to life in the WIPO treaty and in the DMCA.

COPYRIGHT MANAGEMENT INFORMATION

The driving concern behind the "copyright management information" section of the Green Paper, the WIPO treaty, and the DMCA was that in entering the online world copyrighted works will lose their identity, encouraging piracy both witting and unwitting and making it impossible to trace. As will be seen, though, the cure goes well beyond the ostensible disease.[60]

Some of the elements of copyright management information are obvious: the copyright notice placed on a work; any other information that identifies the work, the author, and the copyright owner; the terms and conditions for use of the work. Other elements are not so obvious: if the work is an audiovisual work, any information identifying any writer, performer, or director who is credited in the work; in the case of any other sort of work (principally sound recordings), information identifying any performer whose performance is fixed in the work. Some of this information is relevant to the new performers' rights discussed in chapter 6, but some of it goes beyond that and is responsive to the concern of European countries, many of which give broader rights to film directors and the like than we do. Finally, copyright management information includes "identifying numbers or symbols referring to such information or [hyper]links to such information."

It is now unlawful to do any of the following, *whether in digital mode or in any traditional medium:*

- intentionally remove or alter any copyright management information;
- knowingly provide false copyright management information with intent to induce, enable, facilitate, or conceal infringement (presumably, infringement of any right protected under the copyright laws—although the statute does not explicitly say so, as it does in another context discussed two bullets below);
- knowingly distribute, or import for distribution, copyright management information that has been altered or truncated or that is false;
- distribute works or copies of works, or import them for distribution, knowing that copyright management information has been removed or altered without permission and knowing, or having reason to know, that doing so will induce, enable, facilitate, or conceal infringement of any right protected under the copyright laws, including the moral right and the new performers' rights;
- publicly perform any work knowing that copyright management information has been removed or altered without permission on the work itself, or on the copy of the work that

one is using for the performance, and knowing, or having reason to know, that doing so will induce, enable, facilitate, or conceal infringement of any right protected under the copyright laws.

There is a carve-out for law enforcement, intelligence, and other activities of any level of government—federal, state, or local. There is a sort of carve-out for broadcast and cable transmissions where removal of the information is necessary to prevent degradation of the signal, although Congress evidently anticipates that industry groups will very shortly agree upon standards that will make this carve-out obsolete.

The entire focus of the negotiations on the treaty and on the legislation was on digital technology. However, it is clear that the DMCA does not apply only to digital media. It is also clear that, wittingly or not, Congress has greatly expanded the moral right of attribution beyond the very narrow scope of the moral right section of the statute, discussed in chapter 6. Previously the right to be acknowledged as author of a work, or to remove a false attribution to oneself, applied only to an extremely narrow class of works of fine art. Now it applies to any work whatsoever, and to copies as well as to originals. Furthermore, unlike the express moral right, this *de facto* moral right lasts beyond the life of the author.

The statute says that any person injured by a violation of these provisions may sue for damages and injunctive relief. Damages may be actual damages or statutory damages; the latter may be not less than $2,500 nor more than $25,000 per violation—not per work, as is the case with statutory damages for infringement. Repeat offenders may be subject to treble damages. In addition, the court is empowered to award attorneys' fees to the prevailing party, which may of course be either the plaintiff or the defendant.[61]

If the violator was not aware and had no reason to believe that its acts constituted a violation, the court may reduce or eliminate any damage award; if the violator in these circumstances is a nonprofit library, archive, or educational institution, the court is required to eliminate the damage award.

Although the statute does not say so explicitly, it seems clear that one may recover damages under this section *in addition to* damages for straight copyright infringement. Thus, someone who infringes a work *and* removes copyright management information in so doing is exposed to two different types of damage claims.

Apart from civil penalties, a violator of this section of the statute is liable for criminal penalties if the violation is willful and for purposes of commercial advantage or private financial gain. The penalties are as steep as for copyright infringement, and, as with civil damages, appear to be additional to those for copyright infringement.[62]

What does all this do to fair use? Someone making a transformative use of digital material in the digital environment—a parodist, say—is not likely to retain all of the original copyright owner's copyright management information. Is this person liable for not less than $2,500 statutory damages? Probably not. This portion of the statute does not speak of fair use in so many words (although it does make a rather limp nod of acknowledgment to free speech, which may not be enjoined by a court enforcing these provisions). It does, however, say that alteration or removal of copyright management information is not a violation where permitted by the copyright owner "or the law," and "the law" does of course include fair use. The statute also says that it is not intended to alter in any manner the effect of other statutes designed to protect the privacy of Internet users. Thus, one may not under the guise of enforcing copyright management information do anything that would violate such a privacy statute. These are both welcome, if rather vague, reassurances.

ENCRYPTION AND DECRYPTION

In the digital world an ounce of prevention, if one could get it, would be worth many pounds of cure and many paragraphs of finger-wagging enactments like that described immediately above. The prevention that most interests copyright owners at present is encryption.

The copyright industries are working hard on technological fixes that will enable them to prevent piracy, or at least police it. One technology under development would restrict access to works on any machine, or network, for which the user had not expressly paid a fee; upon leaving that environment, the work would once again become cloaked with protection that could not be removed except by payment of yet another fee.

Encryption, of course, always inspires decryption. To prevent this, the treaty and now the enabling legislation forbid anyone to "manufacture, import, offer to the public, provide, or otherwise traffic in" anything that is designed or produced *primarily* to circumvent technological measures that effectively control access to copyrighted works or that effectively protect the rights of a copyright owner—for example, by making it impossible to copy a work without permission.[63] Technologies that pass this test—i.e., that are not designed or produced primarily for illicit decryption—will nonetheless be banned if their legitimate uses have only limited *commercial* significance (whatever that means). And finally, even if a technology survives both of these cuts, it is unlawful to *market* it as an anticircumvention measure. The only exception to all of this is for measures whose sole purpose is to prevent the access of minors to material on the Internet.

In addition to cutting off the flow of products that could defeat encryption measures, the statute also forbids anyone from personally gaining unauthorized access to a work by circumventing any technological measure that effectively controls access to the work. This particular part of the law does not become effective until October of 2000, and in the meantime the Librarian of Congress and the Register of Copyrights are charged with determining whether there are particular classes of works (whatever that means) to which this part of the law should not apply. Any such classes of works will be excluded for a three-year, renewable period. The determination of which classes, if any, to exclude, is to be made again in 2003 and every third year thereafter. One does not envy the Librarian and the Register this task.

Of course, excluding any works from this part of the statute may be helpful only to the technologically skilled. The rest of us, who could not crack an encrypted work without buying the tools from someone, won't be able to buy the tools.

There are a few exemptions to the broad sweep of this law. One rather odd one permits nonprofit libraries, archives, and educational institutions to gain unauthorized access to works "solely in order to make a good faith determination of whether to acquire a copy." What the librarians and educators thought they were getting by this is hard to say; is any sane copyright owner going to deny a potential customer the right to look at its wares?

More meaningful exemptions apply to law enforcement, intelligence, and other governmental activities. Others cover bona fide encryption research and security testing. Yet another exemption permits computer programmers to circumvent protection so as to reverse-engineer software, to the extent necessary for achieving interoperability with other programs, and permits the sale of technologies for this purpose. This exemption does not take a position on whether reverse engineering of any particular sort is permissible; it places the risk of determining that on the programmer. The risk is not negligible: to the extent that circumvention is used to facilitate reverse engineering that infringes copyright, the circumvention is itself unlawful, with the effect that the programmer concerned may be punished twice for the same course of conduct. (As discussed earlier in this chapter, some cases have blessed some reverse engineering as fair use; beyond the writ of those cases, you're on your own.)

On a plane more of interest to most of us, the law permits circumvention for the sole purpose of disabling a function that collects information on the user. The purpose here is to protect user privacy. The right to disable does not apply to encryption mechanisms that give the user clear warning that personal information will be collected and an opportunity to prevent or restrict such collection. Where one may disable, however, how is one to do that when the statute prevents the sale of technologies that would enable the circumvention? As with the excluded "classes" of works, only the geeks will benefit from this exemption.

The penalties for violation of this section of the statute are substantially the same as for violation of the copyright management information section and, like those, are in addition to damages for infringement.[64] The only difference is that the range of statutory damages, other than for repeat offenders, is between $200 and $2500 "per act of circumvention, device, product, component, offer, or performance of service." It seems right to have a lower range of damages where personal acts of circumvention are concerned, but odd to apply that same range to commercial products. In practice, though, circumvention technologies will probably be dealt with by injunction before they ever get to the stage of causing much damage.

Is fair use dead, as a result of all this? Theoretically, no; the law as such does not in any way limit the defense of fair use. But in practical terms, by restricting access through technological means the law is narrowing the field in which fair use can occur. Furthermore, by controlling access, copyright owners can compel their customers to sign contracts in which the customers give up rights of fair use. Unless the courts begin to hold that fair use is a constitutional right—something no court has yet done, but perhaps only because the issue has not been squarely presented—fair use could become a historical artifact of the analog age.

What about works that are outside of copyright? One of the disturbing things about this statutory scheme, as I have indicated more than once in the foregoing remarks, is that it does not distinguish in its effect between copyrighted material and public domain material. It may well be, for example, that the owners of databases that do not qualify for copyright will lock up their products inside technologies that are used "primarily" by the owners of valid copyrights. Once that happens, the database is effectively given protection by the copyright law—by this odd new part of the copyright law that attempts to control the flow of allegedly dangerous technology.

I am concerned, in short, by the sweeping breadth of this addition to the copyright law. Its conception and birth took place largely out of the public eye, although the public will be directly impacted by it to a major extent. Granted, there were voices speaking up for users of copyrighted materials, but they were special interest groups themselves, and in the end were bought off with some exclusions that don't do much for the ordinary citizen. It seems a mistake for Congress to act so preemptively with regard to new technologies whose nature and impact are still largely unknown.

ONLINE SERVICE PROVIDERS

In addition to pushing laws to protect their technological fixes, the copyright industries have attempted to deter piracy through litigation. However, most infringers on the Internet are highly mobile, even fly-by-night, and the copyright industries soon found it impractical if not impossible to pursue them. Instead, they put pressure on a much easier target: the online service providers (OSPs), through whose servers nearly all infringing material must pass at some point or other. They argued that OSPs should be treated like publishers, because they are involved in transmitting the material—and publishers are always liable for infringing content they publish, even if they publish it innocently.

Thus began another war of analogies, such as digital technology has repeatedly provoked. The OSPs protested that they were not publishers at all, because they exercised no control over what passed through their systems. Instead, they argued, they should be treated like phone companies, who are not liable for unlawful telephone calls.

This dispute might ultimately have sorted itself out through litigation, albeit at great length and expense. But then Congress began work on the DMCA; seeing their chance, the OSPs lobbied hard for their problem to be dealt with in the Act. They bargained intensively with the copyright industries. The result was, as part of the DMCA, a new Section 512 for the Copyright Act, entitled "Limitations on liability relating to material online."

This new section provides, in essence, a safe harbor for OSPs. They may not be held liable for damages, attorneys' fees, or any other monetary relief for infringing uses of their systems so long as they meet certain criteria and abide by certain rules. Failure to comply with these criteria and rules, however, does not deprive OSPs of whatever protection from liability they might otherwise have as a matter of general legal doctrine.

To be able to enter this safe harbor, an OSP must adopt and "reasonably implement" a policy of terminating subscribers who are repeat infringers, in appropriate circumstances. (The statute does not say what "appropriate circumstances" are, or how one must go about "reasonably implementing" one's policy.) The OSP must inform its subscribers and account holders of this policy. (A prudent OSP will include this policy in its subscriber contracts, and in periodic transmissions to all subscribers.) Furthermore, the OSP's system must be compatible with whatever standard technical measures may henceforth be used by copyright owners to identify and protect copyrighted works. Presumably, these measures might include standard forms of encryption and "copyright management information" discussed earlier in this chapter, as well as technologies such as digital "watermarking." However, the statute acknowledges that as of late 1998 such measures do not exist. It imposes an obligation on OSPs only to honor those that are developed "pursuant to a broad consensus of copyright owners and service providers in an open, fair, voluntary, multi-industry standards process," that are available to any person on "reasonable and non-discriminatory terms," and that do not impose substantial costs or burdens on OSPs. In other words, Congress has passed the task of filling in the blanks to the OSPs and copyright industries, while not imposing on the OSPs any obligation to agree to anything.

An OSP that meets these criteria must also follow certain rules to be certain of escaping liability for transmission (including routing and any necessary transient storage), storage, and "system caching" of infringing material on its system. There are separate rules governing each of these activities.

An OSP will be exempt from liability for an infringing transmission if the transmission occurs as part of "an automatic technical process" triggered by instructions from someone other than the OSP itself. The OSP must take no part in selecting or modifying the content of the transmission. It must exercise no say in who receives the transmission.

As regards storage, an OSP will not be liable for innocently allowing others to store infringing material on its system unless it has the right and ability to control infringing use of the material and receives a direct financial benefit from such infringing use. (An example of direct financial benefit would be a per-transaction fee paid to the OSP by the infringer.) The OSP will be considered innocent unless it has actual knowledge of the infringement, or the facts and circumstances that it does know are such that any reasonable person would infer the presence of infringement. Once it has that level of knowledge, it must act "expeditiously" to remove the material or disable access to it.

Third, an OSP will not be liable for referring or linking users to a site that contains infringing material or activity, so long as it meets the same conditions as apply to storage of infringing material (see preceding paragraph).

In the case of storage and linkage, but not mere transmission, the OSP has to meet a further obligation. It must have a designated agent to whom copyright owners can send notice of infringement that they believe is occurring on the OSP's system. The name, address, phone number, and e-mail address of this person must be posted on the OSP's website and sent to the Copyright Office, which is to maintain a directory of such persons and has the right to charge the OSPs a fee for the privilege. Until the Copyright Office adopts official regulations concerning this directory, you should use the draft forms posted on the Office's website (http://lcweb.loc.gov/copyright/forms/formfile). The form to use initially is called "Interim Designation of Agent to Receive Notice of Claimed Infringement." To amend it, use the "Amended Interim Designation [etc.]" form.

If a copyright owner believes that the OSP's system, or a linked site, contains infringing material or activity, the DMCA has choreographed an elaborate three-way dance. The copyright owner starts up the dance by sending a written notice to the OSP's designated agent. This notice must contain a physical or electronic signature of the person sending it, and give his or her contact information—name, address, phone number, and e-mail address. It must identify the work or works infringed. In the case of multiple works, a representative list of the works infringed will suffice. The notice must also identify the offending site and material, or the offending link or reference. Finally, it must state that the complaining party "has a good faith belief that use of the material in the manner complained of is not authorized by the copyright owner, its agent, or the law." It must state that the information in the notice is accurate. Finally, it must state that the signer of the notice is authorized to act on behalf of the owner of the right infringed, and this last statement must be notarized or otherwise made "under penalty of perjury."

If the notice fails to identify the infringed work or the infringing work, or fails to give adequate contact information for the sender, it is null and void and will not be construed as putting the OSP on notice of any infringement. If, however, it is defective in any other respect, the OSP has an obligation to follow up so as to "assist in the receipt of notification that substantially complies" with the foregoing rules.

Upon receipt of a notice that does comply with the rules, the OSP must "expeditiously" remove or disable access to the site or the link. Also, the sender of a fully compliant notice can get a subpoena compelling the OSP to reveal the identity of the alleged infringer.

And to protect OSPs against breach of contract claims by their subscribers, the DMCA provides that an OSP will not be liable to anyone if it removes or disables access to material identified in a valid notice or if the OSP in good faith believes that infringement is apparent, even if it turns out in the end that no infringement has occurred. But of course, in the real world, the OSP has to worry about more than legal liability to its subscribers. It must also worry about their loyalty, and shutting down customers' sites every time third parties claim infringement is not a way to win customer loyalty. The

DMCA recognizes this, though in an oddly backhanded way. For at this point, the focus of the dance shifts to the alleged infringer.

The DMCA provides that in order to be immune to contract claims from a subscriber accused of infringement, the OSP must take reasonable steps to notify the subscriber that it has removed or disabled access to the material that the subscriber has stored on the OSP's system. The subscriber then has the right to send a counternotice. The counternotice must identify the material in question and its former electronic address, and must contain the subscriber's name, address, telephone number, and physical or electronic signature. It must state under penalty of perjury that the subscriber in good faith believes the material was removed or disabled as a result of mistake or misidentification of the material. In this counternotice the subscriber must also consent to the jurisdiction of the Federal district court in the district where the subscriber's address is located, or (if the subscriber is outside the United States) in any district where the OSP may be "found" (i.e., sued), and the subscriber must agree to accept service of legal process from the person who gave the original notice of infringement.

Upon receipt of a counternotice that complies with these rules, the OSP must forward it promptly to the person who provided the original infringement notice, and inform that person that it, the OSP, will replace the removed material or cease disabling it, as the case may be, in ten business days. The OSP is then obligated to replace the removed material or cease disabling it, not less than ten and not more than fourteen business days after receipt of the counternotice, unless the OSP's designated agent first receives notice from the person who submitted the original infringement notice that such person has filed an action seeking a court injunction against the subscriber's infringement on the OSP's system. Here the dance finally ends.

All this is, to say the least, an intricate procedure. It does serve to balance the interests of the copyright owner and the alleged infringer, while keeping the OSP entangled in the middle no longer than necessary. Note, though, that the entire scheme gives a copyright owner the power to obtain, in effect, an injunction shutting down an alleged infringer for several weeks, possibly more, before the owner must finally appear in court, argue its case, and put money at risk.

Such a system could lead to substantial abuse. Anticipating this, Congress built into the law strong incentives to discourage abuse or manipulation. Each party is liable to the other for any knowing and material misrepresentation, in a notice or counternotice, as to whether the material in question is infringing or not infringing. It will also be liable to the OSP for damages and attorneys' fees resulting from the OSP's reliance on the misrepresentation.

The DMCA also provides immunity to OSPs in the matter of "system caching." System caching is the temporary storage on an OSP's system of material that has already been transmitted. Once material has been transmitted through an OSP's network once, to one subscriber, the OSP stores it in system cache for delivery to subscribers who make subsequent requests. By eliminating the need to send those subsequent requests back to the original source, the OSP saves bandwidth and provides faster delivery. This procedure does not hurt the original vendor of the material so long as the OSP does not interfere with the vendor's right to update or "refresh" material and to get full and accurate "hit" information back from buyers. To accommodate all these interests, the Act provides that an OSP will not be liable for system caching provided the OSP does not interfere with the rights of the copyright owner to be paid for usage, to receive user information, and so on, and complies with negotiated industry standards (which, as the statute acknowledges, do not yet exist). Where infringing material in a system cache originated with a subscriber, the rules I have described above concerning storage liability apply, except that the OSP's obligation to remove or disable access to system-cached material arises only if the notice of infringement states that the material has already been, or is under court order to be, removed or disabled at the original source.

All of the above limitations on OSP liability apply to damages and other monetary relief. They do not exempt an OSP from injunctive relief. However, the DMCA does restrict the kinds of injunctions that can be issued. In the context of storage of infringing material, the injunction can force the OSP to deny access to a particular online site, or to shut down specified accounts of a specified individual. In the context of infringing transmission, the injunction may only compel the OSP to terminate specified accounts of a specified individual, or to take reasonable steps to block access to a specified online location outside the United States. These limitations mean that the court cannot by injunction turn the OSP into a police or peace-keeping force.

Finally, it is important to bear in mind that though I have focused largely on Internet OSPs, the statute is not limited in that way. It applies to any online network, including intracompany and educational networks. However, there is a special exemption available to educational institutions that meet certain criteria. Many colleges and universities have developed campuswide electronic networks carrying everything from administrative messages to homework assignments. Often these are linked to the institutions' libraries. Such networks present obvious opportunities for copying and distribution of textbooks, journal articles, and the like without copyright permission.

The educational community argued strenuously that most conduct of this sort is by faculty and graduate teaching assistants acting on their own, without the blessing of the Dean's office. Furthermore they argued, and Congress agreed, that academic freedom requires that institutions forbear from constant monitoring of their faculties' conduct. The compromise they worked out relieves a college or university from liability for infringements committed by its faculty and teaching assistants in the course of genuine teaching and research, if the institution has provided to all users of its system "materials that accurately describe, and promote compliance with," copyright restrictions. In no event does the exemption apply where the professor or teaching assistant puts up on the network anything that he or she recommended or required for any course during the previous three years. (We hear in this an echo of the older rule of "spontaneity" in classroom photocopying.) Furthermore, if the institution receives in any three-year period two or more good faith notices of infringement, of the type I have described above in the commercial context, with respect to any particular teacher, the institution will be liable for any infringements committed by that teacher in the following three years, even if those notices turn out to have been incorrect.

All in all, this is not much of an exemption. To make matters worse, an institution that takes shelter on these terms from a damage award cannot at the same time invoke the limitations on injunctive relief that are granted to other OSPs. This means, among other things, that an institution may be compelled to do more than simply shut down a particular teacher's access to the system. Any court asked for such an injunction must consider other mitigating factors, such as whether restrictions would unduly burden the institution or interfere with access to noninfringing material by other users, and whether "other less burdensome and comparably effective means of preventing access to the infringing material" are available.

As you will have noticed, the statute seems to take as a given that the posting of material on the school's network can be an infringement even if carried out for genuine teaching or research purposes. As far as "teaching" is concerned, this breaks no new ground; the classroom photocopying guidelines spring from the same assumption. But to extend this assumption to research use, in a nonprofit educational institution, is a step no court and no previous Congress has taken. Granted, the new Section 512 contains various platitudes at the end to the effect that nothing in it is intended to limit the doctrine of fair use. But the message of the statute is that in the online world, at least, the sharing of materials among researchers cannot be presumed acceptable.

9 Works Created before 1978

So far I have dealt with the law that applies to works created in 1978 or thereafter. In all respects but one it is also the law that applies to works created but neither published, nor registered with the Copyright Office as unpublished works, before 1978. (The previous federal statute permitted registration of certain works of the performing and visual arts prior to publication.) The one difference has to do with duration of the copyright term. The law makes a special provision for works in this category: no copyright for such a work can expire before December 31, 2002, and, furthermore, if the work is published before that date, its copyright will not expire before December 31, 2047.

Works that were published or registered before 1978 are governed by a different set of rules. Although in many respects the new law applies to those works, several fundamental provisions of the old system that have otherwise been discarded also apply. Since these works are by far the majority of works in existence and will be for many years to come, it is important to know those portions of the old law that are still of concern.

Publication and Notice under the Old Law

Chief among the basic premises of the old copyright system was the division between statutory copyright and common law copyright, a division based on the concept of publication. Common law copyright was, in essence, the right of "first publication"; it entitled its owner to exploit his work exclusively and in almost any manner for an unlimited period of time, so long as he did not publish it, and it entitled him to be the first to publish the work. Beyond that the common law would not go; once you published your work, you either assumed the mantle of federal statutory copyright or, if you did not properly protect yourself, you forfeited your work to the public domain.

At the moment of first publication within the United States, notice became crucial. (What effect notice or lack of notice in foreign publication had is an unresolved dispute.)[1] If you affixed proper notice to the work, you automatically secured statutory copyright. If you failed to affix proper notice, your work went into the public domain.

REQUIREMENTS FOR NOTICE UNDER THE OLD LAW

Notice requirements under the old law[2] were much the same as they are today (as described in chapter 4), with certain important differences:

1. The date of first publication was not required except on printed copies of literary, musical, or dramatic works, and on phonorecords (called "reproductions" in the old law) of sound recordings.

2. On the first publication, only the name of the copyright proprietor could be used. Thus on first publication the person whose name appeared in the notice had to be the owner of the entire copyright.

3. The full name of the copyright owner had to be used except on visual works and sound recordings; abbreviations, trademarks, and other symbols were not acceptable. If the name given in the notice on a visual work was in fact a trademark or other symbol, the full and proper name had to appear somewhere, even if only on the bottom or back of the work.

4. Placement of the notice was strictly regulated. In the case of any printed work other than a periodical, notice had to be placed on the title page or the page immediately following. In the case of a periodical, it had to be placed on the title page or on the first page of text of each separate issue or

under the title heading. In the case of sheet music or other printed musical work, it went on the title page or the first page of music. And in the case of phonorecords and visual works, it went in some "reasonable" place. ("Reasonable" had basically the same meaning as under the 1976 Act.)

5. Any defect in the notice, including omission of any part of proper notice, caused the work to be treated as if notice had been omitted entirely. There were only two exceptions. If, by accident or mistake, the year given in the notice was earlier than the true year of first publication, the copyright term simply began in the earlier year, and if, by accident or mistake, the year given was later than the true year by no more than a year, the fault was overlooked, at least where no innocent person, relying on the faulty notice, had begun to exploit the work thinking it to be in the public domain.[3] (This charitable approach to notices defective by only one year was a comparatively recent development.)

Under the old law, if notice was omitted or given improperly, copyright was lost. There were not all the special indulgences provided in the new law for registration within five years, and so on; what was done could not be undone. There were only two exceptions. First, omission of proper notice had no effect if the copies or phonorecords were distributed without the authority of the copyright owner. Second, omission from a very small number of copies, if caused by accident or mistake (other than mistake as to what the law required), did not affect the copyright; however, an innocent person acting in the belief that the work was in the public domain (having been misled by the lack of notice) would not be liable for damages and could be enjoined from further infringement only if the copyright proprietor agreed to reimburse him for his out-of-pocket expenses.

NOTICE UNDER CURRENT LAW FOR WORKS FIRST PUBLISHED BEFORE 1978

The 1976 Act provides that works first published before 1978 may continue to abide by the old formalities of notice. Any new copies or phonorecords of those works can bear either the notice that was acceptable under the old law or that required by current law. However, the reverse is not true. If copies or phonorecords distributed before 1978 did not carry notice that was proper at the time, the consequences will be governed by the old law, even though the notice might be permissible by post-1977 standards.[4]

"RESTORATION" OF FOREIGN COPYRIGHTS

As part of U.S. adherence to the North American Free Trade Agreement (NAFTA), and later the General Agreement on Tariffs and Trade (GATT), Congress added a new Section 104A to the Copyright Act. This new section grants or restores U.S. copyright to large classes of foreign works. It was billed as solely a restoration of previously lost copyrights, but in many cases it actually creates rights that were never lost because they never existed in the first place. Whether the euphemism of "restoration" was a sop to European pride—for the Europeans pressed hardest for this change in our law—or a sugar-coating for domestic political consumption, who can say? The bottom line is that the United States has made a major change in its treatment of foreign works.

WHAT COPYRIGHTS ARE RESTORED?

The first version of Section 104A, enacted in compliance with NAFTA, restored to copyright a very narrow class of Mexican and Canadian works: films (and any new works, such as original musical scores, incorporated in those films) that were first published on or after January 1, 1978, and before March 1, 1989, and that lost U.S. copyright through omission of proper copyright notice. Restoration was contingent on the copyright owner's filing a statement with the U.S.

Copyright Office during 1994, and became effective on January 1, 1995.

With U.S. adherence to GATT, this rather narrow statute has been replaced with one of much greater breadth and depth—although, as will be seen, much greater textual problems.

The classes of works that are "restored" to copyright under GATT, or at least eligible for restoration, are these:

• Foreign works that forfeited U.S. copyright by failure to use proper notice. (See endnote 1 of this chapter.) Since in most cases such works were never published in the United States, copyright was often forfeited through sheer ignorance of U.S. law on the part of foreign publishers. In this respect restoration seems only fair. However, the broad sweep of restoration will no doubt benefit some foreign works that were published in the United States with inadequate notice, and such works will be granted benefits for which U.S. works with the same defects are not eligible.

• Foreign works that forfeited U.S. copyright by failure to renew after expiration of the first twenty-eight-year term. Here the moral case for restoration seems weaker, since we are speaking of authors who secured proper U.S. copyright in the first term but failed to follow U.S. procedure for the renewal term. Nevertheless their works are restored to copyright where those of U.S. authors who committed the same error are left in the public domain.

• Foreign sound recordings fixed before February 15, 1972. U.S. domestic sound recordings of identical vintage are still denied U.S. copyright, though they may qualify for state law protection. Here is the most extreme example of a whole new grant of rights masquerading as a "restoration."

• Works created in countries that at the time of creation were not parties to any copyright treaty with the United States. Here again are new, not "restored," rights.

All this was, quite explicitly, the price that the United States had to pay to obtain support from other Berne Convention countries for inserting tough intellectual property standards into GATT. What the United States got in return was international commitment to: copyright protection of computer programs and databases; recognition of a rental right for computer programs and sound recordings; protection abroad of existing U.S. sound recordings; a minimum of fifty years' protection for sound recordings; and a minimum of fifty years' protection for motion pictures and other corporate-authored works.

If you are concerned with the copyright status of a work that potentially falls into one of the above categories of restored works, you need to ask the following questions to ascertain if restoration is in fact available:

Who is the author? The simplicity of this question is deceptive. The question must be answered by referring to the law of the "source country" of the work, not to U.S. law. Identifying the source country of a work has its own pitfalls, as will be seen shortly, but so long as the United States is not the "source country" restoration may be available.

If the source country takes a narrower view of work made for hire, for example, than American law, the person entitled to the restored U.S. copyright may be the creative employee, not the employer to whom American law would normally have attributed the right. Or if the source country grants joint authorship only to works where the two authors' contributions are truly inseparable (as is the rule in most countries other than the United States), rather than merely interdependent, there will be two copyrights to deal with, not one.

The one exception to the above lies in the case of sound recordings. Where the work is a sound recording, one should ask not "Who is the author?" but *Who is the right holder?* The "right holder" of a sound recording is whoever first makes an authorized fixation of the sound recording in tangible form, or whoever now owns the rights that that person had. Under American law that person might well also qualify as the "author" of the sound recording, but the statute is deliberately worded to avoid any argument that under foreign law some other person might be regarded as author. Thus, in most cases, we are looking for the recording company or its successor. For convenience, I am going to use the word "author" throughout this analysis, but read "right holder" for "author" wherever a sound recording is concerned.

What is the source country of the work? The answer to this depends in large measure on whether the work is "published" or not. The GATT legislation does not define "publication," so presumably we should apply the normal criteria of U.S. domestic law to ascertain if a work is published. Whether the work is published or not, the source country must be a signatory of one of several copyright treaties, or be subject to a special Presidential proclamation. The treaties are Berne, the World Trade Organization, the World Intellectual Property Organization Copyright Treaty, and the World Intellectual Property Organization Performances and Phonograms Treaty. Most if not all countries that belong to one of the latter two will also belong to Berne or the WTO, and few of those that do not belong will be significant sources of copyrightable works with any value in the American market. But for the sake of completeness I will refer to all foreign countries that fall into any of the above categories as "treaty parties."

If a work is published, then the "source country" of the work is the country where first publication occurred. If the work was first published in two countries (neither being the United States) within thirty days of each other, and each is a treaty party, the country having the most significant connection with the work is the source country. If the work was first published in a treaty party but was then published in the

United States within thirty days thereafter, the work is not eligible for restoration.

If, on the other hand, the work is unpublished, its source country is the nation where the author is a citizen regardless of where the work might have been created and regardless of what the author's citizenship might have been at that time. In the case of a corporation or other business entity, read "domicile" (legal situs) for citizenship.

If an unpublished work has multiple authors who are citizens of or domiciled in more than one country, the source country is whichever of the eligible countries is connected to the majority of authors, unless the majority are U.S. authors, in which case the source country is the country other than the United States having the most significant connection with the work. The statute does not say what would happen if there were no majority to be found—for example, if there were only two authors, each from a different Berne country. Presumably, one would seek to identify the country with the most significant connection to the work.

A circularity is embedded in this regime: the author of an unpublished work is determined under the law of the source country, but the source country is determined by the identity of the author. Fortunately, few restored works are likely to present this difficulty. Although the evidence is only anecdotal, it seems likely that most works eligible for restoration are published works that lost copyright protection due to noncompliance with U.S. formalities.

What was the citizenship or domicile of the author(s) at the time the work was created? Unless at least one of the country or countries you identify in answer to this question is a treaty party, the work will not be eligible for restoration, even if the source country of the work itself meets all eligibility criteria. This requirement seems to have been designed largely to exclude from restoration the oeuvre of American authors first published abroad—a small but culturally significant body of work.

Is the work still subject to copyright in its source country? If not, it is not eligible for restoration.

Assuming one has passed these threshold tests of restoration, one turns next to the mechanics of restoration.

WHEN DOES RESTORATION OF COPYRIGHT OCCUR?

Restoration took effect on January 1, 1996, or on whatever later date the source country became a treaty party. For most countries' works, January 1, 1996, is the operative date.

Restoration is not retroactive. The copyright owner of a restored work cannot sue for uses of the work that occurred before the restoration date. Even an act of infringement that occurs now may be beyond reach if the infringement was "commenced" before the date of restoration, or if certain other conditions (which I will discuss presently) are met.

WHO GETS THE RESTORED COPYRIGHT?

The copyright in a restored work vests originally in the author or the initial right holder. This vesting rule is significant. The statute in effect ignores the intervening history of the restored copyright, and looks all the way back to the time of its birth. Congress evidently wished to give the windfall of a restored U.S. copyright to the author of the work, regardless of who might be the current copyright owner. However, this will not prevent the law of the source country, or the relevant contracts among the interested parties, from reallocating the restored right to the author's heirs or assignees. In fact, the limited statutory history suggests that the drafters of the statute expected the rights to be reallocated from the author or first right holder in this manner to whoever would be their present owner had no forfeiture ever taken place.[5]

Among the interesting anomalies that this vesting rule creates is that the whole elaborate statutory scheme governing who succeeds to the second term of U.S. copyright, where a work is renewed after the author's death, counts for nothing in the case of a restored work. (That scheme is discussed later in this chapter.) The copyright term of a restored work is treated as a unitary whole, of life plus fifty (now seventy) years in most cases, not two terms of twenty-eight years and sixty-seven years, respectively. Here again, Congress has chosen to apply a set of rules to restored foreign works quite different from what applies to the works of U.S. authors, and even to the works of foreign authors who played by U.S. rules and renewed their copyrights.

WHAT HAPPENS TO PEOPLE WHO HAVE BEEN EXPLOITING RESTORED WORKS IN THE UNITED STATES?

The prospect of old copyrights arising from the grave is naturally terrifying to those who have, like the suitors of Odysseus's wife, caroused at the supposedly departed's table. In a partial attempt to address the legitimate interests of such persons, Congress has created a complex, and not altogether comprehensible, transitional scheme. Part of this scheme involves a new legal character known as a "reliance party."

A reliance party is one who:

- engaged in acts that would constitute infringement of a since-restored copyright, prior to December 8, 1994 (or whatever later date the source country of the work becomes a treaty party),[6] and continues to engage in these acts after that date, or
- prior to that date acquired a copy or phonorecord of the work, or
- is a successor in business of such a person, or
- acquired "significant assets" from such a person by assignment or license. The statute does not define "significant assets." The phrase seems designed to protect, for example, a publisher that acquired a whole list of titles from another publisher. An isolated sale or license of a particular work probably will not qualify. This means, among other things,

that a licensee of a reliance party is not necessarily itself a reliance party.

To assert a restored copyright against a reliance party, the owner of all rights or any exclusive right in the work must prepare a "notice of intent to enforce the restored copyright." (See appendix H for the format of this notice.) This notice may be served on a reliance party at any time after restoration. Alternatively, it could be made effective against all reliance parties if filed with the U.S. Copyright Office within two years after the date of restoration of the copyright (i.e., in most cases, before January 1, 1998). The notice must contain, at a minimum, the title of work with an English translation, any other titles known to the owner by which the restored work may be identified (which would presumably include, for example, English title translations used by reliance parties), the name of the owner of the right(s) concerned, and an address and telephone number where that owner can be reached. The notice must be signed by the owner. The owner's agent may sign the notice if authorized in writing to do so. The notice may cover multiple works by the same author. If filed with the Copyright Office, it should be sent to:

URAA/GATT, NIEs
P.O. Box 72400
Southwest Station
Washington, DC 20024.

Publication of the notice by the Copyright Office in the Federal Register, or service of the notice by the copyright owner on the reliance party, begins the running of a twelve-month grace period.[7] During this grace period the reliance party may not make any copies of the work but is otherwise free to make use of the work without liability. After the grace period, any new or continuing use will be an infringement, with one exception. A reliance party may continue to exploit an "existing derivative work" for the duration of copyright so long as it pays a reasonable royalty for the use.

An "existing derivative work" is a derivative work created before (i) December 8, 1994, if the source country of the underlying work was a treaty party on that date, or (ii) in other cases, before the United States has either Berne or WTO treaty relations with the source country of the underlying work.[8] But what if the derivative work has not been completed by the cutoff date: is the derivative work author entitled to finish it according to plan? Does it matter how near completion it is on the cutoff date? There may be room for argument.

Another concern raised by the restoration of copyrights that had been considered dead and gone is the status of contractual commitments regarding the affected works. Those commitments typically include promises by licensees to exploit works, and warranties by licensors of their right to license. To deal with such concerns, Section 104A specifically provides that no one who made a commitment before January 1, 1995, to exploit a work that is now restored to copyright can be held to his promise if that would force him to infringe the copyright. On the other side of the coin, no one who gave a warranty of noninfringement before January 1, 1995, may be held liable under that warranty if it proves false because of the restoration of a copyright. For example, if an author warranted to a publisher in a 1994 contract that her use of old English photographs is noninfringing, she may not now be held to account under that warranty if the copyright in the photographs is restored. Nor, on the other hand, may the publisher be compelled to publish those photographs.

One last quirk of this new statute should be noted in passing. It concerns statutory damages. The general rule, discussed in chapter 7, is that a plaintiff in an infringement suit may elect to recover statutory damages, which are to be determined in the court's discretion, rather than actual damages, which must be proved to the jury. This election may be made so long as the work, if unpublished, has been registered before infringement begins, or, if published, has been registered either before infringement begins or within a grace period of three months after the first publication. With regard to restored works, the new statute provides that an infringement by a reliance party will be deemed to have preceded registration—making the copyright owner ineligible for statutory damages—if the unauthorized use of material from a restored work precedes the date of restoration.

In most instances this provision would be redundant. But it would make a difference if, for example, a foreign work had been registered but had fallen into the public domain through failure to use proper copyright notice. In such a case the earlier registration would be disregarded and the work would be ineligible for statutory damages.

As noted above, the act provides that a reliance party who uses an "existing derivative work" must pay a reasonable royalty. When the reliance party and the copyright owner of the restored underlying work cannot agree on a license fee or royalty terms, the matter may be taken before a federal district judge. How is a judge to be guided in awarding compensation to the copyright owner? The statute says that the compensation—be it a royalty, a one-time fee, or anything else—must "reflect any harm to the actual or potential market for or value of the restored work ... as well as the relative contributions *of expression* of the author of the restored works and the reliance party" (my emphasis). This phrase "relative contributions of expression" is an invitation to endless argument. Courts have grown used, in awarding copyright damages, to assessing the contribution made by an infringer to the commercial value of the infringer's product. In one famous case, no less a judge than Learned Hand (who was no friend of Hollywood) gave Hollywood its due by holding that much of the profits of an infringing movie were due to the stars who played the roles, and similar factors, rather than to the material stolen from the plaintiff's play, and denied the plaintiff that share of profits.[9] But the phrase "contributions of expression" seems to contemplate something very different from contributions of *value*. It threatens to embroil the judge in literary criticism rather than simple market analysis. In fact, it does not appear to permit the court even to consider the economic realities that Learned Hand observed.

Most disconcerting about this provision of the statute is that it does not appear to give any deference to industry custom. A court cannot simply say: standard industry royalties are X percent of gross, so henceforth the reliance party will pay the copyright owner X percent of gross. Perhaps the court will get to that result, but only after beating around the bush weighing "harm to the market" and so on. The best hope is that both parties, contemplating the mysteries of this judicial process, will be moved to settle their differences before submitting to it.

I mentioned above that one type of "reliance party" is a person who made or acquired a copy of a work prior to January 1, 1995 (or the earliest later date that the United States and the source country of the work have treaty relations). A reliance party is free to sell any such copy for a period of twelve months after publication or actual receipt of the copyright owner's "notice of intent to enforce" the copyright. Surprisingly, the prohibition on sale of copies after the twelve-month grace period is binding not only on the reliance party but on persons downstream in the chain of title as well. The "first sale" doctrine, which in general permits endless resale of lawfully acquired copies, does not apply, after the twelve-month grace period, to copies that were made before the publication or service of the copyright owner's notice. In theory, a secondhand bookseller could be infringing copyright by reselling a copy that had not been authorized. It is hard to believe that the drafters of the statute intended such a thing, but that is what they have written.[10]

COPYRIGHT OWNERSHIP UNDER THE OLD LAW

INDIVISIBILITY AND THE PERIODICALS PROBLEM

The problem of notice brought into play another important principle of the old law, one that the new law has gone to great lengths to eliminate: that copyright ownership was indivisible. You could give other people licenses to use your work in one way or another, but you could not sell them any absolute right under the copyright; the only absolute transfer you could make was of the entire copyright as an undivided whole. This concept caused particular difficulties in the area of notice because the old statute specifically stated that notice at the time of first publication had to be in the name of the copyright owner or it would be considered to be no notice at all, and the work would go into the public domain. Thus if you gave a magazine permission to make first publication of a story, but neither transferred copyright ownership to the magazine nor insisted that separate notice be inserted in your own name, copyright notice in the name of the magazine would not protect your copyright.

Over the course of time courts made many inroads in this rather rigid formalism, primarily by finding that an author had in fact conveyed all of his rights to the magazine, but that the magazine held them in trust for him, with a promise to reconvey them after publication. In 1970 the Second Circuit Court of Appeals (generally a bellwether court in copyright matters) simply abandoned the whole doctrine of indivisibility, so far as notice was concerned, at least where the author has shown no intention of abandoning his copyright.[11] Thus if you made any sale or license of magazine rights after 1970, the chances are great, even though a court will be obliged to apply the old law to your case, that you will be protected by whatever notice was put on the magazine as a whole. Indeed in most cases the Second Circuit's view could probably be applied to pre-1970 situations as well.

Presumably this 1970 opinion swept away another old doctrine as applied to periodicals: that if a publisher, having secured copyright in its own name, conveyed its rights to someone else, the name in any copyright notice on the work could not be changed until the conveyance had been recorded with the Copyright Office.[12]

Not only was copyright indivisible in itself; before first publication or federal registration it generally traveled with the tangible object in which the work was fixed, assuming that object was the unique fixation of the work. Sale of an unpublished manuscript or painting, for example, carried with it the sale of common law copyright in the work unless the seller expressed some clear intent to the contrary.[13] This rule was reversed by statute (at least as to works of fine art, though not as to manuscripts) in New York in 1966 and in California in 1976.[14] ("Fine art" in the New York law meant paintings, sculpture, drawings, or graphic art. In California it meant any kind of visual art.) It is not clear, however, what would happen if the case were to arise now concerning a sale carried out in either of those states before their laws were changed or in any state other than California and New York before 1978. Perhaps the old rule would be ignored, but I can offer no guarantee.

WORKS MADE FOR HIRE

The old law was much looser than the new law in its approach to works made for hire. Whether a work fell under the rule depended entirely on the intent of the persons involved. This meant that most commissioned works were regarded as works made for hire, but it meant also that an employer and employee could agree to waive the rule and could do so either orally or in writing.

There was some disagreement in the case of a commissioned work as to whether the commissioning party was to be treated as the author or only as the owner of the first-term copyright. The latter seems to be the prevailing view.[15] However, since the intent of the persons involved is a factor here as well, the question is open to litigation.

Whether a work was made for hire, and whether in the case of a commissioned work the hirer got the entire copyright or only the first-term copyright, will be particularly important questions in the context of termination rights. They will also continue to affect the ownership of renewal rights.

JOINT WORKS

In most respects the old law governing joint works does not differ from current law. However, the 1976 Act rejected one doctrine that still has validity for pre-1978 works. This doctrine, first stated in what is known as the "12th Street Rag" case, is that intent to create a joint work can arise after one of the joint authors has already completed his part of the work.[16] Euday L. Bowman had composed "12th Street Rag" as an instrumental piano solo and then assigned his rights to a publisher. The publisher commissioned lyrics for it. Bowman had no notion of setting words to his music; it was entirely the publisher's idea; nonetheless the court held that the resulting song was a joint work, giving the lyricist copyright in the music as well as the lyrics.

The court stressed that what mattered was the intent of whoever owned the copyright at the time the contributions were brought together, not the intent of either author at the time of creation. Effectively it permitted someone to trade exclusive rights in a work for joint ownership in a larger work. The doctrine would not extend, for example, to someone who sold movie rights in a novel to a producer, for in that case the seller does not intend that the novel will become merely a part of a movie.

Limited as it may be, this "12th Street Rag" doctrine will continue to affect royalty rights and renewal rights even under present law, and will also have repercussions for the termination rights created by the 1976 Act. It should therefore be taken into account whenever you are dealing with a pre-1978 work that can be interpreted as a joint work.

SPECIAL RULES FOR PRE-1978 SOUND RECORDINGS AND PHONORECORDS

The copyright status of sound recordings under the 1909 Act presented thorny questions for decades. Just before enactment of the 1909 Act, the Supreme Court had issued an opinion holding that player piano rolls could not be considered infringing "copies" of a musical work because the musical work could not be perceived visually from them.[17] From this it followed, more or less logically, that the original piano rolls—and by extension, in the following decades, vinyl albums and cassette tapes—were themselves not copyrightable because they embodied no work that could be visually perceived from them.

Congress had little incentive, in those early days, to wade into this issue. So it said nothing about sound recordings in the original version of the 1909 Act. It was left to the states to pass record piracy laws, and many of them did.[18] However, as of February 15, 1972, federal law was amended so as to apply to sound recordings published on or after that date. The new law largely carries this forward, with certain changes in the terms of the compulsory license. But sound recordings made before February 15, 1972, will continue to be protected by state piracy laws until February 15, 2047, after which date they will be protected by federal laws or not at all.[19]

For pre-1972 sound recordings, copyrightability was not the only question. A related concern was whether sale of phonorecords (as they are now called) of those sound recordings could be said to "publish" the underlying musical work, with all the consequences that entailed. The prevailing view for decades was that it would not, and accordingly that no copyright notice regarding the music should be placed on phonorecords. But in 1995 the Ninth Circuit Court of Appeals ruled to the contrary. Since this ruling, if carried through, would have plunged a good many valuable musical works into the public domain, the music industry lobbied strenuously to have it overturned. Ultimately, in 1998, the Copyright Act was amended specifically to overturn the Ninth Circuit opinion. Thus, the rule is now clear that pre-1972 phonorecords did not "publish" their underlying musical works.[20]

COPYRIGHT TERM FOR PRE-1978 WORKS

Under the old law copyright lasted for a twenty-eight-year term, but could be "renewed" for a second twenty-eight-year term. Thus, for example, a copyright secured on May 12, 1932, would have run through May 11, 1960. If a copyright was not renewed in the last year of its first term, it went into the public domain. If it was renewed, it went into the public domain at the end of the second term. However, during the years that Congress was deliberating over the new statute, the expiration of second-term copyright was repeatedly postponed. Any work still in its renewal term on September 19, 1962, remained covered as of January 1, 1978. On January 1, 1978, the renewal term of any work then under copyright was extended from twenty-eight years to forty-seven years, with ramifications I will discuss presently. And in 1998, the renewal term was extended by a further twenty years, for those works published in 1923 or later, for a total protected term of ninety-five years. (The twenty-year extension does not apply to works whose forty-seven-year renewal term had expired before 1998.)

The law governing the mechanics of renewal were also substantially changed, effective January 1, 1992. Depending on when a work first came under federal copyright protection, the method and the impact of renewal varies substantially. I will describe the old regime first, and then describe how it has changed—and not changed.

RENEWAL BEFORE 1992

Renewal of copyright was accomplished by filing an application for renewal with the Copyright Office in the last year of the original twenty-eight-year copyright term. This application could be filed by anyone, or on behalf of anyone, who was or might be entitled to the renewal term. Whether the person entitled had to be alive on the day that the renewal term was to begin, or merely to survive long enough to file for renewal in the twenty-eighth year of the first term, was a matter of dispute between the courts—a dispute that the 1976 Act did nothing to resolve.[21] Whichever might be the magic date, if the person entitled to the renewal did not live to see that date the renewal copyright would go to someone else. The right to renew was thus a mongrel sort of creation—rather like the termination right created by the new law—possessed only as long as you lived. If you died before your renewal right vested, the right to renew your copyright might pass to your heirs, and someone who had purchased the renewal copyright from you would be out of luck.

The provision for renewal, like that for termination under the new law, was designed to protect artists from themselves—and from the impossibility of knowing the true value of a work when it is first created—by giving them a chance to regain their copyrights after twenty-eight years. Unfortunately this noble purpose never was fulfilled. Those who wished to exploit artists, and those artists who preferred a dollar in hand to an uncertain hope of future riches, began to arrange sales and licenses of the renewal term in advance. (Generally these sales had to be explicit to be enforceable. A sale by an author of "all my right, title, and interest" in a work was usually interpreted not to include a sale of the renewal copyright.)[22] Moreover, because the sale would be worthless if the artist died before having a chance to renew his copyright, it became common for spouses and children of artists to make ends meet by selling in advance whatever rights they might get if the artist died prematurely.[23]

Sales by authors and their families of the renewal term copyright have not always been upheld. If the seller can show that the sale was made under "such coercion of circumstances that enforcement would be unconscionable," a court will not enforce the bargain.[24] This reflects a tendency on the part of courts to invalidate unconscionable contracts of all kinds, and is not strictly a doctrine of copyright law.

The question of who was entitled to the renewal copyright was rather complicated. If an author died before applying for renewal—or, in the view of some courts, before the renewal term actually began—the right to renew went to his surviving spouse and children, or as many of them as were living, as a group. Any one of them or all of them could then apply for renewal, and the copyright would belong to as many of the family as were alive at the critical time, in equal *per capita* shares. (The surviving spouse retained the renewal right regardless of remarriage.)[25] For example, if a novelist died before renewal, leaving a husband and three children, any one of those four persons could apply for renewal and each of them would receive a 25 percent share in the new copyright. The owners of these various shares were regarded as tenants in common. Each of them could make a transfer of the copyright, but would have to account to the other owners for a fair share of the profits.

The law spoke only of children; more remote descendants were not mentioned. (Whether illegitimate children could take advantage of the statute used to depend on state law regarding the rights of illegitimate children, but it appears that illegitimate children can renew under the new law.)[26] The omission of more remote descendants meant that if the novelist in the example died leaving no family except grandchildren, the renewal copyright would go to the executor of her estate, who would then pass it on to whoever was entitled to receive it by the terms of her will.[27] If the novelist left no will, the copyright would go to her next of kin, who in this case would be the grandchildren. If, however, the novelist was survived only by her husband and her grandchildren, the husband would get the entire copyright, and the grandchildren would get nothing. If she was survived by a child and by children of a deceased child, those grandchildren would not even take a *per stirpes* share. The rule seems harsh, but it has never been changed.

Because an application for renewal could be made "on behalf of" the person or corporation entitled to renewal, anyone who wished to could apply for renewal, as long as he did so in the name of the person entitled by law to renew. For example, if the author had sold his right to the renewal term, he was still entitled by law to file the claim for renewal, but people who purchased the renewal copyright from an author rarely relied on the author to make the renewal claim; instead they filed the claim themselves on his behalf. Thus also a magazine contributor whose contribution had been registered only as part of a magazine issue could still apply for renewal, as long as he did so in the name of the owner of copyright in the magazine.[28] In this manner he could protect his renewal copyright without having to depend on the publisher.

In the case of a joint work, any one of the authors could file for renewal, and the general rule has been to give all of the joint authors full ownership of the renewal term.[29]

There were four exceptions to the rule that an author or his surviving family, or his estate, or his heirs, were entitled to the renewal copyright. For four categories of works, ownership of the original copyright brought with it entitlement to the renewal copyright as well.

The first category was that of so-called posthumous works. What was a posthumous work? For a long time it was believed that a posthumous work was one not published before the author's death. However, though this definition fit in with familiar usage and conventional wisdom, it had the effect of disinheriting the author's spouse and children, for it meant that if an author before his death sold his copyright to someone else and died before publication, the purchaser would own the renewal right without having paid a dime for it. Responding to this clear inequity, the Second Circuit Court of Appeals in 1975 decreed that henceforth it would regard as posthumous only works in which the author had not, during his life, made any contract for exploitation of his copyright by publication, performance, or otherwise.[30] This meant that the only person who would have the right to renew copyright in a posthumous work would be the person who inherited the copyright from the author. That of course still left it open to the author to bequeath his common law copyright by will to some unrelated person, but the practical effect of the new rule has generally been a real benefit to the families of authors. This definition of posthumous works has been adopted by Congress for all renewals made after January 1, 1978.[31]

The second category was of works published without separate notice in a magazine or other "composite work." The author of the contribution did not possess the renewal right unless his work bore a separate copyright notice.[32] However, the practical significance of this was minimal, because if the publisher held the original copyright in trust for the author, as courts have recently tended to declare, it would also hold the renewal copyright in trust.

The third and fourth categories were closely related. The third comprised works made for hire. As noted above, though, where such works were *commissioned,* some courts have awarded the renewal term to the creator. The fourth comprised works in which copyright originally belonged to a corporate body (for example, a company, a board of trustees, or a charitable society). Since this would not be so if the corporate body was not itself the author of the work, in most cases this fourth exception simply overlapped with the work-made-for-hire exception.

RENEWAL IN 1992 AND THEREAFTER

The requirement that renewal had to be actively sought, through registration, created a trap for the unwary. Authors and their families were often ignorant of the law; publishers and production houses might know the law but lose track of a work after twenty-eight years, or go out of business. For example, copyright in the movie *It's a Wonderful Life* expired after twenty-eight years because the movie company that owned it had gone bankrupt and the residual copyright interest had gotten lost in the shuffle.

Congress has now largely deactivated this trap. As discussed earlier in this chapter, foreign works that fell into the public domain for failure to renew have been restored to copyright. And for both U.S. and foreign works due to be renewed in 1992 or thereafter—i.e., for works that first came under federal copyright between January 1, 1964, and December 31, 1977—renewal is now automatic. No application for renewal need be filed; indeed, the work does not even need to have been registered in its first term to be renewed for a second.[33]

Should no one bother, then, to apply for renewal? Not so. To encourage copyright owners to apply "proactively," so to speak, the new rules create several compelling incentives. First, if you apply for renewal instead of waiting for it to happen, your renewal will vest at the time you apply; but if you let renewal occur automatically, the renewal right will vest in the person(s) who could have applied on the last day of the first term. Thus, if an author actually renews his copyright and then dies during the last year of the first term, the copyright is his to license or bequeath as he wishes. But if he dies in that last year without having applied for renewal, the renewal term will pass to those of his wife and children who are living at the end of the year. (If there are none it will pass to his heirs by will or intestacy.)

The second incentive to apply for renewal is that it gives your registration for the renewal term the same *prima facie* evidentiary value as a first-term registration. If you let things simply take their course, any registration you make thereafter (for example, to be able to sue an infringer) will have only such weight as a court may choose to give it.

The third and perhaps the greatest incentive is that unless you actively apply for renewal, any licensee who has made a derivative work during the first term of copyright will be entitled to continue exploiting that derivative work—although not to make any new derivative work—during the second term of copyright. This is a significant departure from prior law, which held that a derivative work licensee had no rights in the renewal term unless he had obtained a license from whoever actually came to own the renewal term copyright.[34] To understand what this may mean in practice, consider the case of a work of fiction that has been made into a famous movie. If the novelist applies for renewal, the owner of the movie will be unable to show the movie in the renewal term without obtaining a new license, probably on terms much more favorable than the novelist got the first time around. If by contrast nature is allowed to take its course, the novel copyright will be automatically renewed but so will the movie owner's rights. If the first two incentives for proactive renewal are sticks, this can be a carrot of major dimensions.

If you miss the twenty-eighth year deadline for renewal and your work was not registered during the first copyright term, it is still advisable to file a late renewal registration, which the law permits you to do, so as to be eligible for attorneys' fees and statutory damages in a suit against a subsequent infringer.[35]

MECHANICS OF APPLYING FOR RENEWAL

The application form for renewal is form RE. (See appendix F for the fee.) If the work has not previously been registered, an Addendum to form RE must be submitted, setting forth much of the same information as would have been required for registration, and deposit of the same type as for normal registration must be made. If a minor error is made, it can be corrected by filing a supplemental registration at any time. Major errors, however, such as errors in identifying the renewal claimant or the basis for the renewal claim, generally cannot be corrected once the renewal term has begun, unless you can convince the Copyright Office that the error was inadvertent. If you are not allowed to correct the error, the copyright will be treated as if not timely renewed, with all the consequences that that entails.[36]

RENEWING A GROUP OF WORKS

As I have mentioned, since 1978 it has been possible for an author to register a number of contributions to collective works on the same form. Since 1978 there has been a similar provision where renewal is concerned. In the case of the works of an individual author, renewal registration may be made on a single form and for a single fee if these conditions are met:

• If the renewal claimant or claimants are the same for each work. For example, if a magazine owns two of the renewal rights and the author's family own the other two, the same registration form cannot be used for all four works.

• If the basis of the claim is the same for each work. This will be the case in all but a very few circumstances. An example to the contrary would be if the publisher is entitled to renew some works because their renewal terms were assigned to it by the author and entitled to renew others because they were works made for hire; in both cases the publisher is the proper renewal claimant, but it cannot use the same form to renew all of these works.

• If the works were all copyrighted at the time of their first publication, either by separate notice and registration or by virtue of a copyright notice having been affixed to the periodical issue as a whole, regardless of whether that issue was registered.

• If all the works were first published in the same calendar year.

• If the application identifies each work and states the name and date of the periodical issue in which it was first published.[37]

LENGTH OF RENEWAL TERM

As I mentioned earlier, the renewal term for pre-1978 works now runs for a total of sixty-seven years.[38] It might seem unfair that authors of works copyrighted before 1978 should not get the benefit of the life-plus-fifty (now life-plus-seventy) term, but Congress felt that altering the structure of existing copyrights to that extent would upset the financial expectations of people who had invested in them and would cause numerous other difficulties and contradictions. Instead Congress added to the renewal term of copyright for works in their first term as of January 1, 1978: originally nineteen years, later augmented by a further twenty years. Those works, if renewed, are now protected for a total of ninety-five years from the year of first publication.

The renewal term for works that were already in their second term when the new law went into effect, or for which a timely renewal application was still pending on December 31, 1977, has also been lengthened by thirty-nine years. Those works too will thus be protected for a total of ninety-five years from the year of first publication.

In all cases the copyright term for pre-1978 works that were still under copyright on January 1, 1978, runs through the end of the *calendar* year in which it would otherwise expire. This is a great improvement over prior law.

The addition of thirty-nine years is intended to benefit authors, not the people to whom they may have sold their rights. To ensure that this will in fact be the result, the new law has adopted a procedure for terminating renewal term grants, and that includes not only grants of the renewal right but also any grant or license that applies to the renewal term. The procedure is similar in most respects to that for terminating transfers of post-1977 copyrights (discussed in chapter 3).

TERMINATING PRE-1978 RENEWAL RIGHTS

The right to terminate transfers of renewal copyright[39] applies only to transfers made before January 1, 1978, of copyright in works published before that date. No grant or license concerning the renewal term made after December 31, 1977, can be terminated, nor can any grant made before 1978 of a work that was not under federal copyright as of December 31, 1977. The right is not available for works made for hire, and it does not affect grants made by will or grants of rights in foreign countries. Furthermore it affects only the thirty-nine-year extension period, not the basic twenty-eight-year renewal term.

GRANTS MADE BY PERSONS OTHER THAN THE AUTHOR

It is now possible for an author's spouse or children to terminate grants of renewal rights that they have made. It is also possible for them to terminate any grant that takes effect during the renewal term. Termination must be made by all of the grantors who are still alive. Thus if three children joined in making a grant of renewal rights and two of them die, the remaining child can effect termination all by himself. But if all three children are still alive, all three must join in making the termination. The heirs of a deceased grantor other than the author have no termination rights. Thus, in my example, if two children die before having a chance to take part in the termination, the remaining child is the only person who can effect termination; a deceased child's children have no rights in this respect. Nor do they have any rights once termination has been carried out. However, from the moment that the copyright reverts to the persons who terminated the grant, which it does on the date the termination becomes effective, it becomes property; it is no longer personal to the grantor but can be inherited. Thus if a child dies after taking part in the termination, his heirs will get an equal share of the copyright. This distinction seems unfair, but it is nonetheless the law.

GRANTS MADE BY THE AUTHOR

Termination of grants of renewal rights made by the author may be made by him alone, if he is living. If the author is dead, the termination right is owned and may be exercised by his family. His spouse has the entire right if there are no children or grandchildren; his children and grandchildren have the entire right if there is no spouse; if there are both a spouse and children or grandchildren, the spouse has half the termination right and the children and grandchildren have the other half, divided among them in equal shares *per stirpes*. The share of a deceased child can be exercised only by a majority of his children. And if neither the author nor any of these family members is living, the author's "executor, administrator, personal representative, or trustee" owns the termination right. In short, apportionment of the termination rights is identical to that provided for grants of copyright in post-1977 works.

GRANTS OF RENEWAL IN JOINT WORKS

Any author who joined in a grant of rights regarding the renewal term may terminate the grant to the extent of his share of the rights. (If he is dead, his termination right may be exercised by his family.) This provision for joint works differs substantially from the rule covering grants of copyright in post-1977 works. The rule in the latter case is that a majority of authors who signed the original grant must join in giving notice of termination; but in the case of renewal term grants made before January 1, 1978, each of the joint authors can terminate his own individual share of the grant. This may lead to inequitable results. If one of the joint owners pulls out, he can make a grant to someone else; is the person who has the original grant stuck paying royalties to the other joint authors but without any longer having an exclusive license, or is he free at that point to cancel the contract, leaving the other joint authors by the roadside?

OWNERSHIP OF COPYRIGHT AFTER TERMINATION

When a grant is terminated, the copyright reverts on the date termination becomes effective. However, the ownership of the rights that are to revert becomes fixed ("vested," in the legal phrase) on the date the notice of termination is given. The reverting right goes to those persons who could have signed the termination notice. Thus, if the author made the grant and is terminating it, the right (or whatever share of the right the author owned) reverts to the author. If the author made the grant and someone else is terminating it, the reversion goes to the author's surviving family, in the same *per stirpes* shares as they owned the termination right. If the grant was made by someone other than the author, the right reverts to as many of the grantors as are living on the date the notice is sent. Note that the reversion goes to whoever could have signed the notice, whether they did so or not. For example, a deceased author's child who did not sign the termination notice still receives a proportionate share of the copyright when it reverts.

Once the reversion has vested, the expectancy interest in the copyright becomes ordinary property that may be bequeathed or given within the family. However, no new grant of the reverting right may be made until after the effective date of the termination. Any new grant of a reverted right is valid only if it is in writing and only if it is signed by at least the same number of persons, and by persons representing at least the same proportion of ownership, as were required to carry out termination. This is so whether the new grant is exclusive or nonexclusive. (A new grant of a right originally granted by persons other than the author does not have to meet these number and proportion requirements.)

An example may help to demonstrate these rules. Suppose that termination rights in a work are owned 50 percent by the author's widow and 25 percent by each of two daughters. Termination would have to be carried out by at least two persons (the widow and at least one daughter). At the time of notice the right to reversion of the copyright vests in the widow and daughters in the same proportions. Suppose that one of the daughters then dies, leaving her share of the copyright to her alma mater. (She was able to make this bequest because ownership of the copyright had vested in her.) For a new grant of the copyright to be valid, it must be signed by at least two persons, who must represent at least the same percentage of the right as was required for termination. But they need not be the same persons who terminated the original grant. Thus the statute is satisfied if the grant is signed by the widow and the college.

The new grant binds and benefits even those who did not participate in it. Thus the daughter who does not sign the new grant is still legally bound by it, and the buyer is obligated to pay her a share of the royalties.

MECHANICS FOR TERMINATING A RENEWAL TERM GRANT

The following rules apply to all terminations of renewal right grants, whether the grants were made by the author or by his family:[40]

1. In most cases, termination may take effect at any time during the five-year period beginning fifty-six years after the date copyright was first obtained (normally, the actual date the work was first published, or any earlier date on which it was registered.) That remains the case. However, when Congress extended the renewal term by a further twenty years, in October 1998, it recognized that some persons might have missed their opportunity to terminate and that the twenty-year extension would prove a windfall to their licensees. Accordingly, the Act provides that if, back before the new twenty-year extension of copyright was enacted, you missed the deadline for termination, you may terminate as to the new twenty-year extension at any time in the first five years after the seventy-fifth anniversary of the date copyright was first secured.

2. Notice of termination, which must be in writing and signed by all persons whose consent is required for termination, must be given not more than ten years and not fewer than two years before the date that termination is to take effect.

3. A copy of the notice must be recorded in the Copyright Office before the date of termination, or the termination becomes null and void. See appendix F for the recording fees.

4. As with the termination of grants of post-1977 copyrights, no new grant, and no agreement to make a new grant, can be made until the date termination becomes effective, except that renegotiation of an existing grant may be made as soon as notice is given. Rights under a renegotiated contract do not ripen until termination takes effect.

5. As with the termination of post-1977 copyrights, termination of renewal grants does not affect the ongoing use

of any derivative work prepared by a grantee prior to termination. For example, if a novelist terminates a grant to a film producer, that will only prevent the producer from making a new film of the same story, not from performing a film already made.

A notice of termination must contain certain basic information:

1. The name of the persons whose rights are being terminated and the address to which the notice is being sent. If you are sending notice to more than one address, list all of them.
2. The title of the work.
3. The name of at least one author of the work.
4. The date that copyright was secured.
5. The copyright registration number, if possible.
6. The exact nature of the grant you are terminating.
7. The date that termination is to become effective.
8. If the grant was made by someone other than the author, a list of all persons who made the original grant and who are still alive.
9. If the grant was made by the author, but is being terminated by his family, a list of all the persons who are entitled to take part in termination (whether they are actually doing so or not) and their relationships to the author. Indicate on the list which persons actually are taking part in the termination and what their percentage shares of the termination right are.

If you are not sure of all this information, put down as much as you know and explain why you are uncertain as to the rest.

The notice must be signed by all persons taking part. Each signature should be accompanied by the person's name and address, in legible form. The notice must also contain a statement that to the best of their knowledge those persons have among them a sufficiently large share of the termination right to entitle them to terminate.

The notice must be delivered by hand or by first-class mail. It is your duty to make reasonably sure that the person to whom you are giving the notice is still the owner of the right and has not granted it to someone else, and also that you have the correct address. This means that you should write to the Copyright Office and request a search for recordations of any transfers. (See appendix F for search fees.) In the case of musical works, you should also check with the performing rights societies, ASCAP, BMI, and SESAC.

If you fail to comply with any of these requirements and if your errors or omissions cause other people to be misled to their disadvantage, your notice of termination may be judged legally ineffective.

THE RELATION BETWEEN DERIVATIVE WORKS AND THE UNDERLYING SOURCE WORKS

Although pre-1978 law recognized that a derivative work has a separate copyright from the underlying work, it did not apply this rule where the underlying work was not *federally* copyrighted. Thus, for example, release of a motion picture would be deemed to "publish" all material in it, such as the screenplay, that might have been subject to a common law copyright, and when the motion picture entered the public domain, so did those preexisting works. If, however, the underlying work had been published, or registered with the Copyright Office, loss of copyright in the movie would have no impact on copyright in the original. This disparate treatment shows the federal law's bias against common law copyrights, which were potentially eternal in duration.[41]

10 TAX TREATMENT OF COPYRIGHTS

Authors generally have two tax problems: how to report their income and how to deduct their expenses. Other copyright owners have similar problems but from a different perspective. For them the problems are not much different from those of someone who buys a machine or farm. For an author, though, Congress has created a veritable funhouse of rules.

THE AUTHOR AS OWNER: WHEN IS AN ASSET NOT AN ASSET?

The author's trouble arises principally from governmental ambivalence as to whether a copyright is a capital asset in the hands of its creator. In many respects an author is like someone who builds houses rather than like someone who buys them: his profit is taxed as ordinary income. Nonetheless, if he is a professional author he must treat some of his expenses as capital investments, and if he is not he must treat them all as capital investments. When and how those expenses can later be deducted also depends on whether the author is a professional.

As you can see, this is not an area where common sense or logic will necessarily be of help. The thing to have is a map and a rulebook, and I hope what follows will serve.

THE AMATEUR

An amateur author cannot deduct any of the expenses of his hobby unless and until he sells the work.[1] An amateur author is one who is not engaged in the trade or business of creating copyrighted works. For example, someone who paints for recreation is an amateur for tax purposes, however good the paintings may be.

The question that decides whether someone is an amateur or a professional is whether the activity is carried on primarily for livelihood or profit or primarily for recreation. Dim hopes of future glory will not convert a hobby into a trade. On the other hand financial failure does not brand one as an amateur, if one has made a genuine effort to sell one's creations.[2] Nor is it necessary that the activity be one's sole pursuit in life: painting on weekends may still be a profession if you are actively trying to sell the results. The regularity with which you pursue an activity will help determine whether you are a professional or an amateur.[3] The tortoise is more professional than the hare.

THE PROFESSIONAL

Generally, if you are a professional author, costs relating to your title in a copyright cannot be deducted in the year you incur them. Instead they have to be capitalized—that is, treated as investments—and depreciated over the useful life of a copyright. Other expenses, such as travel, secretarial help, or supplies, may be deducted in the year they are incurred. The basic principles are these:

Costs relating to title. This phrase covers the cost of copyright registration, including legal fees. It also covers all expenses, including legal fees, that you may incur in defending your copyright against someone who accuses you of infringing or in suing an infringer yourself. However, it does not include expenses incurred or damages won in defending or asserting a right to income. By the same token, damages that are in the form of profits are taxed as ordinary income. Damages that relate to title are not taxable as income but the amount of them must be subtracted from the capital basis on which you compute depreciation.

This is the sort of hairsplitting that has earned the Internal Revenue Code a bad name. Suppose you become involved in a complicated infringement suit, where not only the basic title to copyright but also the right to royalties is at stake. How do you decide where title ends and the right to royalties begins? The best you can do is to ask the court to apportion the damages it awards you between the two and apply the same ratio to your legal costs and to the damages you win. Sometimes your attorney will be able to give you an itemized bill, but this method of allocating legal costs runs a risk of being overruled by the IRS.

The foregoing applies only if you win. If the court decides your claimed copyright is invalid and you lose, all of your expenses will be deductible in the year the decision is handed down, and you will also be able to deduct the dollar value of the title you have lost (but not the value of projected income) in the year the decision is handed down. Expenses that arise from litigation over income will be deductible when paid.

Other expenses. The deductibility of expenses incurred in creating a work is subject to complex rules. For a brief period Congress tried to subject all authors' expenses to the so-called uniform capitalization rules, so that all of these expenses would have to be capitalized rather than deducted. In response to an outcry from authors' groups, Congress quickly retreated, but left in place the following:

- In general, no current deduction is allowed unless you are self-employed.
- Writers, composers, photographers, and artists are allowed to deduct most expenses in the year incurred, but it appears, somewhat ambiguously, that this is not allowed to filmmakers.
- Expenses relating to printing, photographic plates, motion picture films, videotapes, or similar items are not deductible but must be capitalized. Just what are "similar items" is unclear, but judging by the items listed one would have to extend this rule to, say, the costs a sculptor incurs in casting in bronze.
- No current deduction is allowed to an artist—as distinct from an author or photographer—unless the individual is "engaged in the business of being an artist." In this seemingly

redundant provision a troublesome value judgment lurks: Congress does not regard anyone as an "artist" for tax purposes unless the aesthetic value of the work produced "predominates" over the utilitarian value. Thus, for example, says the legislative report accompanying the statute, "an expense that is incurred in producing jewelry, silverware, pottery, furniture, or other similar household items generally is not considered as being paid or incurred in the business of an individual being an artist." This presumptuous generalization practically invites litigation.

• Artists who do not qualify for current deduction treatment are given a "safe harbor"; they can deduct 50 percent of their expenses in the year incurred and 25 percent in each of the next two years.[4]

Depreciation. The tax laws permit an author to take a deduction each year for a portion of the capital value of a copyright, until it is reduced almost to zero. Depreciation should be taken over the useful life of the copyright. The presumption is that copyright will retain its value for its entire duration: life plus seventy years, or whatever the applicable term is. However, if you can prove that your copyright has a market life of only a few years, you can speed up your depreciation. Thus if you have written a textbook with a predictable market life of only six years, you can deduct one-sixth of your capital costs in each of those six years, starting with the year of first publication.[5] The general rule for depreciation is that it cannot begin until the asset is "placed in service." With works that are not published but are exploited by performance or display, depreciation would begin when exploitation begins. An interesting question, to which no one has the answer, is whether an unpublished work is "placed in service" when derivative works based upon it are published. I tend to think it should be so treated.

I use the phrase "almost to zero" because until you dispose of your copyright you cannot depreciate it below what is termed "salvage value."[6] Salvage value is, basically, what you could get for the copyright, even after income has dwindled away, by selling it to some optimistic buyer who hopes for a backswing in the pendulum of public taste or who wants to be able to use parts of your work without threat of suit. In most cases salvage value will be negligible. If your copyright is valuable, though, salvage may be a factor. You should consult your tax advisor on this point as on many of the other points noted here.

Matching depreciation to income. If you sell your copyright for a flat fee, you can deduct the remaining balance of your capital value in the year of sale. However, if you sell on a royalty basis, you should take your depreciation deductions against royalty income. In such a case the rules differ depending on whether you can predict your income flow. If you can, you should adjust your depreciation accordingly. For example, if you can predict that income will be $20,000 in the first year, $10,000 in the second year, $5,000 in the third, and zero in the fourth, for a total of $35,000, you can deduct twenty thirty-fifths of your capital value in the first year, ten thirty-fifths in the second, and the remaining five thirty-fifths in the third (always, of course, allowing for salvage value).[7] If you cannot predict your income flow, you can deduct for depreciation in any given year only up to the amount of income you receive.[8]

Deduction for loss. If you abandon or forfeit your copyright, if it is taken away from you in a lawsuit, or if it becomes valueless, you can deduct the remaining balance of your capital value in the year the loss occurs.[9]

Special problems for sculpture, paintings, and plates. This discussion has so far dealt with the copyright itself, an intangible property right. A sculptor or painter, however, produces something tangible as well, quite apart from the copyright in the work. So does a printmaker or photographer. So too does a publisher.

The physical object has a value quite separate from that of the copyright. It is a capital-type asset. Because of this, the costs of the materials and so on that go into it must be capitalized, even though they might otherwise be regarded as business expenses. Sometimes this will lead to allocation problems. For example, if you weld steel sculptures in your garage, what part of your electricity costs has to be attributed to the object? Your guess is probably as good as the IRS's so long as you guess in good faith. Depreciation cannot be taken unless the object is likely to deteriorate noticeably in the owner's lifetime. Sale of the object by the author will produce ordinary income, against which the author can deduct any remaining capital basis.

JOINT AUTHORS

Where there are two or more joint authors, the depreciation basis must be divided among them in the same proportions as their ownership. Unless there is an agreement to the contrary, each joint author will take an equal share of the basis.

GIFT AND ESTATE TAXES

When an author makes a private gift of a copyright, it is valued for gift tax purposes not at its capital basis value but at its fair market value. It may have a basis of only $200, but if its market value (based on projected income) is $20,000, the author is treated as making a gift of $20,000. However, a gift to *charity* will be valued not at fair market value but at the author's capital value.

Whether a gift other than to charity will actually incur gift tax depends on the number of donees, whether the author's spouse joins in making the gift, and whether the author has used up his "unified credit against gift and estate taxes." These are complex questions and outside the scope of this book. If you are making a gift to any one person of a copyright with a probable market value of over $10,000—the limit on tax-free gifts in any given year—you should consult a tax advisor.

A gift of royalty interest will not circumvent this rule. Indeed, a gift of a royalty interest, without any transfer of ownership, will not even suffice to make the income taxable to the donee rather than the author, although it will nonetheless be taxed as a gift.[10] This problem is frequently encountered by authors who wish to shift the future income stream of a work to their children, or to trusts for their children. The usual solution is to assign all copyright interest to the donee and, if the work is under contract for publication, to assign the *entire* contract, not merely the right to royalties.

Although unified with the gift tax laws in some respects, the estate tax laws as they apply to copyrights differ from the scheme I have described for gifts. A copyright is valued in the author's estate at its market value, no matter whether it is left to private persons or to charity. Thus if a copyright is left to charity—for example, as Shaw left his copyrights to the National Gallery of Ireland—the estate reports the full value in its inventory and receives as an offset a charitable deduction for the full value.

SPECIAL RULES FOR CORPORATIONS

Copyright in a film or other work produced by a large corporation, whose creative staff are paid a salary and have no financial stake in the corporation, in many cases will be treated as a capital asset if the corporation is in the trade or business of exploiting it rather than of selling or brokering it.[11]

COPYRIGHT AS CAPITAL ASSET: PERSONS OTHER THAN THE AUTHOR

A different set of rules applies to a person to whom the author gives, bequeaths, or sells his copyright. The basis for such a person depends on which type of transfer occurs.

BASIS IN AN ACQUIRED COPYRIGHT

Donees. Basis in a gift is determined by looking at what lawyers call the owner's "chain of title." If you obtain a copyright by gift, your basis depends on who gave it to you. If you got it from the author, your basis is the author's basis, less any depreciation already taken before it reaches you. The same is true if you got it from someone who was given it by the author. There can be any number of gifts, but if the chain began with the author, the author's basis (as adjusted along the way) will be the basis for every owner in the chain. However, if someone in the chain of title purchased or inherited the copyright, the basis you get is that purchase price, or the estate value, less any depreciation taken on it since then. Each purchase or inheritance in a chain of title establishes a new basis for the copyright.

Inheritors. The tax laws give a break to someone who receives a copyright by inheritance. Basis is "stepped up" to the value of the copyright in the author's estate. Admittedly this makes a strange distinction between, say, a child of an author who is given a copyright and a child who gets it by inheritance. This distinction is sometimes overlooked by well-meaning parents; here, again, it is wise to seek the advice of a tax lawyer.

Purchasers. If you purchase a copyright, your basis will be what you paid for it. However, for there to have been a purchase, there has to have been a sale. The term "sale," as used in the tax laws, has special meaning. Because a copyright is a bundle of distinct rights, there can be a sale of one of those rights even if the others are retained. For example, you can have a sale of the publication right alone. However, if the transferor retains too much control over the right, there is no sale even though, for purposes of the copyright law, there has been an exclusive transfer.

The only controls that a seller can safely retain without running afoul of this rule are the right to sue for infringement and the right to rescind the transfer for failure to make royalty payments or because the transferee has gone bankrupt, or because the transferee fails to market the property. The general principle here is that a transfer is a sale so long as rescission can occur only because of some event that is not in the seller's control.[12] The statutory right to terminate a transfer (see chapters 3 and 9) does not affect the status of a "sale."

A transfer may be limited in geographical scope. If it is, it should be paid for not on a royalty basis but in a lump sum, or it will be treated as a license and not a sale. Conversely, if paid for on a royalty basis it will be considered a sale only if the exclusive rights given are without geographical limitation.[13] And all of this is without regard to whether the arrangement would be called a transfer of ownership for copyright purposes.

In many cases, a purchaser will want to have a transfer characterized as a license so that he can deduct his payments as a cost of doing business instead of capitalizing them. The seller is just as likely to want the opposite. When the transaction is ambiguous, this will be an important bargaining point for both sides.

DEPRECIATION

A donee or inheritor of a copyright can take depreciation only if a copyright is producing income. A purchaser of a copyright, assuming that the purchaser has acquired the property for investment purposes and not as a broker or trader in copyrights, can take depreciation regardless of whether income is being received. A broker or trader in copyrights holds the copyrights as inventory and cannot take depreciation at all.

The depreciation rules for someone who receives a copyright by gift or inheritance are generally the same as for an author: depreciation may be taken against income in any of the ways discussed. A purchaser of a copyright must also follow these rules if he holds the copyright for investment purposes, except that he can take a deduction in a year of no income. All three types of persons can take a deduction for loss or forfeiture.

Where a copyright is acquired as part of the acquisition of a business, it must be depreciated over a fourteen-year period.[14]

11 International Copyright Protection

If you know something of the life of Charles Dickens, you know something also of the chaos that existed in the early days of bulk printing, when, in the view of the U.S. Government, copyrights stopped at the borders of an author's native land. Dickens and other popular English writers suffered wholesale piracy of their works by American printers, until at last the U.S. Senate, against strong domestic pressure, agreed by treaty to recognize English copyrights.

Copyright is intrinsically a creature of national law. However, there are now few countries that do not have treaty arrangements for the international protection of copyrights. Most of these countries are members of either or both of the two great conventions, as they are called: the Berne Convention and the Universal Copyright Convention (UCC). These conventions are essentially multilateral agreements to give certain recognition to copyrights that arise in other member countries. Neither of these conventions requires a member nation to protect copyright in sound recordings. There is a separate treaty on this subject: the Convention for the Protection of Producers of Phonograms Against Unauthorized Duplication of Their Phonograms. However, the membership of this phonogram convention is comparatively small.

The United States was one of the founding members of the UCC in the early 1950s, but did not join Berne until 1989. The United States pushed for the formation of the UCC as an alternative to Berne; it declined for decades to join Berne out of a reluctance to abandon the notice requirement and certain other formalities and to extend copyright duration to meet Berne standards. It has finally succumbed, with the results I have described in preceding chapters.

Nearly every country in the world belongs to one of the two conventions; most belong to both. A few holdouts remain, but the trend is toward wider membership, and through this and other methods copyright piracy has been substantially reduced. Most of our major trading partners belong to Berne. Even China, Russia, and some other former Communist bloc countries have now joined Berne. Berne membership has widened to the point that the UCC may soon die of irrelevance.[1]

Both Berne and the UCC live largely by two key precepts: "national treatment" and the setting of minimum standards of protection by which all treaty members must abide. National treatment requires that every member nation extend the protection of its laws to works that originate in other member nations. Thus an American sculptor must receive in Italy the same copyright treatment as an Italian sculptor, and the Italian must receive in the United States the same treatment as her American counterpart.

There are two qualifications to this. The first is the "rule of the shorter term," which is, in practice, more an exception than a rule. It permits the United States to protect foreign photographs, for example, only for as long as they would be protected in their countries of origin. To some this seems perverse, like denying Babe Ruth a homer to left in Wrigley Field if the ball wouldn't have cleared the wall at Fenway Park. To others it seems eminently fair; after all, if the author's own government doesn't care to protect him, why should any other?

Under Berne the rule of the shorter term can be applied on a case-by-case basis. Thus, for example, if an American film has gone into the public domain because of failure to renew, other countries will not be obliged to protect it thereafter. (Most will anyway.) Under the UCC the rule can be invoked only if the foreign work belongs to a *class* of works that receives shorter protection in the country of origin.[2] In some countries the situation is further complicated by bilateral treaties with the United States that apply somewhat different rules in cases not governed by Berne or the UCC.[3]

The United States has never invoked the rule, even as to works where it could easily have done so. For many years it protected photographs and sound recordings, for example, much longer than many Berne countries, but it always gave such countries' authors the same treatment as its own. This generosity was not always reciprocated. The disparity continues despite earnest talk of harmonization. When the European Union countries extended their copyright terms to life of the author plus seventy years, Congress followed suit. But in Europe, this extension applies only to literary, dramatic, musical, and artistic works, and (with some minor modification) to motion pictures. In the United States, it applies to all works.

The other qualification to national treatment favors developing countries. Both Berne and the UCC give these countries the right to reproduce foreign works for teaching purposes, on a sort of compulsory license basis, if no edition is generally available in those countries at a "reasonable price." Both also give some developing countries the right to publish unauthorized translations. The conditions that must be met for either of these rights to be invoked are complicated,[4] and I will not explicate them here. I will allow myself the observation that though the purpose of these provisions is laudable, the method seems unfair. Steel companies are not told that they must sell their steel at a discount to developing countries; if they do so, one government or the other subsidizes them. Why should copyright owners bear a different burden?

National treatment governs fundamental issues of copyrightability. For example, a foreign country might grant copyright to a factual compilation that, under the *Feist* doctrine, is not eligible for U.S. copyright. American courts will not protect such a work; under the Constitution, they cannot.

However, national treatment does not govern issues of ownership. When it comes to ownership, our courts will in general defer to the law of the place where the work was created.[5] Thus, if a work is regarded in its country of origin as a joint work, our courts will treat the authors as being the joint owners of copyright within our borders, even though the relationship between the authors might be one that we would consider a work-for-hire relationship if the parties were U.S. citizens. The reason for this rule is that, since the work was not created here, the United States has little interest in regulating the relationship between the parties; the country of origin has a much greater interest in that. And even though the United States does have an interest in regulating the duration of copyrights, our courts would probably, for the sake of consistency, look to the country of origin in determining whether a work should have a joint-author term (longest life plus seventy years) or a work-for-hire term (ninety-five years from first publication, etc.).

These issues involve a legal doctrine called "conflicts of laws," and the courts of various nations do not necessarily agree on how to determine which country's law to apply in such situations. Furthermore, different legal systems are built on different concepts, and it may be asking too much to ask a foreign court to apply our concepts, or vice versa. For example, in European countries a work may be considered a "joint work" only if the authors' contributions are truly inseparable. The idea that a lyricist and a composer may be joint authors of a song is alien to them, because the lyrics and the music are capable of existing independent of each other. Would an English court, then, treat an American song as a joint work, or as a collective work? To do the former might create problems in administering the copyright within England. Nor is this the only point of disagreement over joint works. Most if not all European countries require any license, even a nonexclusive license, of a joint work to be signed by both authors. Would a French court honor a license signed by just our lyricist? The answer in that particular case seems to be no: French courts will treat any such license as invalid, to the extent that it purports to give publication rights in France, even if the work is a U.S. work and the license is executed in the United States.[6] Would other European countries follow suit? I hesitate to say. Would a U.S. court honor a nonexclusive license signed in France by just one of two French authors? If tit-for-tat is the rule, then the answer is no, and yet there would seem to be no good reason not to honor such a license, at least within our borders.

How all this will shake out as the Internet promotes cross-border collaborations, as multinational companies increasingly create and traffic in copyrightable works, will be interesting to watch. For example, if an American and a German collaborate on a work, under circumstances that U.S. law would categorize as a work-for-hire relationship but German law would categorize as a joint-author relationship, who wins? No one knows. In this particular example, the problem can be avoided if the two individuals reduce their understanding to writing, and choose the law by which they wish to be governed, for most countries will give great weight to any contractual choice of law. Where contract conflicts with a perceived public policy, though, this relative certainty disappears.

An example of such a public policy lies in regulation of contracts. In some countries rights of reversion are given to authors on moral grounds, rights that U.S. law does not give. Such a country might well insist on enforcing the reversion, at least within its borders, no matter what the contract says—especially if the author were one of its own citizens and the assignee an American. Our own law has rights of termination that are inalienable; the case has not arisen, but I would not be surprised to see an American court enforce the termination within our borders even if the country where the contract was signed has no such provision. Or to take another example: in the United States, one may grant rights in future technologies by referring to "all media now known or hereafter discovered." In some countries, however, a grant of rights will not be extended to cover technologies that did not exist at the time of the grant, no matter how the grant is worded. Here, too, a court might perceive a public policy needing to be enforced.

Or take the matter of renewal. In the case of, say, a work by a deceased English author, there is really no good reason why the ownership of copyright within the United States should revert to his widow after twenty-eight years while ownership elsewhere in the world remains with his publisher—but our courts would very likely enforce such a result. Indeed, it is hard to see how they could avoid it.

These anomalies complicate international dealings in copyright. One is reminded of the early days of railroads, when rail gauges were not uniform across borders. There have always been differences among nations in economic regulation. But when such differences impede commerce, which, like the railroads, is designed for travel across borders, they are difficult to justify. Copyright is an area where justification runs particularly thin. The Internet makes possible simultaneous worldwide exploitation of rights. That exploitation ought not to be subject to a hundred different legal standards, however reasonable any of them might be in isolation.

Although it might not seem so in light of the preceding discussion, the second key concept of Berne and the UCC is, as I mentioned, the setting of standards. Berne requires longer terms of protection and eschews formalities; Berne is also more broadly favorable to authors in the area of moral rights. The UCC, though it does not encourage formalities, is more tolerant. In particular, although it does not require copyright notice, it establishes "© [name] [year of first publication]" as a sort of international form of copyright notice for those who wish to use it. It is therefore prudent, when using copyright notice, to use this particular form.

The setting of standards is an ongoing process. As of 1997, the United States and other members of the Berne Convention had agreed on the text of two treaties expanding and clarifying the treatment of certain copyrights. Both have yet to be fully adopted by the U.S. Senate, and after Senate approval enabling legislation will have to be adopted. In both cases, the legislation will probably, if the recent past is any guide, generate some discord, confusion, and bad draftsmanship.

The first of these treaties is a "Treaty on Certain Questions Concerning the Protection of Literary and Artistic Works." It requires all Berne countries to do certain things that the United States has already done: ensure that copyright owners of computer programs and sound recordings can control the rental of their works; protect computer programs as literary works; and protect copyright in photographs for the same term as other types of works (Berne at present requires only twenty-five years' protection). It makes clear that copyright owners control the right to disseminate their works electronically. There was an effort to add a provision confirming that copyright owners control the right to make digital reproduction of their works, but this went down due to an inability to reach consensus on whether temporary storage of a work in the digital memory of, say, an Internet service provider infringes the copyright owner's reproduction right.

The treaty also contains important provisions concerning technological anti-infringement devices. These have been enacted, in the Digital Millennium Copyright Act, as have the provisions regarding "rights management information."

Another possibly noteworthy provision of the treaty is one requiring signatory nations to give copyright owners of cinematographic works (i.e., movies) the right to control commercial rental of their works. However, the treaty says that this right does not have to be enacted unless commercial rental of movies has "led to widespread copying of such works materially impairing the exclusive right of reproduction." This escape clause has in effect been used by Congress, which shows no greater inclination than previously to give movie producers a video rental right. The provision may someday benefit our movie industry, but more likely overseas than at home. In theory, if the industry were able to prove that commercial rental in developing countries has caused it serious financial loss, the United States could through treaty enforcement mechanisms compel the offending countries to enact rental right legislation.

The second treaty concerns sound recordings. It requires all parties to recognize the rights of reproduction and distribution of sound recordings that U.S. law has long recognized. If fully implemented, however, it will involve two changes in our law, one of them quite dramatic in its impact.

The most important of these changes would be the creation of a performance right for sound recordings. The United States already recognizes such a right, subject to limitations, where digital transmission is concerned. The treaty, though, applies to both analog and digital performance. In essence, performers of music would be treated the same way as the copyright owners of music: they would receive "equitable remuneration" from radio stations, discotheques, and others who perform their recordings publicly. The treaty does not make this mandatory, however; any nation can choose to opt out of this particular requirement.[7]

This treaty would also require the United States to enact federal law preventing unauthorized fixation of aural performances. As noted in chapter 1, this requirement goes beyond GATT, which required such legislation as to musical performances but not all aural performances generally.

The trend, as I have noted, is toward wider membership in copyright conventions, enhanced standards of protection, greater uniformity of law (for the most part), and less piracy. Overall we now operate in an international system that ensures American copyright owners reasonably predictable and uniform protection throughout most of the world. GATT has reinforced this system, openly acknowledging the link between copyright and free trade. By this and other agreements, nations have been compelled to honor copyright as a cost of access to markets. As international trade in copyrights becomes more and more valuable—in science, software, and entertainment—this system will likely prove to have been not merely fair-minded but foresighted as well.

Copyright and the Information Society: A Few Parting Thoughts

Information is power, as we are often told. But like most other kinds of power, it has no value except in use. We as a society benefit from that use and so we encourage authors as best we know how, realizing, as Samuel Johnson once put it, that "nobody but a blockhead ever wrote except for money."

However, as international copyright law demonstrates, people outside the free-market democracies do not view this equation in the same way. Our economies require raw materials; what the economies of developing countries require from us above all else—more than consumer goods and fancy weapons and the other vanities of modem life—is information. If they are to modernize, they must have access to our technical and scientific literature. Some have agreed to pay for it only under extreme pressure.

The international copyright system works reasonably well at the moment. But there are difficulties ahead. As computer software increases the sophistication of our technology, the gap that separates the haves from the have-nots may widen. Will the developing countries honor the claims of our authors in this field, or will they encourage the growth of a black market? And what sort of example will we set, given the pushes and pulls within our own society?

In 1909, when the predecessor to our current Copyright Act was passed, few if any foresaw the phenomenal development of radio, television, or sound recording. Yet these three media have radically changed our culture, and for many people they have greater importance than the printed word. Few if any foresaw the advent of photocopying, which seemed for a time to pose a true threat to the publishing industry. In each case lawyers and their clients found themselves having to discuss new concepts in an old language. As Congress dickered and delayed, the courts were obliged to apply a sometimes outmoded statute as best they could. The results were uneven, but copyright survived.

Now we have caught up, but one wonders for how long. As cable and telephone companies scramble to wire the country, electronic dissemination of copyrighted material is poised for an expansion of unprecedented speed and scope. Copyright owners are understandably filled with anxiety, for the risks and rewards are equally enormous. Never before has technology placed seller and buyer, and the would-be pirate, on so equal a footing.

I have discussed at the end of chapter 8 the complex laws enacted to clamp down—so their promoters hope—on electronic piracy. These laws, protecting "copyright management information" and outlawing decryption devices, have the air about them of a Victorian schoolmaster pounding his cane on his desk for order. I respectfully suggest that prevention of electronic piracy will require a combination of better technology, better pricing, and better education. Technology will have to make it easy to get a lawful copy, and to monitor the intake of each consumer on the Internet. Devices now in an advanced stage of development will enable every office and living room to download online digitized works on demand, and pay through an automatic debit-card or credit-card mechanism. These techniques can control, through encryption and decryption, first-time access by an authorized user. Whether any technique can acceptably control unauthorized reuse and redistribution remains to be seen. Technologies being developed in some quarters for permanently marking information will, should they prove feasible, be controversial with the public, for the sort of data they can give back to the copyright owner would be highly invasive of the user's privacy. They may also shut off fair use in ways the public will not accept.

Pricing will have to be reasonable; people will be far less tempted to steal if they can buy conveniently and at what they consider a fair price. Finally, education will have to instill in the public a greater understanding of why we have a copyright system, and how the public benefits from the incentives it provides to authors.

These observations are as embryonic as the information superhighway itself. It is impossible to predict all the challenges that the digital world will make to our established ways of thinking, just as it must have been impossible to predict the ramifications of photography in its infancy, and later of sound recording. The task of copyright will be to stake a moral and technological claim to its due rewards, without appearing to present a roadblock to progress. Copyright owners must price uses of their material at a level that is intuitively fair, for they will gain in goodwill and volume what they lose in unit price. Users, for their part, need to recognize more than ever that unless they pay a fair price for the use of copyrighted material, they will choke off the source of the very goods they covet. There is a great deal of learning to be done on both sides.

One way or another the copyright law has managed to adapt and survive past challenges. Some doctrines have been abandoned in the process; new ones have been acquired; others have scarcely changed in 200 years. There is a real virtue in this process, for it makes us focus on principles. Perhaps, as time goes on, we are developing a sense of what may be jettisoned in the cause of progress and what may not.

My main purpose in writing this book has been to acquaint you with the law as it is. However, if information really is power, what I have said may help you to contribute to the growth and orderly change of that law. That would be a benefit to all of us.

Appendix A Methods of Affixation and Positions of the Copyright Notice on Various Types of Works [37 C.F.R. Ch. II §201.20]

(a) *General.* (1) This section specifies examples of methods of affixation and positions of the copyright notice on various types of works that will satisfy the notice requirement of section 401(c) of Title 17 of the United States Code, as amended by Pub. L. 94-553. A notice considered "acceptable" under this regulation shall be considered to satisfy the requirement of that section that it be "affixed to the copies in such manner and location as to give reasonable notice of the claim to copyright." As provided by that section, the examples specified in this regulation shall not be considered exhaustive of methods of affixation and positions giving reasonable notice of the claim of copyright.

(2) The provisions of this section are applicable to copies publicly distributed on or after December 1, 1981. This section does not establish any rules concerning the form of the notice or the legal sufficiency of particular notices, except with respect to methods of affixation and positions of notice. The adequacy or legal sufficiency of a copyright notice is determined by the law in effect at the time of the first publication of the work.

(b) *Definitions.* For the purposes of this section:

(1) The terms *audiovisual works, collective works, copies, device, fixed, machine, motion picture, pictorial, graphic, and sculptural works*, and their variant forms, have the meanings given to them in section 101 of title 17.

(2) *Title 17* means Title 17 of the United States Code, as amended by Pub. L. 94-553.

(3) In the case of a work consisting preponderantly of leaves on which the work is printed or otherwise reproduced on both sides, a *page* is one side of a leaf; where the preponderance of the leaves are printed on one side only, the terms "page" and "leaf" mean the same.

(4) A work is published in *book form* if the copies embodying it consist of multiple leaves bound, fastened, or assembled in predetermined order as, for example, a volume, booklet, pamphlet, or multipage folder. For the purpose of this section, a work need not consist of textual matter in order to be considered published in "book form."

(5) *A title page* is a page, or two consecutive pages facing each other, appearing at or near the front of the copies of a work published in book form, on which the complete title of the work is prominently stated and on which the names of the author or authors, the name of the publisher, the place of publication, or some combination of them, are given.

(6) The meaning of the terms *front, back, first, last,* and *following,* when used in connection with works published in book form, will vary in relation to the physical form of the copies, depending on the particular language in which the work is written.

(7) In the case of a work published in book form with a hard or soft cover, the *front page* and *back page* of the copies are the outsides of the front and back covers; where there is no cover, the "front page" and "back page" are the pages visible at the front and back of the copies before they are opened.

(8) A *masthead* is a body of information appearing in approximately the same location in most issues of a newspaper, magazine, journal, review, or other periodical or serial, typically containing the title of the periodical or serial, information about the staff, periodicity of issues, operation, and subscription and editorial policies of the publication.

(9) A *single-leaf work* is a work published in copies consisting of a single leaf, including copies on which the work is printed or otherwise reproduced on either one side or on both sides of the leaf, and also folders which, without cutting or tearing the copies, can be opened out to form a single leaf. For the purpose of this section, a work need not consist of textual matter to be considered a "single-leaf work."

(c) *Manner of Affixation and Position Generally.* (1) In all cases dealt with in this section, the acceptability of a notice depends on its being permanently legible to an ordinary user of the work under normal conditions of use, and affixed to the copies in such manner and position that, when affixed, it is not concealed from view upon reasonable examination.

(2) Where, in a particular case, a notice does not appear in one of the precise locations prescribed in this section but a person looking in one of those locations would be reasonably certain to find a notice in another somewhat different location, that notice will be acceptable under this section.

(d) *Works Published in Book Form.* In the case of works published in book form, a notice reproduced on the copies in any of the following positions is acceptable:

(1) The title page, if any;

(2) The page immediately following the title page, if any;

(3) Either side of the front cover, if any; or, if there is no front cover, either side of the front leaf of the copies;

(4) Either side of the back cover, if any; or, if there is no back cover, either side of the back leaf of the copies;

(5) The first page of the main body of the work;

(6) The last page of the main body of the work;

(7) Any page between the front page and the first page of the main body of the work; if: (i) There are no more than ten pages between the front page and the first page of the main body of the work; and (ii) the notice is reproduced

prominently and is set apart from other matter on the page where it appears;

(8) Any page between the last page of the main body of the work and the back page, if: (i) There are no more than ten pages between the last page of the main body of the work and the back page; and (ii) the notice is reproduced prominently and is set apart from the other matter on the page where it appears.

(9) In the case of a work published as an issue of a periodical or serial, in addition to any of the locations listed in paragraphs (d)(1) through (8) of this section, a notice is acceptable if it is located: (i) As a part of, or adjacent to, the masthead; (ii) on the page containing the masthead if the notice is reproduced prominently and is set apart from the other matter appearing on the page; or (iii) adjacent to a prominent heading, appearing at or near the front of the issue, containing the title of the periodical or serial and any combination of the volume and issue number and date of the issue.

(10) In the case of musical work, in addition to any of the locations listed in paragraphs (d)(1) through (9) of this section, a notice is acceptable if it is located on the first page of music.

(e) *Single-Leaf Works.* In the case of single-leaf works, a notice reproduced on the copies anywhere on the front or back of the leaf is acceptable.

(f) *Contributions to Collective Works.* For a separate contribution to a collective work to be considered to "bear its own notice of copyright," as provided by 17 U.S.C. 404, a notice reproduced on the copies in any of the following positions is acceptable:

(1) Where the separate contribution is reproduced on a single page, a notice is acceptable if it appears: (i) Under the title of the contribution on that page; (ii) adjacent to the contribution; or (iii) on the same page if, through format, wording,

or both, the application of the notice to the particular contribution is made clear;

(2) Where the separate contribution is reproduced on more than one page of the collective work, a notice is acceptable if it appears: (i) Under a title appearing at or near the beginning of the contribution; (ii) on the first page of the main body of the contribution; (iii) immediately following the end of the contribution; or (iv) on any of the pages where the contribution appears if: (A) The contribution is reproduced on no more than twenty pages of the collective work; (B) the notice is reproduced prominently and is set apart from other matter on the page where it appears; and (C) through format, wording, or both, the application of the notice to the particular contribution is made clear;

(3) Where the separate contribution is a musical work, in addition to any of the locations listed in paragraphs (f)(1) and (2) of this section, a notice is acceptable if it is located on the first page of music of the contribution.

(4) As an alternative to placing the notice on one of the pages where a separate contribution itself appears, the contribution is considered to "bear its own notice" if the notice appears clearly in juxtaposition with a separate listing of the contribution by title, or, if the contribution is untitled, by a description reasonably identifying the contribution: (i) on the page bearing the copyright notice for the collective work as a whole, if any; or (ii) in a clearly identified and readily-accessible table of contents or listing of acknowledgments appearing near the front or back of the collective work as a whole.

(g) *Works Reproduced in Machine-Readable Copies.* For works reproduced in machine-readable copies (such as magnetic tapes or disks, punched cards, or the like), from which the work cannot ordinarily be visually perceived except with the aid of a machine or device,[1] each of the following constitute examples of acceptable methods of affixation and position of notice:

(1) A notice embodied in the copies in machine-readable form in such a manner that on visually perceptible printouts it appears either with or near the title, or at the end of the work;

(2) A notice that is displayed at the user's terminal at sign on;

(3) A notice that is continuously on terminal display;

(4) A legible notice reproduced durably, so as to withstand normal use, on a gummed or other label securely affixed to the copies or to a box, reel, cartridge, cassette, or other container used as a permanent receptacle for the copies.

(h) *Motion Pictures and Other Audiovisual Works.* (1) The following constitute examples of acceptable methods of affixation and positions of the copyright notice on motion pictures and other audiovisual works: A notice that is embodied in the copies by a photomechanical or electronic process, in such a position that it ordinarily would appear whenever the work is performed in its entirety, and that is located (i) with or near the title; (ii) with the cast, credits, and similar information; (iii) at or immediately following the beginning of the work; or (iv) at or immediately preceding the end of the work.

(2) In the case of an untitled motion picture or other audiovisual work whose duration is sixty seconds or less, in addition to any of the locations listed in paragraph (h)(1) of this section, a notice that is embodied in the copies by a photomechanical or electronic process, in such a position that it

1. Works published in a form requiring the use of a machine or device for purposes of optical enlargement (such as film, filmstrips, slide films, and works published in any variety of microform) and works published in visually perceptible form but used in connection with optical scanning devices, are not within this category.

ordinarily would appear to the projectionist or broadcaster when preparing the work for performance, is acceptable if it is located on the leader of the film or tape immediately preceding the beginning of the work.

(3) In the case of a motion picture or other audiovisual work that is distributed to the public for private use, the notice may be affixed, in addition to the locations specified in paragraph (h)(1) of this section, on the housing or container, if it is a permanent receptacle for the work.

(i) *Pictorial, Graphic, and Sculptural Works.* The following constitute examples of acceptable methods of affixation and positions of the copyright notice on various forms of pictorial, graphic, and sculptural works:

(1) Where a work is reproduced in two-dimensional copies, a notice affixed directly or by means of a label cemented, sewn, or otherwise attached durably, so as to withstand normal use, to the front or back of the copies, or to any backing, mounting, matting, framing, or other material to which the copies are durably attached, so as to withstand normal use, or in which they are permanently housed, is acceptable.

(2) Where a work is reproduced in three-dimensional copies, a notice affixed directly or by means of a label cemented, sewn, or otherwise attached durably, so as to withstand normal use, to any visible portion of the work, or to any base, mounting, framing, or other material on which the copies are durably attached, so as to withstand normal use, or in which they are permanently housed, is acceptable.

(3) Where, because of the size or physical characteristics of the material in which the work is reproduced in copies, it is impossible or extremely impracticable to affix a notice to the copies directly or by means of a durable label, a notice is acceptable if it appears on a tag that is of durable material, so as to withstand normal use, and that is attached to the copy

with sufficient durability that it will remain with the copy while it is passing through its normal channels of commerce.

(4) Where a work is reproduced in copies consisting of sheet-like or strip material bearing multiple or continuous reproductions of the work, the notice may be applied: (i) To the reproduction itself; (ii) to the margin, selvage, or reverse side of the material at frequent and regular intervals; or (iii) if the material contains neither a selvage nor a reverse side, to tags and labels, attached to the copies and to any spools, reels, or containers housing them in such a way that a notice is visible while the copies are passing through their normal channels of commerce.

(5) If the work is permanently housed in a container, such as a game or puzzle box, a notice reproduced on the permanent container is acceptable.

APPENDIX B FORM TX

FEE CHANGES
Registration filing fees are effective through June 30, 1999. For information on the fee changes, write the Copyright Office, check http://www.loc.gov/copyright, or call (202) 707-3000. Beginning as early as January 1, 2000, the Copyright Office may impose a service charge when insufficient fees are received.

FORM TX
For a Nondramatic Literary Work
UNITED STATES COPYRIGHT OFFICE

REGISTRATION NUMBER

TX TXU

EFFECTIVE DATE OF REGISTRATION

Month Day Year

DO NOT WRITE ABOVE THIS LINE. IF YOU NEED MORE SPACE, USE A SEPARATE CONTINUATION SHEET.

1

TITLE OF THIS WORK ▼

How To Make Money in Internet Stocks

PREVIOUS OR ALTERNATIVE TITLES ▼

PUBLICATION AS A CONTRIBUTION If this work was published as a contribution to a periodical, serial, or collection, give information about the collective work in which the contribution appeared. **Title of Collective Work ▼**

If published in a periodical or serial give: **Volume ▼** **Number ▼** **Issue Date ▼** **On Pages ▼**

2

a NAME OF AUTHOR ▼
Delessa Fool

DATES OF BIRTH AND DEATH
Year Born ▼ 1975 Year Died ▼

Was this contribution to the work a "work made for hire"? ☐ Yes ☐ No

AUTHOR'S NATIONALITY OR DOMICILE
Name of Country
OR { Citizen of ▶ USA / Domiciled in ▶ }

WAS THIS AUTHOR'S CONTRIBUTION TO THE WORK
Anonymous? ☐ Yes ☒ No
Pseudonymous? ☐ Yes ☐ No
If the answer to either of these questions is "Yes," see detailed instructions.

NATURE OF AUTHORSHIP Briefly describe nature of material created by this author in which copyright is claimed. ▼
Entire Work

b NAME OF AUTHOR ▼

DATES OF BIRTH AND DEATH
Year Born ▼ Year Died ▼

Was this contribution to the work a "work made for hire"? ☐ Yes ☐ No

AUTHOR'S NATIONALITY OR DOMICILE
Name of Country
OR { Citizen of ▶ / Domiciled in ▶ }

WAS THIS AUTHOR'S CONTRIBUTION TO THE WORK
Anonymous? ☐ Yes ☐ No
Pseudonymous? ☐ Yes ☐ No
If the answer to either of these questions is "Yes," see detailed instructions.

NATURE OF AUTHORSHIP Briefly describe nature of material created by this author in which copyright is claimed. ▼

c NAME OF AUTHOR ▼

DATES OF BIRTH AND DEATH
Year Born ▼ Year Died ▼

Was this contribution to the work a "work made for hire"? ☐ Yes ☐ No

AUTHOR'S NATIONALITY OR DOMICILE
Name of Country
OR { Citizen of ▶ / Domiciled in ▶ }

WAS THIS AUTHOR'S CONTRIBUTION TO THE WORK
Anonymous? ☐ Yes ☐ No
Pseudonymous? ☐ Yes ☐ No
If the answer to either of these questions is "Yes," see detailed instructions.

NATURE OF AUTHORSHIP Briefly describe nature of material created by this author in which copyright is claimed. ▼

NOTE

Under the law, the "author" of a "work made for hire" is generally the employer, not the employee (see instructions). For any part of this work that was "made for hire" check "Yes" in the space provided, give the employer (or other person for whom the work was prepared) as "Author" of that part, and leave the space for dates of birth and death blank.

3

a YEAR IN WHICH CREATION OF THIS WORK WAS COMPLETED
1998 ◀ Year
This information must be given in all cases.

b DATE AND NATION OF FIRST PUBLICATION OF THIS PARTICULAR WORK
Complete this information ONLY if this work has been published.
Month ▶ January Day ▶ 18 Year ▶ 1999
◀ Nation

4

COPYRIGHT CLAIMANT(S) Name and address must be given even if the claimant is the same as the author given in space 2. ▼
AirNet Press
One Speculator's Way
Las Vegas, NV 99999

See instructions before completing this space.

TRANSFER If the claimant(s) named here in space 4 is (are) different from the author(s) named in space 2, give a brief statement of how the claimant(s) obtained ownership of the copyright. ▼
Written transfer of all rights from author

DO NOT WRITE HERE OFFICE USE ONLY
APPLICATION RECEIVED
ONE DEPOSIT RECEIVED
TWO DEPOSITS RECEIVED
FUNDS RECEIVED

MORE ON BACK ▶ • Complete all applicable spaces (numbers 5-9) on the reverse side of this page.
• See detailed instructions. • Sign the form at line 8.

DO NOT WRITE HERE
Page 1 of ______ pages

EXAMINED BY

FORM TX

CHECKED BY

☐ CORRESPONDENCE Yes

FOR COPYRIGHT OFFICE USE ONLY

DO NOT WRITE ABOVE THIS LINE. IF YOU NEED MORE SPACE, USE A SEPARATE CONTINUATION SHEET.

5

PREVIOUS REGISTRATION Has registration for this work, or for an earlier version of this work, already been made in the Copyright Office?

☒ Yes ☐ No If your answer is "Yes," why is another registration being sought? (Check appropriate box.) ▼

a. ☐ This is the first published edition of a work previously registered in unpublished form.

b. ☐ This is the first application submitted by this author as copyright claimant.

c. ☒ This is a changed version of the work, as shown by space 6 on this application.

If your answer is "Yes," give: **Previous Registration Number** ▼ TX 369248 **Year of Registration** ▼ 1997

6

DERIVATIVE WORK OR COMPILATION

a **Preexisting Material** Identify any preexisting work or works that this work is based on or incorporates. ▼

How They Made Money in Tulip Bulbs, by Delessa Fool and Lotta Nerv.

b **Material Added to This Work** Give a brief, general statement of the material that has been added to this work and in which copyright is claimed. ▼

Description of strategies and market context has been updated and chapter on new technology has been added.

See instructions before completing this space.

7

a DEPOSIT ACCOUNT If the registration fee is to be charged to a Deposit Account established in the Copyright Office, give name and number of Account.

Name ▼ Account Number ▼

b CORRESPONDENCE Give name and address to which correspondence about this application should be sent. Name/Address/Apt/City/State/ZIP ▼

AirNet Press, Inc.
One Speculator's Way
Las Vegas, NV 99999

Area code and daytime telephone number ▶ 010-011-1010 Fax number ▶ 010-011-1100

Email ▶ admin@airnet.com

8

CERTIFICATION* I, the undersigned, hereby certify that I am the

Check only one ▶

☐ author
☐ other copyright claimant
☐ owner of exclusive right(s)
☒ authorized agent of AirNet Press, Inc.

Name of author or other copyright claimant, or owner of exclusive right(s) ▲

of the work identified in this application and that the statements made by me in this application are correct to the best of my knowledge.

Typed or printed name and date ▼ If this application gives a date of publication in space 3, do not sign and submit it before that date.

Burstyn Bubble Date ▶ February 1, 1999

Handwritten signature (X) ▼

X Burstyn Bubble

Registration filing fees are effective through June 30, 1999. After that date, please write the Copyright Office, check the Copyright Office Website at http://www.loc.gov/copyright, or call (202) 707-3000 for the latest fee information.

9

Mail certificate to:

Certificate will be mailed in window envelope

Name ▼
AirNet Press, Inc.

Number/Street/Apt ▼
One Speculator's Way

City/State/ZIP ▼
Las Vegas, NV 99999

YOU MUST:
- Complete all necessary spaces
- Sign your application in space 8

SEND ALL 3 ELEMENTS IN THE SAME PACKAGE:
1. Application form
2. Nonrefundable filing fee in check or money order payable to *Register of Copyrights*
3. Deposit material

MAIL TO:
Library of Congress
Copyright Office
101 Independence Avenue, S.E.
Washington, D.C. 20559-6000

*17 U.S.C. § 506(e): Any person who knowingly makes a false representation of a material fact in the application for copyright registration provided for by section 409, or in any written statement filed in connection with the application, shall be fined not more than $2,500.

July 1998—

PRINTED ON RECYCLED PAPER

☆U.S. GOVERNMENT PRINTING OFFICE: 1998-

"Best Edition" of Published Copyrighted Works for the Collections of the Library of Congress*

The copyright law (title 17, United States Code) requires that copies or phonorecords deposited in the Copyright Office be of the "best edition" of the work. The law states that "The 'best edition' of a work is the edition, published in the United States at any time before the date of deposit, that the Library of Congress determines to be most suitable for its purposes." (For works first published only in a country other than the United States, the law requires the deposit of the best edition as **first** published.)

When two or more editions of the same version of a work have been published, the one of the highest quality is generally considered to be the best edition. In judging quality, the Library of Congress will adhere to the criteria set forth below in all but exceptional circumstances.

Where differences between editions represent variations in copyrightable content, each edition is a separate version and "best edition" standards based on such differences do not apply. Each such version is a separate work for the purposes of the copyright law.

The criteria to be applied in determining the best edition of each of several types of material are listed below in descending order of importance. In deciding between two editions, a criterion-by-criterion comparison should be made. The edition which first fails to satisfy a criterion is to be considered of inferior quality and will not be an acceptable deposit. Example: If a comparison is made between two hardbound editions of a book, one a trade edition printed on acid-free paper, and the other a specially bound edition printed on average paper, the former will be the best edition because the type of paper is a more important criterion than the binding.

Under regulations of the Copyright Office, potential depositors may request authorization to deposit copies or phonorecords of other than the best edition of a specific work (e.g.,a microform rather than a printed edition of a serial), by requesting "special relief" from the deposit requirements. All requests for special relief should be in writing and should state the reason(s) why the applicant cannot send the required deposit and what the applicant wishes to submit instead of the required deposit.

*This excerpt is taken from Volume 54, No. 198 of the *Federal Register* for Monday, October 16, 1989 (pp. 42299-42300).

I. PRINTED TEXTUAL MATTER

A. Paper, Binding, and Packaging:

1. Archival-quality rather than less-permanent paper.
2. Hard cover rather than soft cover.
3. Library binding rather than commercial binding.
4. Trade edition rather than book club edition.
5. Sewn rather than glue-only binding.
6. Sewn or glued rather than stapled or spiral-bound.
7. Stapled rather than spiral-bound or plastic-bound.
8. Bound rather than looseleaf, except when future looseleaf insertions are to be issued. In the case of looseleaf materials, this includes the submission of all binders and indexes when they are part of the unit as published and offered for sale or distribution. Additionally,the regular and timely receipt of all appropriate looseleaf updates, supplements, and releases including supplemental binders issued to handle these expanded versions, is part of the requirement to properly maintain these publications.
9. Slip-cased rather than nonslip-cased.
10. With protective folders rather than without (for broadsides).
11. Rolled rather than folded (for broadsides).
12. With protective coatings rather than without (except broadsides, which should not be coated).

B. Rarity:

1. Special limited edition having the greatest number of special features.
2. Other limited edition rather than trade edition.
3. Special binding rather than trade binding.

C. Illustrations:

1. Illustrated rather than unillustrated.
2. Illustrations in color rather than black and white.

D. Special Features:

1. With thumb notches or index tabs rather than without.
2. With aids to use such as overlays and magnifiers rather than without.

E. Size:

1. Larger rather than smaller sizes. (Except that large-type editions for the partially-sighted are not required in place of editions employing type of more conventional size.)

II. PHOTOGRAPHS

A. Size and finish, in descending order of preference:
   1. The most widely distributed edition.
   2. 8 x10-inch glossy print.
   3. Other size or finish.

B. Unmounted rather than mounted.

C. Archival-quality rather than less-permanent paper stock or printing process.

III. MOTION PICTURES

A. Film rather than another medium. Film editions are listed below in descending order of preference.
   1. Preprint material, by special arrangement.
   2. Film gauge in which most widely distributed.
   3. 35 mm rather than 16 mm.
   4. 16 mm rather than 8 mm.
   5. Special formats (e.g., 65mm) only in exceptional cases.
   6. Open reel rather than cartridge or cassette.

B. Videotape rather than videodisc. Videotape editions are listed below in descending order of preference.
   1. Tape gauge in which most widely distributed.
   2. Two-inch tape.
   3. One-inch tape.
   4. Three-quarter-inch tape cassette.
   5. One-half-inch tape cassette.

IV. OTHER GRAPHIC MATTER

A. Paper and Printing:
   1. Archival quality rather than less-permanent paper.
   2. Color rather than black and white.

B. Size and Content:
   1. Larger rather than smaller size.
   2. In the case of cartographic works, editions with the greatest amount of information rather than those with less detail.

C. Rarity:
   1. The most widely distributed edition rather than one of limited distribution.
   2. In the case of a work published only in a limited, numbered edition, one copy outside the numbered series but otherwise identical.
   3. A photographic reproduction of the original, by special arrangement only.

D. Text and Other Materials:
   1. Works with annotations, accompanying tabular or textual matter, or other interpretative aids rather than those without them.

E. Binding and Packaging:
   1. Bound rather than unbound.
   2. If editions have different binding, apply the criteria in I.A.2-I.A.7, above.
   3. Rolled rather than folded.
   4. With protective coatings rather than without.

V. PHONORECORDS

A. Compact digital disc rather than a vinyl disc.
B. Vinyl disc rather than tape.
C. With special enclosures rather than without.
D. Open-reel rather than cartridge.
E. Cartridge rather than cassette.
F. Quadraphonic rather than stereophonic.
G. True stereophonic rather than monaural.
H. Monaural rather than electronically rechanneled stereo.

VI. MUSICAL COMPOSITIONS

A. Fullness of Score:
   1. Vocal music:
      a. With orchestral accompaniment—
         i. Full score and parts, if any, rather than conductor's score and parts, if any. (In cases of compositions published only by rental, lease, or lending, this requirement is reduced to full score only.)
         ii. Conductor's score and parts, if any, rather than condensed score and parts, if any. (In cases of compositions published only by rental, lease, or lending, this requirement is reduced to conductor's score only.)
      b. Unaccompanied: Open score (each part on separate staff) rather than closed score (all parts condensed to two staves).

   2. Instrumental music:
      a. Full score and parts, if any, rather than conductor's score and parts, if any. (In cases of compositions published only by rental, lease, or lending, this requirement is reduced to full score only.)

b. Conductor's score and parts, if any, rather than condensed score and parts, if any. (In cases of compositions published only by rental, lease, or lending, this requirement is reduced to conductor's score only.)

B. Printing and Paper:

1. Archival-quality rather than less-permanent paper.

C. Binding and Packaging:

1. Special limited editions rather than trade editions.
2. Bound rather than unbound.
3. If editions have different binding, apply the criteria in I.A.2-I.A.12, above.
4. With protective folders rather than without.

VII. MICROFORMS

A. Related Materials:

1. With indexes, study guides, or other printed matter rather than without.

B. Permanence and Appearance:

1. Silver halide rather than any other emulsion.
2. Positive rather than negative.
3. Color rather than black and white.

C. Format (newspapers and newspaper-formatted serials):

1. Reel microfilm rather than any other microform.

D. Format (all other materials):

1. Microfiche rather than reel microfilm.
2. Reel microfilm rather than microform cassettes.
3. Microfilm cassettes rather than micro-opaque prints.

E. Size:

1. 35 mm rather than 16 mm.

VIII. MACHINE-READABLE COPIES*

A. Computer Programs

1. With documents and other accompanying material rather than without.
2. Not copy-protected rather than copy-protected (if copy-protected then with a back up copy of the disk(s)).
3. *Format:*
   a. PC-DOS or MS-DOS (or other IBM compatible formats, such as XENIX):
      (i) 5 1/4" Diskette(s).
      (ii) 3 1/2" Diskette(s).
      (iii) Optical media, such as CD-ROM—best edition should adhere to prevailing NISO standards.
   b. Apple Macintosh:
      (i) 3 1/2" Diskette(s).
      (ii) Optical media such as CD-ROM—best edition should adhere to prevailing NISO standards.

B. Computerized Information Works, Including Statistical Compendia, Serials, or Reference Works:

1. With documentation and other accompanying material rather than without.
2. With best edition of accompanying program rather than without.
3. Not copy-protected rather than copy-protected (if copy-protected then with a backup copy of the disk(s)).
4. *Format:*
   a. PC-DOS or MS-DOS (or other IBM compatible formats, such as XENIX):
      (i) Optical media, such as CD-ROM—best edition should adhere to prevailing NISO standards.
      (ii) 5 1/4" Diskette(s).
      (iii) 3 1/2" Diskette(s).
   b. Apple Macintosh:
      (i) Optical media, such as CD-ROM—best edition should adhere to prevailing NISO standards.
      (ii) 3 1/2" Diskette(s).

*This best edition requirement applies only to the deposit of copies for the Library of Congress under §407 and does not apply to deposits submitted under §408 for registration of claims to copyright.

IX. WORKS EXISTING IN MORE THAN ONE MEDIUM

Editions are listed below in descending order of preference.

A. Newspapers, dissertations and theses, newspaper-formatted serials:

1. Microform.
2. Printed matter.

B. All other materials:

1. Printed matter.
2. Microform.
3. Phonorecord.

(Effective October 16, 1989.)

For further information on Copyright Office deposit regulations, see Part 202 of 37 CFR, Chapter II, or write to the Register of Copyrights, Library of Congress, Washington, D.C. 20559.

The rules set out in the above circular have been augmented by proposed rules governing published architectural works.[1] For such works, the best edition consists of the most finished form of presentation drawing in the following descending order of preference:

(1) original format, or best-quality form of reproduction, including offset or silk-screen printing;

(2) xerographic or photographic copies on good-quality paper;

(3) positive photos or photodirect positive;

(4) blue-line copies (diazo or ozalid process).

If photographs are submitted, they should be 8 x 10 inch and should clearly show several exterior and interior views. The deposit should disclose the name(s) of the architect(s) and draftsperson(s) and the site of the building.

1. Proposed amendment of 37 C.F.R., chapter II, §202.19, dated 9/12/91 and published at 56 Fed. Reg. 48137.

Appendix D Registration of Computer Programs and Databases

The general rule and accepted practice in registering computer programs and databases is to deposit "identifying material"—source code or data entries sufficient to give the flavor of what you are registering without disclosing too much. If you have questions about what to do, you can reach a Copyright Office information specialist at (202) 707-3000.

Computer Programs

1. In the case of a program, the general rule is to deposit the first 25 pages or equivalent units and the last 25 pages or equivalent units, in visually perceptible form, along with, if the work is published, the page or other unit containing the copyright notice (if any). "Visually perceptible form" means on paper or microform.

2. If you are registering a program and refer specifically to the screen displays on the application, you should deposit identifying material for those screen displays as well. Where authorship in the program is primarily literary, this may consist of printouts, photographs, or drawings, which must be less than 3 x 3 inches and not greater than 9 x 12 inches in dimension. Where the authorship is primarily audiovisual, the proper identifying material may instead be a ½-inch VHS videotape of the screen display sequence, provided this records what is actually fixed in the program and not what the user creates. The Copyright Office will not accept a videotape that is essentially a demonstration of how the program works. In no case will the Copyright Office accept a user manual as identifying material.

This distinction between "predominantly literary" and "predominantly audiovisual" is somewhat misleading. A video game clearly falls in the latter camp, and a complicated signal processing system in the former. But in between is a gray area of large dimensions. What of a computer-aided design program with a heavy visual component but no sound? It would probably be placed in the "literary" camp by default. The true distinction here is that only screen displays that are audiovisual works qualify for videotape deposit.

3. If the program you are depositing is a revision of a preexisting program, the deposit must be representative of the revisions that have been made. If the first 25 and the last 25 pages are not, then you should deposit any 50 representative pages.

4. If the program you are registering contains trade-secret information—as most do—you can take advantage of certain special exceptions:

a. You can block out the trade-secret portions, so long as the blocked out portions are "proportionately less" than what remains and an "appreciable amount of original computer code" is visible.

b. You can deposit the first 10 and last 10 pages with nothing blocked out.

c. You can deposit the first 25 and last 25 pages, with portions blocked out, plus 10 pages with nothing blocked out. If the program is a revised version, and the first 25 and last 25 pages are not representative of the new material, you can deposit 20 pages with nothing blocked out or 50 pages with block-outs, so long as in either case the pages are representative and, if you use block-outs, the material that remains is proportionately more than what you have blocked out and contains an appreciable amount of original code.

5. If the above strategies are undesirable for some good reason, you can apply to the Copyright Office for "special relief," in other words, a special dispensation from these requirements.

6. As an alternative to the above methods in trade-secret situations, you can deposit the first and last 25 pages of binary code rather than source code. The problem with this is that your registration is then made under the "rule of doubt." This means that the Copyright Office, in granting registration, is expressing no opinion on whether the binary code actually embodies the work being registered. The registration is thus more open to attack than one for which identifying material has been deposited.

DATABASES

The deposit requirements for automated databases (those that are available in CD-ROM, online, or other electronic format) are these:

1. For a database on any single subject, the first 25 and last 25 pages or equivalent units, in visually perceptible form, are sufficient. Where the work is a revised version, the rule requires 50 pages that are representative of the revisions made.

2. For a database made up of data files covering two or more separate and distinct subjects, you must deposit either 50 complete data records from each file or the entire file, whichever is less, in visually perceptible form. A "data file" for these purposes is any group of data records, regardless of their size, that pertain to a common subject matter. You must also submit a descriptive statement, typed or printed, containing this information:

- the title of the database;
- a subtitle, date of creation or publication, or other information that will distinguish any separate or distinct data file for cataloguing purposes;

• the name and address of the copyright claimant;
• the name and content of each separate file, including subject matter, origin of the data (if the file is a revised version), and the approximate number of records in the file;
• if the work is published, an exact description of the copyright notice (if any) that is put on the work and the manner or frequency with which it is displayed—for example, at the user's terminal only at sign-on, or on printouts, or whatever.

A procedure has been made available for registration of so-called dynamic databases—those that are updated frequently. The procedure permits registration of all revisions to the database that occur over any three consecutive months in one calendar year, for a single fee and using a single TX form. Special instructions are available from the Copyright Office for the completion of the form; they are complicated and some staff at the Copyright Office believe that in the end a new form will need to be developed. Do not hesitate to call the Office for help in any instance.

Group registration is available only if all of the updates and other revisions are owned by the same copyright claimant, have the same general title, and are similar in subject, content, and organization.

Deposit for a group registration must include 50 pages or equivalent units, or 50 data records, that are representative as of any one date of publication (or if the database is considered unpublished, as is often the case with online databases, one date of fixation). They must also be representative of the revisions generally and must either contain nothing but new material or be marked to show the new material added.

The statement accompanying deposit for a group registration must include, in addition to the usual information required for databases, a description of the nature and frequency of changes to the database, and it must identify at least in a general way the location within the database or the separate data files where the revisions are to be found.

Note that the representative date you choose for the deposit is also the date you must list as the publication date, in the case of a published database. However, as noted in the text, the Copyright Office is agnostic as to whether an online database is "published" or not.

APPENDIX E WARNINGS OF COPYRIGHT FOR USE BY CERTAIN LIBRARIES AND ARCHIVES

WARNING OF COPYRIGHT FOR LIBRARY PHOTOCOPY MACHINES [37 C.F.R. CH. II §201.24]

(a) *Definitions.* (1) A "Display Warning of Copyright" is a notice under paragraphs (d)(2) and (e)(2) of section 108 of Title 17 of the United States Code as amended by Pub. L. 94-553. As required by those sections the "Display Warning of Copyright" is to be displayed at the place where orders for copies or phonorecords are accepted at certain libraries and archives.

(2) An "Order Warning of Copyright" is a notice under paragraphs (d)(2) and (e)(2) of section 108 of Title 17 of the United States Code as amended by Pub. L. 94-553. As required by those sections the "Order Warning of Copyright" is to be included on printed forms supplied by certain libraries and archives and used by their patrons for ordering copies or phonorecords.

(b) *Contents.* A Display Warning of Copyright and an Order Warning of Copyright shall consist of a verbatim reproduction of the following notice, printed in such size and form and displayed in such manner as to comply with paragraph (c) of this section:

NOTICE

WARNING CONCERNING COPYRIGHT RESTRICTIONS

The copyright law of the United States (Title 17, United States Code) governs the making of photocopies or other reproductions of copyrighted material.

Under certain conditions specified in the law, libraries and archives are authorized to furnish a photocopy or other reproduction. One of these specified conditions is that the photocopy or reproduction is not to be "used for any purpose other than private study, scholarship, or research." If a user makes a request for, or later uses, a photocopy or a reproduction for purposes in excess of "fair use," that user may be liable for copyright infringement.

This institution reserves the right to refuse to accept a copying order if, in its judgment, fulfillment of the order would involve violation of copyright law.

(c) *Form and Manner of Use.* (1) A Display Warning of Copyright shall be printed on heavy paper or other durable material in type at least 18 points in size, and shall be displayed prominently, in such manner and location as to be clearly visible, legible, and comprehensible to a casual observer within the immediate vicinity of the place where orders are accepted.

(2) An Order Warning of Copyright shall be printed within a box located prominently on the order form itself, either on the front side of the form or immediately adjacent to the space calling for the name or signature of the person using the form. The notice shall be printed in type size no smaller than that used predominantly throughout the form, and in no case shall the type size be smaller than 8 points. The notice shall be printed in such manner as to be clearly legible, comprehensible, and readily apparent to a casual reader of the form.

WARNING OF COPYRIGHT FOR SOFTWARE LENDING BY NONPROFIT LIBRARIES [CONDENSED FROM 37 C.F.R. CH. II §201.24]

Whenever a nonprofit library lends a copy of a computer program the copy must have the following notice affixed to its packaging:

NOTICE
WARNING OF COPYRIGHT RESTRICTIONS

The copyright law of the United States (Title 17, United States Code) governs the reproduction, distribution, adaptation, public performance, and public display of copyrighted materials.

Under certain conditions specified in law, nonprofit libraries are authorized to lend, lease, or rent copies of computer programs to patrons on a nonprofit basis and for nonprofit purposes. Any person who makes an unauthorized copy or adaptation of the computer program, or redistributes the loan copy or publicly performs or displays the computer program, except as permitted by Title 17 of the United States Code, may be liable for copyright infringement.

This institution reserves the right to refuse to fulfill a loan request if, in its judgment, fulfillment of the request would lead to violation of the copyright law.

This Warning of Copyright Restrictions must be affixed to the packaging that contains the copy of the computer program, by means of a label cemented, gummed, or otherwise durably attached to the copies or to a box, reel, cartridge, cassette, or other container used as a permanent receptacle for the copy of the computer program. The notice must be printed in such manner as to be clearly legible, comprehensible, and readily apparent to a casual user of the computer program.

For any sort of database, if you affix a visually perceptible notice to the work or to the container in which you publish it, you should include a sample of that notice with your deposit. This is mandatory for registrations of multifile databases and for group registrations and is strongly advised, if not actually mandatory, for all others.

APPENDIX F COPYRIGHT FEES

IN GENERAL

The Copyright Act of 1976 (Title 17, United States Code) established statutory fees for services provided by the Copyright Office. These services include registering claims to copyright and renewal of claims, as well as recordation of documents, searches of copyright records, and other services. For each registration and renewal you will receive a certificate bearing the Copyright Office seal.

The Copyright Office has been instructed to bring its fees to cost-recovery level, so at least some fees are likely to increase by mid-1999. Check the Office's website for up-to-date information.

All remittances should be in the form of drafts (that is, checks, bank money orders, or bank drafts) payable to: Register of Copyrights. Do not send cash.

Drafts must be redeemable without service or exchange fees through a U.S. institution, must be payable in U.S. dollars, and must be imprinted with American Banking Association routing numbers. International Money Orders and Postal Money Orders that are negotiable only at a post office are not acceptable.

If a check received in payment of the filing fee is returned to the Copyright Office as uncollectible, the Copyright Office will cancel the registration and will notify the remitter.

The fee for processing an original, supplementary, or renewal claim is nonrefundable, whether or not copyright registration is ultimately made.

The Copyright Office cannot assume any responsibility for the loss of currency sent in payment of copyright fees.

For further information about copyright registration procedures, request Circular 1, "Copyright Basics," from:
Publications Section, LM-455
Copyright Office
Library of Congress
Washington, DC 20559-6000.

You may also order circulars and application forms 24 hours a day. Call the Copyright Office Forms Hotline at (202) 707-9100.

REGISTRATION OF COPYRIGHT CLAIMS

Filing fees for copyright claims: $20 for Forms TX, VA, PA, SR, CA, SE, Short Forms TX, VA, PA, SE, Form MW, and Form RE; $40 for Form G/DN; $10 per issue for Form SE/Group (minimum fee $20).

RECORDATION OF DOCUMENTS

For each recordation you will receive a certificate bearing the Copyright Office seal.

A document that relates to any disposition of a copyright, such as a transfer, will, or license, may be recorded in the Copyright Office. When processing is completed, the submitted document(s) will be returned with a certificate of recordation for each document. The basic fee is $20 for the recordation, under section 205, of a document of any length containing one title. Additional titles are $10 for each group of 10 or fewer. The Copyright Office will verify title counts. For more information about recordation of documents, write:
Documents Unit, LM-462
Copyright Office
Library of Congress
Washington, DC 20559-6000
Tel: (202) 707-1759

or call the Copyright Office Forms Hotline at (202) 707-9100 and request Circular 12, "Recordation of Transfers and Other Documents."

CERTIFICATIONS

The fees for certified copies of the record of registration, including certifications of Copyright Office records, are as follows: $8 for a certified copy of the record of registration, including certifications of Copyright Office records; $20 for other certifications, including certifications of photocopies of Copyright Office records.

Fees are cumulative. Certification fees are in addition to any other applicable fees such as search fees or photoduplication fees. There is an additional charge of $20 for each hour or fraction of an hour required to locate all Copyright Office records, except where the requestor supplies the Copyright Office with the registration number and year of registration.

For more information about this service, write:

Certifications and Documents Section, LM-402
Copyright Office
Library of Congress
Washington, DC 20559-6000
Tel: (202) 707-6787
or call the Copyright Office Forms Hotline at (202) 707-9100 and request Circular 6, "Obtaining Access to and Copies of Copyright Office Records and Deposits."

SEARCHES

For each search you will receive a report. The Reference and Bibliography Section will, upon request, estimate the fee required for a search; the fee must be received before the search is undertaken. Please note that searches are not made (and are not necessary under the copyright law) to determine whether a similar work has already been registered. The fee is

$20 per hour (or fraction thereof) for searching or locating the official records and for making and reporting a search.

For more information about this service, write:
Reference and Bibliography Section, LM-450
Copyright Office
Library of Congress
Washington, DC 20559-6000
Tel: (202)707-6850
or call the Copyright Office Forms Hotline at (202) 707-9100 and request Circular 22, "How to Investigate the Copyright Status of a Work."

FILING OF NOTICE OF INTENTION TO MAKE AND DISTRIBUTE PHONORECORDS

The fee is $12 for the filing, under Section 115(b), of a notice of intention to make and distribute phonorecords.

RECEIPT FOR DEPOSITS

The fee is $4 for the issuance under Section 407, mandatory deposit for the Library of Congress, of a receipt for deposit. Normally, the certificate of registration will serve as a record of receipt for claims submitted under Section 408.

OTHER FEE PROVISIONS

Section 708(a)(11) authorizes the Register to fix additional fees, on the "basis of the cost of providing the service," "for any other special services requiring a substantial amount of time or expense."

SPECIAL HANDLING

Expedited processing of an application for registration of a claim to copyright, a mask work claim, or a request for recordation of documents pertaining to a copyright is granted at the discretion of the Register of Copyrights.

The registration fee in this case is $330 for each application plus the $20 filing fee. There is an additional fee of $50 for each claim given special handling if a single deposit copy covers multiple claims and special handling is requested only for one. This charge may be avoided by submitting a separate deposit copy.

For recordation of a document the fee is $330 for each document plus the recordation fee of $20 for a document of any length containing one title.

Additional titles are $10 for each group of 10 or fewer. Requests for special handling should be made in person in the Public Information Office, LM-401, Library of Congress, or by mail to:

Library of Congress
Department 100
Washington, DC 20540.

Requests for special handling must include details that support the basis for the request. Examples of situations where a special handling request may be approved include pending or prospective litigation, cases involving the U.S. Customs Service, contractual matters, or publishing deadlines. The request must include a written certification, that is, a signed statement that the details are correct to the best of the requestor's knowledge.

For more information about special handling, call the Copyright Office Forms Hotline at (202) 707-9100 and ask for Circular 10, "Special Handling." To speak with an information specialist, call (202) 707-3000, TTY (202) 707-6737.

FULL-TERM RETENTION OF COPYRIGHT DEPOSITS

The fee is $270 for the full-term retention of copyright deposits under Section 704(e). The Copyright Office policy is to retain published copyright deposits for five years; unpublished deposits, however, are ordinarily kept for the full copyright term. Registrants who wish to ensure that the Copyright Office will keep their published deposits for the full length of the copyright term (assumed to be ninety-five years) must pay a fee to cover storage costs. Requests for full-term retention should be made to:

Chief, Information and Reference Division
Copyright Office
Library of Congress
Washington, DC 20559-6000
Attention: Full-term Retention Request.

For further information on full-term retention, call the Copyright Office Forms Hotline at (202) 707-9100 and request Circular 96, Section 202.23, "Full-Term Retention of Copyright Deposits."

SURCHARGE FOR EXPEDITED CERTIFICATIONS AND DOCUMENTS SERVICES

Anyone may request an additional certificate of registration, copies of the copyright application, correspondence, and other documents related to copyright. These services may be provided under certain conditions on an expedited basis. Copies of the copyright deposit will be provided only when (1) written authorization is received from the copyright claimant of record or his/her designated agent or from the owner of any of the exclusive rights in the copyright; (2) the Copyright Office Litigation Statement Form is completed and received from an attorney or authorized representative in connection with actual or prospective litigation involving the copyrighted work; or (3) a court order is issued for a reproduction of a deposited article, facsimile, or identifying portion which is the subject of litigation in the court's jurisdiction.

The new fees for expedited services are surcharges and will be added to the regular charge for the service provided (minimum 1 hour). The fees are per hour or fraction of an hour:

- $50 per hour for additional certificates;
- $50 per hour for in-process searches;
- $50 per hour for a copy of an assignment;
- $50 per hour for certification;
- $70 for the first hour and $50 for each additional hour to retrieve a copy of a deposit stored off-site;
- $70 for the first hour and $50 for each additional hour to retrieve a copy of a correspondence file stored in the Madison Building or at an off-site storage facility.

SURCHARGE FOR EXPEDITED REFERENCE AND BIBLIOGRAPHIC SEARCHES

This service involves researching Office records for information on copyright registrations, renewals, and transfers and other documents. It may be provided on an expedited basis under certain conditions. The new fees for expedited service will be in addition to the $20 statutory fee for each hour (or fraction of an hour). The fee is $100 for the first hour and $50 for each additional hour.

REFUNDS

Filing fees remitted to the Copyright Office for basic, supplementary, or renewal registration and for special handling will not be refunded. Payments in excess of the statutory fee will be refunded, but refunds of $50 or less will only be made upon request.

Appendix G Digest of CONFU Draft on Fair Use Guidelines

The full text of the draft guidelines can be found in *BNA's Patent, Trademark & Copyright Journal* vol. 53, December 19, 1996, pp. 125–137.

The Inclusion of Protected Works in Educational Multimedia Projects

The guidelines under this heading apply to the use, without permission, of portions of lawfully acquired copyrighted works in educational multimedia projects created by educators or students "as part of a systematic learning activity by nonprofit educational institutions." The term "educational, multimedia projects" refers to work that "incorporate[s] students' or educators' original material, such as course notes or commentary, together with various copyrighted media formats including, but not limited to, motion picture media, music, text material, graphics, illustrations, photographs and digital software which are combined into an integrated presentation." The term "systematic learning activities" includes use in connection with "non-commercial curriculum-based learning and teaching activities" at nonprofit educational institutions. Just what sort of thing the phrase "curriculum-based" is meant to exclude is not clear.

One of the interesting and novel things about these particular guidelines is that for the first time copyright owners have attempted to place implicit limits on what students can do; previous fair use guidelines have been focused exclusively on the activities of teachers and institutions. The guidelines say:

[2.1] Students may incorporate portions of lawfully acquired copyrighted works when producing their own educational multimedia projects for a specific course.

---

and

[3.1] Students may perform and display their own educational multimedia projects created under Section 2 of these guidelines for educational uses in the course for which they were created and may use them in their own portfolios as examples of their academic work for later personal uses such as job and graduate school interviews.

It seems remarkable that anyone thought it necessary to reassure anyone on these points. Not surprisingly, though, most of the guidelines are aimed at teacher activities.

[2.2] Educators may incorporate portions of lawfully acquired copyrighted works when producing their own educational multimedia projects for their own teaching tools in support of curriculum-based instructional activities at educational institutions.

Other excerpts follow.

3.2 Educator Use for Curriculum-Based Instruction. Educators may perform and display their own educational multimedia projects created under Section 2 for curriculum-based instruction to students in the following situations:

3.2.1 for face-to-face instruction,

3.2.2 assigned to students for directed self-study,

3.2.3 for remote instruction to students enrolled in curriculum-based courses and located at remote sites, provided over the educational institution's secure electronic network in real-time, or for after class review or directed self-study, provided there are technological limitations on access to the network and educational multimedia project (such as a password or PIN) and provided further that the technology prevents the making of copies of copyrighted material.

If the educational institution's network or technology used to access [a lawfully made educational multimedia project] cannot prevent duplication of copyrighted material, students or educators may use the multimedia educational projects over an otherwise secure network for a period of only 15 days after its initial real-time remote use in the course of instruction or 15 days after its assignment for directed self-study. After that period, one of the two use copies of the educational multimedia project may be placed on reserve in a learning resource center, library or similar facility for on-site use by students enrolled in the course. Students shall be advised that they are not permitted to make their own copies of the educational multimedia project.

3.3 Educator Use for Peer Conferences. Educators may perform or display their own educational multimedia projects created under Section 2 of these guidelines in presentations to their peers, for example, at workshops and conferences.

3.4 Educator Use for Professional Portfolio. Educators may retain educational multimedia projects...in their personal portfolios for later personal uses such as tenure review or job interviews.

4. Limitations: Time, Portion, Copying and Distribution

The preparation of educational multimedia projects incorporating copyrighted works... [is] subject to the limitations noted below.

4.1 Time Limitations. Educators may use their educational multimedia projects...for a period of up to two years after the first instructional use with a class. Use beyond that time period, even for educational purposes, requires permission for each copyrighted portion incorporated in the production....

4.2 Portion Limitations.... These limitations apply cumulatively to each educator's or student's multimedia project(s) for the same academic semester, cycle or term. All students should be instructed about the reasons for copyright protection and the need to follow these guidelines. It is understood, however, that students in kindergarten through grade six may not be able to adhere rigidly to the portion limitations in this section in their independent development of educational multimedia projects. In any event, each such project retained under Sections 3.1 and 4.3 should comply with the portion limitations in this section.

4.2.4 Illustrations and photographs. The reproduction or incorporation of photographs and illustrations is more difficult to define with regard to fair use because fair use usually precludes the use of an entire work. Under these guidelines a photograph or illustration may be used in its entirety but no more than 5 images by an artist or photographer may be reproduced or otherwise incorporated as part of an educational multimedia project created under Section 2. When using photographs and illustrations from a published collective work, not more than 10% or 15 images, whichever is less, may be reproduced or otherwise incorporated as part of an educational multimedia project created under Section 2.

4.3 Copying and Distribution Limitations. Only a limited number of copies, including the original, may be made of an educator's educational multimedia project. For all of the uses permitted by Section 3, there may be no more than two use copies only one of which may be placed on reserve as described in Section 3.2.3. An additional copy may be made for preservation purposes but may only be used or copied to replace a use copy that has been lost, stolen, or damaged. In the case of a jointly created educational multimedia project, each principal creator may retain one copy but only for the purposes described in Sections 3.3 and 3.4 for educators and in Section 3.1 for students.

5.2 Duplication of Multimedia Projects beyond Limitations Listed in These Guidelines. Even for educational uses, educators and students must seek individual permissions for all copyrighted works incorporated in their personally created educational multimedia projects before replicating or distributing beyond the limitations listed in Section 4.3. [Note: the use of the word "must" here, and at certain other places in the excerpts that follow, is somewhat at odds with the general intent that these guidelines are "safe harbor" guidelines, not the last word on the topic.]

6.2 Attribution and Acknowledgment. Educators and students are reminded to credit the sources and display the copyright notice and copyright ownership information if this is shown in the original source, for all works incorporated as part of educational multimedia projects prepared by educators and students, including those prepared under fair use....

The credit and copyright notice information may be combined and shown in a separate section of the educational multimedia project (e.g. credit section) except for images incorporated into the project for the uses described in Section 3.2.3. In such cases, the copyright notice and the name of the creator of the image must be incorporated into the image when, and to the extent, such information is reasonably available; credit and copyright notice information is considered "incorporated" if it is attached to the image file and appears on the screen when the image is viewed. In those cases when displaying source credits and copyright ownership information on the screen with the image would be mutually exclusive with an instructional objective (e.g. during examinations in which the source credits and/or copyright information would be relevant to the examination questions), those images may be displayed without such information being simultaneously displayed on the screen. In such cases, this information should be linked to the image in a manner compatible with such instructional objectives.

6.3 Notice of Use Restrictions. Educators and students are advised that they must include on the opening screen of their multimedia project and any accompanying print material a notice that certain materials are included under the fair use exception of the U.S. Copyright Law and have been prepared according to the educational multimedia fair use guidelines and are restricted from further use.

6.5 Integrity of Copyrighted Works: Alterations. Educators and students may make alterations in the portions of the copyrighted works they incorporate as part of an educational multimedia project only if the alterations support specific instructional objectives. Educators and students are advised to note that alterations have been made.

———

Appendix H Notice of Intent to Enforce a Copyright Restored under the Uruguay Round Agreements Act

Format--Notice of Intent to Enforce a Copyright Restored under the Uruguay Round Agreements Act (URAA)

1. Title:____

   (If this work does not have a title, state "No title.")

   OR

   Brief description of work (for untitled works only):

   ____

2. English translation of title (if applicable):

   ____

3. Alternative title(s) (if any):________________________

   ____

4. Type of work:______________________________________

   ____

   (e.g. painting, sculpture, music, motion picture, sound recording, book)

5. Name of author(s):__________________________________

   ____

6. Source country:____________________________________

7. Approximate year of publication:______________________

8. Additional identifying information:____________________

   ____

   (e.g. for movies: director, leading actors, screenwriter, animator; for photographs: subject matter; for books: editor, publisher, contributors,subject matter).

9. Name of copyright owner:____________________________

   (Statements may be filed in the name of the owner of the restored copyright or the owner of an exclusive right therein.)

10. If you are not the owner of all rights, specify the rights you own:____

    (e.g. the right to reproduce/distribute/publicly display/publicly perform the work, or to prepare a derivative work based on the work)

11. Address at which copyright owner may be contacted:

____

____

____

(Give the complete address, including the country and an "attention" line, or "in care of" name, if necessary.)

12. Telephone number of owner:______________________________________.

13. Telefax number of owner:______________________________________

14. Certification and Signature:

I hereby certify that, for each of the work(s) listed above, I am the copyright owner, or the owner of an exclusive right, or the owner's authorized agent, the agency relationship having been constituted in a writing signed by the owner before the filing of this notice, and that the information given herein is true and correct to the best of my knowledge.

Signature:______________________________________

Name (printed or typed):______________________________________

As agent for (if applicable):______________________________________

Date:______________________________________

NOTE: Notices of Intent to Enforce must be in English, except for the original title, and either typed or printed by hand legibly in dark, preferably black, ink. They must be on 8 1/2 by 11 inch white paper of good quality, with at least a 1-inch (or 3 cm) margin.

Notes

CHAPTER 1

1. 17 U.S.C. §102(a).

2. 17 U.S.C. §301.

3. *See, e.g.,* Hoehling v. Universal City Studios, Inc., 618 F.2d 972 (2d Cir. 1980), *cert. denied* 449 U.S. 841 (1980); Miller v. Universal City Studios, Inc., 650 F.2d 1365 (5th Cir. 1981).

4. Sheldon v. Metro-Goldwyn Pictures Corp., 81 F.2d 49, 54 (2d Cir. 1936).

5. 17 U.S.C. §101.

6. Alfred Bell & Co. v. Catalda Fine Arts, Inc., 191 F.2d 99 (2d Cir. 1951), *aff'g* 74 F.Supp. 973 (S.D.N.Y. 1947); Alva Studios, Inc. v. Winninger, 177 F.Supp. 265 (S.D.N.Y. 1959). One case has held that affixing an art print to a ceramic tile creates a derivative work, but this is almost certainly an aberration. Mirage Editions, Inc. v. Albuquerque A.R.T. Co., 856 F.2d 1341 (9th Cir. 1988).

7. 17 U.S.C. §103(b).

8. L. Batlin & Son, Inc. v. Snyder, 536 F.2d 436 (2d Cir. 1976); Durham Industries, Inc. v. Tomy Corp., 630 F.2d 905 (2d Cir. 1980); Gracen v. Bradford Exchange, 698 F.2d 300 (7th Cir. 1983); Sunset House Distrib. Corp. v. Doran, 304 F.2d 251 (9th Cir. 1962), *aff'g* 197 F.Supp. 940 (S.D.Cal. 1961). *See also* Knickerbocker Toy Co., Inc. v. Winterbrook Toy Corp., 216 U.S.P.Q. 621 (D.N.H. 1982). A return to a more generous standard may be visible in Kramer Mfg. Co. v. Andrews, 783 F.2d 421 (4th Cir. 1986), and in Norma Ribbon & Trimming Inc. v. Little, 51 F.3d 45, 48 (5th Cir. 1995).

9. A lucid and interesting discussion of this problem may be found in Oppenheimer, "Originality in Art Reproductions: 'Variations' in Search of a Theme," *Bull. Copr. Soc.* vol. 26, no. 1, 1978.

10. Gilliam v. American Broadcasting Companies, Inc., 538 F.2d 14 (2d Cir. 1976).

11. 111 S.Ct. 1282 (1991).

12. I discuss this issue in detail in "Database Protection after Feist v. Rural Telephone Co.," *Jrnl. Copr. Soc.* vol. 42, no. 1, 1994.

13. 101 U.S. 99 (1880).

14. Harcourt, Brace & World Inc. v. Graphic Controls Corp., 329 F.Supp. 517 (S.D.N.Y. 1971); Manpower, Inc. v. Temporary Help of Harrisburg, Inc., 246 F.Supp. 788 (E.D.Pa. 1965).

15. Morrissey v. Procter & Gamble Co., 379 F.2d 675 (1st Cir. 1967).

16. 17 U.S.C. §102(a).

17. Leon v. Pacific Tel. & Tel. Co., 91 F.2d 484 (9th Cir. 1937); Amsterdam v. Triangle Publications, Inc., 189 F.2d 104 (3rd Cir. 1951).

18. *See, e.g.,* Becker v. Loew's, Inc., 133 F.2d 889 (7th Cir. 1943); CCM Cable Rep. Inc. v. Ocean Coast Properties, Inc., 97 F.3d 1513, 1519 (1st Cir. 1996); *compare* John Muller & Co. v. New York Arrows Soccer Team, Inc., 231 U.S.P.Q. 319 (8th Cir. 1986), *with* Reader's Digest Association, Inc. v. Conservative Digest, Inc., 821 F.2d 800 (D.C. Cir. 1987).

19. Paramore v. Mack Sennett, 9 F.2d 66 (S.D.Cal. 1925); *cf.* Duff v. Kansas City Star Co., 229 F.2d 320 (8th Cir. 1962). The scope of the law on unfair competition has been severely limited in recent years. Federal copyright law now preempts state laws in the field, to the extent that they purport to protect rights equivalent to rights under copyright in works fixed in tangible form, whether or not they are copyrightable. 17 U.S.C. §301; H.R. Rep. No. 94-1476, 94th Cong., 2d Sess., at pp. 130–133 (1976). (This, the House of Representatives Report for the Copyright Act of 1976, will be referred to hereafter as "H. Rep.") This does not apply quite so broadly to causes of action arising before 1978. There is no reason to feel it would restrict protection of titles, because titles are regarded as trademarks under federal law, not as works of authorship.

20. H. Rep., pp. 53–54.

21. The leading toy case is Gay Toys, Inc. v. Buddy L Corp., 703 F.2d 970 (6th Cir. 1983). The Copyright Office guidelines are at 56 Fed.Reg. 56530. The recent masquerade case is Whimsicality Inc. v. Maison Joseph Battat Ltee, 97 Civ. 7871, 11/24/98, 57 PTCJ 141 (S.D.N.Y. 1998).

22. H. Rep., p. 55.

23. Brandir International, Inc. v. Cascade Pacific Lumber Co., 834 F.2d 1142 (2d Cir. 1987).

24. *Ibid.;* 17 U.S.C. §§101, 113(b); H. Rep., p. 105.

25. H. Rep., p. 55.

26. H.R. Rep. No. 101-735, 101st Cong., 2d Sess., at pp. 20–21.

27. 17 U.S.C. §101.

28. H.R. Rep. No. 101-735, 101st Cong., 2d Sess., p. 20.

29. 37 C.F.R. Ch. II, §202.11. One court has also held that a structure must be freestanding to be a building: a store inside a mall, even if it looks like a building, is not one. The Yankee Candle Company, Inc. v. New England Candle Co., 14 F.Supp.2d 154 (D.Mass. 1998). However, this judgment was ultimately vacated by consent and so its force as precedent is somewhat weakened. 1998 U.S.Dist. LEXIS 21434.

30. 37 C.F.R. Ch. II, §202.11.

31. *See, e.g.,* Nichols v. Universal Pictures Corp., 45 F.2d 119 (1930), *cert. denied* 282 U.S. 902 (1931).

32. Warner Bros. Pictures, Inc. v. Columbia Broadcasting System, Inc., 216 F.2d 945 (9th Cir. 1954); *see* Borroughs v. Metro-Goldwyn-Mayer, Inc., 683 F.2d 610 (2d Cir. 1982).

33. Williams Electronics, Inc. v. Artic International, Inc., 685 F.2d 870 (3rd Cir. 1982); Apple Computer, Inc. v. Franklin Computer Corp., 714 F.2d 1240 (3rd Cir. 1983), *cert. denied* 464 U.S. 1033 (1984); Apple Computer, Inc. v. Formula International Inc., 562 F.Supp. 775 (N.D.Cal. 1983).

34. Final Report of the National Commission on New Technological Uses of Copyrighted Works (CONTU) (1978), pp. 9–38. Prior law had held that if a work was not intelligible, even with magnification, to the human eye, it neither infringed copyright nor was entitled to copyright. White-Smith Music Publishing Co. v. Apollo Co., 209 U.S. 1 (1908); Corcoran v. Montgomery Ward & Co., Inc., 121 F.2d 572 (9th Cir. 1941). At first it was thought that this doctrine might apply to object code. Data Cash Systems, Inc. v. JS&A Group, Inc., 480 F.Supp. 1063 (N.D.Ill. 1979), *aff'd on other grounds* 628 F.2d 1038 (7th Cir. 1980). *See* Stern, "Another Look at Copyright Protection of Software: Did the 1980 Act Do Anything for Object Code?" *Computer Law Jrnl.* vol. 3, no. 1, Fall 1981, pp. 1–17.

35. Final Report of CONTU, at pp. 19–21.

36. Chamberlin v. Uris Sales Corp., 150 F.2d 512 (2d Cir. 1945); *see* Brief English Systems v. Owen, 48 F.2d 555 (2d Cir. 1931), and Universal Athletic Sales Co. v. Salkeld, 511 F.2d 904 (3rd Cir. 1975); *cf.* the factually ambiguous case of Runge v. Lee, 441 F.2d 479 (9th Cir. 1971) and Justice Douglas's dissent to the denial of certiorari thereon, 404 U.S. 887 (1971).

37. 797 F.2d 1222 (3d Cir. 1986).

38. Computer Associates Int'l Inc. v. Altai Inc., 982 F.2d 693 (2d Cir. 1992).

39. Diamond v. Diehr, 450 U.S. 175 (1981); *see also* Diamond v. Bradley, 600 F.2d 807 (C.C.P.A. 1979), *aff'd by an equally divided court* 450 U.S. 381 (1981).

40. This and several other patented algorithms are described in a story in the *New York Times,* February 15, 1989, p. D1. Indeed, the scope of patent protection for software continues to grow, because the courts have given their blessing to patent claims for software where a "machine" (i.e., a computer) is identified as a component. On this basis, for example, a patent was recently upheld for algorithms used in running a hub-and-spoke mutual fund arrangement. State Street Bank & Trust Co. v. Signature Financial Group, 149 F.3d 1368 (Fed. Cir. 1998).

41. Lotus Development Corp. v. Paperbook Software Int'l, 740 F.Supp. 37 (D.Mass. 1990).

42. 53 Fed.Reg. 21817–21820 (6/10/88); *cf.* Digital Communications Associates, Inc. v. Softklone Distributing Corp., 659 F.Supp. 449 (N.D.Ga. 1987).

43. Manufacturers Technologies, Inc. v. Cams, Inc., 706 F.Supp. 984 (D.Conn. 1989).

44. Lotus Development Corp. v. Borland International, Inc., 49 F.3d 807 (1st Cir. 1995), *aff'd by an equally divided court* 116 S.Ct. 804 (1996). The statutory reference is to 17 U.S.C. §102.

45. For interesting analyses of this topic, see Clifford, "Intellectual Property in the Era of the Creative Computer Program: Will the True Creator Please Stand Up?," *Tulane L. Rev.*, vol. 17, 1997, pp. 1675, 1682–1683; Miller, "Computers and Copyright Protection," *Harv. L. Rev.*, vol. 106, 1993, pp. 977, 1042–1073.

46. 17 U.S.C. §901 *et seq.*

47. 17 U.S.C. §906(a). Brooktree Corp. v. Advanced Micro Devices, Inc., 705 F.Supp. 491 (S.D.Cal. 1988).

48. 17 U.S.C. §1101. For state law to the same effect see, *e.g.*, Metropolitan Opera Association, Inc. v. Wagner-Nichols Recorder Corp., 199 Misc. 786, 101 N.Y.S.2d 483 (1950), *aff'd* 279 App.Div. 632, 107 N.Y.S.2d 795 (1951). The new §1101 expressly does not preempt state laws.

49. 18 U.S.C. Ch. 113, §2319A.

50. I am indebted to William F. Patry, a leading author and commentator in this field, for this observation. I am informed by Marybeth Peters, the Register of Copyrights, that a definite term of protection was supposed to have been included in the statute but was overlooked by the drafters. As time goes by, hope dwindles that this omission may be cured by remedial legislation.

51. Midler v. Ford Motor Co., 849 F.2d 460 (9th Cir. 1988). *See* Lennon v. Pulsebeat News, Inc., 143 U.S.P.Q. 309 (N.Y.Sup.Ct. 1964); Sinatra v. Goodyear Tire & Rubber Co., 435 F.2d 711 (9th Cir. 1979); Booth v. Colgate-Palmolive Co., 362 F.Supp. 343 (S.D.N.Y. 1973).

CHAPTER 2

1. 17 U.S.C. §101.

2. Shapiro, Bernstein & Co. v. Jerry Vogel Music Co., Inc., 161 F.2d 406, 410 (2d Cir. 1946, 1947), *cert. denied* 331 U.S. 820 (1942).

3. H. Rep., p. 120.

4. Childress v. Taylor, 945 F.2d 500 (2d Cir. 1991).

5. Thomson v. Larson, 147 F.3d 195 (2d Cir. 1998).

6. Childress v. Taylor, *supra*; Ashton-Tate Corp. v. Ross, 916 F.2d 516 (9th Cir. 1990); Erickson v. Trinity Theater Inc., 13 F.3d 1061 (7th Cir. 1994). *See* Andrien v. Southern Ocean County Chamber of Commerce, 927 F.2d 132 (3d Cir. 1991), for a perhaps more expansive view of what it means to "contribute" copyrightable expression.

7. Sweet Music, Inc. v. Melrose Music Corp., 189 F.Supp. 655, 659 (S.D.Cal. 1960).

8. Melville B. Nimmer, *Nimmer on Copyright* (New York: Matthew Bender, 1980), §6.10[C].

9. Marshall v. Miles Laboratories, Inc., 647 F.Supp. 1326, 1330 (N.D.Ind. 1986). *See generally* Artec Systems Inc. v. Peiffer, 30 U.S.P.Q.2d 1365 (4th Cir. 1994).

10. *See* Avedon v. Exstein, 141 F.Supp. 278 (S.D.N.Y. 1956); Lumiere v. Pathe Exchange, 275 Fed. 428 (2d Cir. 1921).

11. Brattleboro Publishing Co. v. Winmill Publishing Corp., 369 F.2d 565 (2d Cir. 1966); May v. Morganelli-Heumann & Associates, 618 F.2d 1363, 1368 (9th Cir. 1980).

12. Aldon Accessories Ltd. v. Spiegel, Inc., 738 F.2d 548 (2d Cir. 1984); *accord,* Brunswick Beacon, Inc. v. Schock-Hopchas Publishing Co., 810 F.2d 410 (4th Cir. 1987); Evans Newton, Inc. v. Chicago Systems Software, 793 F.2d 889 (7th Cir. 1986), *cert. denied* 107 S.Ct. 434 (1986).

13. Town of Clarkstown v. Reeder, 566 F.Supp. 137 (S.D.N.Y. 1983).

14. 815 F.2d 323 (5th Cir. 1987).

15. Community for Creative Non-Violence v. Reid, 846 F.2d 1485 (D.C. Cir. 1988).

16. Dumas v. Gommerman, 865 F.2d 1093 (9th Cir. 1989).

17. Community for Creative Non-Violence v. Reid, 490 U.S. 730 (1989).

18. Aymes v. Bonelli, 980 F.2d 857 (2d Cir. 1992).

19. *Ibid.*

20. Marco v. Accent Publishing Co., 969 F.2d 1547 (3d Cir. 1992).

21. 17 U.S.C. §109(c).

22. *See* Yojna, Inc. v. American Medical Data Systems, Inc., 667 F.Supp. 446 (E.D.Mich. 1987).

23. *See* 17 U.S.C. §301(a).

24. 17 U.S.C. §201(b).

25. Van Cleef & Arpels, Inc. v. Schechter, 308 F.Supp. 674 (S.D.N.Y. 1969); Scherr v. Universal Match Corp., 417 F.2d 497 (2d Cir. 1969).

26. Playboy Enterprises, Inc. v. Dumas, 53 F.3d 549 (2d Cir. 1995), *cert. denied* 116 S.Ct. 567 (1995). *But see* Armento v. The Laser Image, Inc., 40 U.S.P.Q.2d 1874 (W.D.N.C. 1996).

27. 17 U.S.C. §201(b).

28. *See* Lulirama Ltd. Inc. v. Axxess Broadcast Services, Inc., 128 F.3d 872 (5th Cir. 1997).

29. Schiller & Schmidt, Inc. v. Nordisco Corp., 23 U.S.P.Q.2d 1762 (7th Cir. 1992).

30. Playboy Enterprises, Inc. v. Dumas, *supra.*

31. Oddo v. Ries, 743 F.2d 630 (9th Cir. 1984). One court has held that for a partnership agreement to create co-ownership of copyright, it must be in writing. Konigsberg International Inc. v. Rice, 16 F.2d 355 (9th Cir.

1994). This is in keeping with the general rule, discussed in chapter 3, that an assignment of an interest in copyright must be in writing. In essence, the author is assigning copyright to the partnership of which she is a member, and that assignment must be in writing.

32. 17 U.S.C. §101.

33. *See* Ringer and Flacks, "Applicability of the Universal Copyright Convention to Certain Works in the Public Domain of Their Country of Origin," *Bull. Copr. Society* vol. 27, no. 3, 1980.

34. *See, e.g.,* Public Affairs Associates, Inc. v. Rickover, 268 F.Supp. 444 (D.D.C. 1967); Bell v. Combined Registry Co., 536 F.2d 164 (7th Cir. 1976).

35. 17 U.S.C. §103(a).

36. 17 U.S.C. §201(d)(2).

37. 17 U.S.C. §202.

38. 17 U.S.C. §109(b).

39. This was the holding of the trial court in Community for Creative Non-Violence v. Reid. The issue was not discussed at the appellate or Supreme Court levels (see notes 15 and 17 *supra*).

40. *In re* Marriage of Worth, 4 U.S.P.Q.2d 1730 (Cal.Ct.App. 1987); Rodrigue v. Rodrigue, BNA PTCJ Vol. 57, No. 1415 (E.D.La., No. 95-2862, 2/12/99).

41. 17 U.S.C. §904.

42. 17 U.S.C. §302(b).

43. 17 U.S.C. §302(c).

CHAPTER 3

1. 17 U.S.C. §201(e).

2. See P.L. 101-650 §805, 104 Stat. 5136, and 37 C.F.R. Ch. II §201.26.

3. ProCD, Inc. v. Zeidenberg, 86 F.3d 1447 (7th Cir. 1996). *Compare* Vault Corporation v. Quaid Software, Ltd., 847 F.2d 255 (5th Cir. 1988).

4. David Grossman Designs, Inc. v. Bortin, 347 F.Supp. 1150 (N.D.Ill. 1972); Gerlach-Barklow Co. v. Morris & Bendien, 23 F.2d 159 (2d Cir. 1927).

5. 17 U.S.C. §204(a).

6. *See, e.g.*, with regard to time limitations, 17 U.S.C. §203(b)(6); Viacom Int'l, Inc. v. Tandem Productions, Inc., 368 F.Supp. 1264 (S.D.N.Y. 1974), *aff'd* 526 F.2d 593 (2d Cir. 1975).

7. *See, e.g.*, Bartsch v. Metro-Goldwyn-Mayer, Inc., 391 F.2d 150 (2d Cir. 1968); Ettore v. Philco Television Broadcasting Corp., 229 F.2d 481 (3rd Cir. 1956). Prof. Nimmer lists many more of these cases at §10.10[B] of Nimmer, *op. cit.*

8. 17 U.S.C. §201(c).

9. Tasini v. New York Times Co., 972 F.Supp. 804 (S.D.N.Y. 1997).

10. Mills Music v. Cromwell Music, 126 F.Supp. 54 (S.D.N.Y. 1954); cf. Viacom Int'l, Inc. v. Tandem Productions, Inc., *supra.*

11. 17 U.S.C. §204(a).

12. Nimmer, *op. cit.*, §10.09. See further discussion in chapter 9.

13. Folsom v. Marsh, 9 Fed.Cas. 342, No. 4901 (C.C.Mass. 1841).

14. 17 U.S.C. §204(b).

15. 17 U.S.C. §204(a). Eden Toys v. Florelee, 697 F.2d 27 (2d Cir. 1982); Magnuson v. Video Yesteryear, 85 F.3d 1424 (9th Cir. 1996). I infer the third-party reliance exception from Schiller & Schmidt, Inc. v. Nordisco Corp., 23 U.S.P.Q.2d 1762 (7th Cir. 1992), which is otherwise out of step with prevailing opinion.

16. 17 U.S.C. §405(a)(3).

17. 17 U.S.C. §205(c).

18. 17 U.S.C. §205(e).

19. *Ibid.*

20. 17 U.S.C. §205(f).

21. National Peregrine, Inc. v. Capitol Federal Savings and Loan Association of Denver, 116 B.R. 194 (C.D.Cal. 1990).

22. 17 U.S.C. §203(a)(5).

23. 17 U.S.C. §§203(a), 203(b)(5).

24. *Ibid.*

25. 17 U.S.C. §203(b)(1); Mills Music, Inc. v. Snyder, 469 U.S. 153 (1985).

26. 17 U.S.C. §§101, 203(a).

27. 17 U.S.C. §203(a)(3).

28. *See generally* 17 U.S.C. §203.

29. 17 U.S.C. §203(b).

30. 17 U.S.C. §203(b)(4).

31. 17 U.S.C. §203(b)(3).

32. *Ibid.*

CHAPTER 4

1. 17 U.S.C. §401(d), added by P.L. 100-568, 102 Stat. 2853.

2. 17 U.S.C. §101, Jewelers' Mercantile Agency, Ltd. v. Jewelers' Weekly Pub. Co., 155 N.Y. 241, 49 N.E. 872 (1897).

3. Gottsberger v. Aldine Book Pub. Co., 33 Fed. 381 (C.C.D.Mass. 1887); Bobbs-Merrill Co. v. Straus, 147 Fed. 15 (2d Cir. 1906), *aff'd* 210 U.S. 339 (1908).

4. 17 U.S.C. §101.

5. Grandma Moses Properties, Inc. v. This Week Magazine, 117 F.Supp. 348 (S.D.N.Y. 1953); *cf.* remarks of Rep. Kastenmeier, 122 Cong. Rec. No. 10, 874–875 (daily ed. Sept. 22, 1976).

6. 17 U.S.C. §101.

7. 17 U.S.C. §101; White v. Kimmell, 193 F.2d 744 (9th Cir. 1952).

8. Marvin Worth Prods. v. Superior Films Corp., 319 F.Supp. 1269 (S.D.N.Y. 1970); *see generally* Nimmer, *op. cit.,* §4.10.

9. 17 U.S.C. §101.

10. 17 U.S.C. §404(a). This does not apply to ads inserted on behalf of the copyright owner of the collective work.

11. 17 U.S.C. §404(b).

12. 17 U.S.C. §909(b).

13. 17 U.S.C. §§401(b)(2), 909(b).

14. 17 U.S.C. §§401(b)(3), 408(a).

15. Tonka Corp. v. Tsaisun, Inc., 1 U.S.P.Q.2d 1387 (D.Minn. 1986); *see also* Koontz v. Jaffarian, 787 F.2d 906 (4th Cir. 1986).

16. 17 U.S.C. §406(a).

17. Russell v. Price, 448 F.Supp. 303 (C.D.Cal. 1977).

18. Charles Garnier, Paris v. Andin International Inc., 36 F.3d 1214 (1st Cir. 1994), *aff'g* 30 U.S.P.Q.2d 1612 (D.R.I. 1994). The not entirely convincing proposition that works properly published before Berne need not bear notice after Berne is found in Encore Shoes v. Bennett Industries Inc., 18 U.S.P.Q.2d 1874 (D.Mass. 1991).

19. It has been held that omission from 1 percent of 40,000 copies was permissible, whereas omission from 22 to 37 percent of 1,335 copies was not. Original Appalachian Artworks, Inc. v. The Toy Loft, Inc., 684 F.2d 821 (11th Cir. 1982); King v. Burnett, CCH Copr.L.Dec. ¶25,489 (D.D.C. 1982).

20. *Compare* Charles Garnier, Paris v. Andin International Inc., note 18 above, and Shapiro & Son Bedspread Corp. v. Royal Mills Associates, 764 F.2d 69 (2d Cir. 1985), *with* Forry, Inc. v. Neundorfer, Inc., 837 F.2d 259 (6th Cir. 1988) and cases cited therein.

21. Charles Garnier, Paris v. Andin International Inc., note 18 above.

22. 17 U.S.C. §103(b); Grove Press, Inc. v. Greenleaf Publishing Co., 247 F.Supp. 518 (S.D.N.Y. 1965); Russell v. Price, 612 F.2d 1123 (9th Cir. 1979), *cert. denied* 446 U.S. 952 (1980).

23. 17 U.S.C. §506(c).

24. 17 U.S.C. §406(a).

25. 17 U.S.C. §406(b).

26. Note the negative implication of 17 U.S.C. §402(d). If this merely refers to the innocence defenses under §§405(b) and 406(a), it is simply redundant.

CHAPTER 5

1. 17 U.S.C. §411(a).

2. 17 U.S.C. §412. The special exemption for films first fixed at time of broadcast is only available if advance notice is given to an infringer. 17 U.S.C. §411(b), 37 C.F.R. Ch. II §201.22.

3. 17 U.S.C. §910.

4. The tests described *infra* are embodied in the definitions of the "Berne Convention work" and "country of origin," in 17 U.S.C. §101, as amended by P.L. 100-568, 102 Stat. 2853.

5. The statute is poorly drafted in this respect. Interpreted literally, it would waive registration for any unpublished audiovisual work of which not all authors are legal entities headquartered in the United States; in other words, even if all authors are U.S. citizens, it would waive registration because the authors are not "legal entities." This is clearly not the statutory intent, however.

6. 17 U.S.C. §409.

7. 17 U.S.C. §506(e). *See* Ashton-Tate Corp. v. Fox Software Inc., 760 F.Supp. 831 (C.D.Cal. 1990), rescinded by Order dated Apr. 18, 1991, 1991 U.S.Dist. LEXIS 6577. *See also* Whimsicality, Inc. v. Rubie's Costumes Co. Inc., 891 F.2d 452 (2d Cir. 1989).

8. 17 U.S.C. §407.

9. 37 C.F.R. Ch. II §202.19(f).

10. 17 U.S.C. §407(d).

11. 37 C.F.R. Ch. II §202.19.

12. 37 C.F.R. Ch. II §202.20.

13. A motion picture is not considered to be published for these purposes merely because a nonprofit institution has been given a license to make a fixation of it. For example, if a school is given permission to videotape a television broadcast, the television program is still unpublished for deposit purposes though not for other purposes.

14. 37 C.F.R. Ch. II §202.21.

15. 17 U.S.C. §408(c)(2).

16. 37 C.F.R. Ch. II §202.3(b).

17. Benham Jewelry Corp. v. Aron Basha Corp., 55 PTCJ 1352, 97 Civ. 3841 (RWS) (S.D.N.Y. 10/14/97).

18. 17 U.S.C. §710; 37 C.F.R. Ch. II §201.15.

CHAPTER 6

1. The first two of these three limitations are contained in 17 U.S.C. §114(d); the third is in 17 U.S.C. §112. Under §112, those transmitters who transmit sound recordings to business establishments (for background music, basically) must pay a compulsory license fee to exercise this right. (The amount of the fee, and other particulars, were under negotiation as of January 1999.) Note also that in the case of *digital* transmitters who have rights under §112, copyright owners are supposed to supply decryption technology to them for purposes of making lawful copies, "if it is technologically feasible and economically reasonable" for the copyright owners to do so. If they do not, then the transmitters are

released from that part of the statute which makes it illegal to decrypt copyrighted material. The topic of decryption is treated in chapter 8.

2. 17 U.S.C. §117.

3. 17 U.S.C. §120. The case is Leicester v. Warner Bros., C.D.Cal., No. CV95-4058-HLH (5/29/98).

4. 17 U.S.C. §109.

5. Quality King Distrib., Inc. v. L'Anza Research Int'l, 118 S.Ct. 1125 (1998).

6. Technically, the restrictions regarding software apply to anyone in possession of a copy of a program, not just the "owner" of a copy. It is odd that Congress thought it necessary to state this, since the first sale doctrine of §109(a) explicitly applies only to copies of which *ownership* has passed from the copyright owner. Despite the appearances this may create, no negative inference should be drawn from the wording of §109(b): the first sale doctrine exempts rental, lease, and lending *only* where title to the object has passed to the lessor or lender.

7. 17 U.S.C. §114(a). In addition to the exceptions discussed *infra,* Congress has specifically provided that one who owns a lawfully made copy of a video game has the right to perform the game publicly without the copyright owner's permission. This presumptive right does not apply to works incorporated in the visual part of the game unless those works are owned by the same copyright owner. 17 U.S.C. §109.

8. 17 U.S.C. §106(6).

9. All exceptions under this heading are in 17 U.S.C. §110 unless otherwise noted.

10. 17 U.S.C. §111(a),(b).

11. 17 U.S.C. §504(d).

12. 17 U.S.C. §112(b).

13. 37 C.F.R. Ch. II §201.13.

14. 17 U.S.C. §112(d).

15. All exceptions under this heading are in 17 U.S.C. §110 unless otherwise noted. As with the performance right, the display right for video games is not effective against owners of lawfully made copies. See note 7 above.

16. 17 U.S.C. §110(3).

17. 17 U.S.C. §113(c).

18. 17 U.S.C. §106A.

19. Carter v. Helmsley-Spear Inc., No. 94 Civ. 2922 (S.D.N.Y. 8/31/94); and the earlier decision in the same case, 852 F.Supp. 228 (S.D.N.Y. 1994).

20. 17 U.S.C. §106A(c)(2). This provision is quite illogical, since intent is clearly required for actionable modification, and the statute specifically distinguishes between intent and gross negligence. See §106A(a)(3)(A) and (B). Nevertheless, we are obliged to take it seriously. The statutory history loses sight of the limitation, further muddying the waters. See H.R. Rep. No. 101-514 at p. 16, under the heading "State of Mind."

21. Carter v. Helmsley-Spear Inc., *supra.*

22. 17 U.S.C. §113(d).

23. In this sentence, I am deviating somewhat from the statutory language, as I believe the statute intends to say more than it does and is poorly drafted. My departure is to speak here of works "incorporated in" a building. Technically, this part of the statute, §113(d)(2), addresses only works that are "part of" buildings, a term that purports to be different from "incorporated in" (see §113(d)(1)(A)). But the distinction (if there is one) seems contrary to the intent of the statute; furthermore, the section of the statute that provides a registry for artists' names for purposes of notice under §113(d)(2)—namely, §113(d)(3)—speaks of works "incorporated in or made part of" buildings.

24. 37 C.F.R. Ch. II §201.25.

25. See H.R. Rep. No. 101-514 at p. 19.

26. See Karlin, "Joint Ownership of Moral Rights," *Jrnl. Copr. Soc.* vol. 38, no. 4, 1991.

27. Both of these problems appear to have been created by floor amendments to the bill. Compare the statute as enacted with H.R. Rep. No. 101-514 at p. 19.

28. For the state laws just referred to, see: Gen. Stat. of Conn., Title 42 §42-116s *et seq.;* La. Rev. Stat. §51:2151c *et seq.;* 27 Maine Rev. Stat. §303; Mass. Gen. Laws Ch. 231 §85S; N.J. Stat. Title 2A, Ch. 24A; N.Y. General Business Law, Art. 12-J, §228 m–q; 73 Penn. Stat. §2101–2110; and Gen. Laws of R.I., Title 5, Ch. 62.

29. Calif. Civil Code §986.

CHAPTER 7

1. 17 U.S.C. §115. For the royalty rates see 37 C.F.R. Ch. II §307.3.

2. 37 C.F.R. Ch. II §201.18.

3. *Ibid.*

4. 17 U.S.C. §114(d),(e),(f).

5. 17 U.S.C. §115(c).

6. §1(e) of the 1909 Act *(i.e.,* of Title 17 as amended prior to enactment of the Copyright Act of 1976); 17 U.S.C. §116(a).

7. Fortnightly Corp. v. United Artists Television, Inc., 392 U.S. 390 (1968).

8. 17 U.S.C. §111. The royalty rates are found at 37 C.F.R. Ch. III §308.2. The license is not available to satellite carriers, even if they are passive retransmitters. Satellite Broadcasting and Communications Association of America v. Oman, 17 F.3d 344 (11th Cir. 1994). The license was extended to "wireless" television by P.L. 103-369.

9. 17 U.S.C. §501(b),(c),(d).

10. See 43 PTCJ 510.

11. 17 U.S.C. §118.

12. 37 C.F.R. Ch. III Part 304.

13. 17 U.S.C. §119.

14. 17 U.S.C. Ch. 10.

15. 17 U.S.C. §512.

CHAPTER 8

1. A stimulating discussion of this is Prof. Benjamin Kaplan's book, *An Unhurried View of Copyright* (New York: Columbia Univ. Press, 1967).

2. Judge Learned Hand, writing in Nichols v. Universal Pictures Corp., 45 F.2d 119 (2d Cir. 1930), *cert. denied* 282 U.S. 902 (1931).

3. *See, e.g.,* Harold Lloyd Corp. v. Witwer, 65 F.2d 1 (9th Cir. 1933); Twentieth Century Fox-Film Corp. v. Stonesifer, 140 F.2d 579 (9th Cir. 1944).

4. Sheldon v. Metro-Goldwyn Pictures Corp., 81 F.2d 49 (2d Cir. 1936).

5. *See, e.g.,* Computer Associates Inc. v. Altai Inc., 982 F.2d 693 (2d Cir. 1992).

6. Sid & Marty Krofft Television Prods., Inc. v. McDonald's Corp., 562 F.2d 1157 (9th Cir. 1977).

7. For cases where these evils have arisen, see Dawson v. Hinshaw Music, Inc., 905 F.2d 731 (4th Cir. 1990), in which the court finds that music sold only to choral directors should be judged by what a choral director would perceive, never bothering to inquire what the ultimate audience might perceive; and Original Appalachian Artworks, Inc. v. Blue Box Factory (USA) Ltd., 577 F.Supp. 625 (S.D.N.Y. 1983), in which Dr. Joyce Brothers was allowed to opine on how the works in question would be perceived by juvenile customers.

8. Romm Art Creations Ltd. v. Simcha Int'l Arts Inc., 786 F.Supp. 1126 (E.D.N.Y. 1992).

9. Bleistein v. Donaldson Lithographing Co., 188 U.S. 239 (1903).

10. Burrow-Giles Lithographic Co. v. Sarony, 111 U.S. 53 (1884).

11. Concrete Machinery Co., Inc. v. Classic Lawn Ornaments, Inc., 843 F.2d 600 (1st Cir. 1988).

12. Shapiro, Bernstein & Co. v. H. L. Green Co., 316 F.2d 304 (2d Cir. 1963).

13. Merchant v. Levy, 92 F.3d 51 (2d Cir. 1996), *cert. denied* 136 L.Ed.2d 833 (1997).

14. 17 U.S.C. §501(b).

15. *Ibid.*

16. 17 U.S.C. §504(b).

17. 17 U.S.C. §504(c). Feltner v. Columbia Pictures Television, Inc., __ U.S. __ (1998). In the past, one has been able to elect statutory damages at any time up until actual entry of judgment. Branch v. Ogilvy & Mather, 772 F.Supp. 1359 (S.D.N.Y. 1991); Oboler v. Goldin, 714 F.2d 211 (2d Cir. 1983). Whether this interpretation has survived the Supreme Court's determination in *Feltner* that there is a right to trial by jury in statutory damage cases, it is too early to say. Technically, these two concepts seem compatible.

18. 17 U.S.C. §505. Rosciszewski v. Arete Associates, Inc., 1 F.3d 225 (4th Cir. 1993); Fogerty v. Fantasy Inc., 114 S.Ct. 1023 (1994).

19. Woods v. Universal City Studios, 920 F.Supp. 62 (S.D.N.Y. 1996).

20. Chavez v. Arte Publico Press, 53 F.3d 539 (5th Cir. 1998); College Savings Bank v. Florida Prepaid Postsecondary Education Expense Board, No. 97-1246 (Fed. Cir. 6/30/98). The Fifth Circuit granted *en banc* review on October 1, 1998. 56 PTCJ 695 (10/15/98).

21. 17 U.S.C. §506(a), as amended by P.L. 105-145. The fines are found in 18 U.S.C. §3571, and it should be noted that the fine can be greater: up to twice the defendant's pecuniary gain or twice the copyright owner's pecuniary loss. It should also be noted that copyright infringement has been brought within the scope of the Racketeering and Corrupt Practices Act, which exposes a defendant to yet greater penalties: 18 U.S.C. §1961.

22. 17 U.S.C. §107. On the first criterion, see Rubin v. Boston Magazine Co., 645 F.2d 80 (1st Cir. 1981). On the fourth, see New Boston Television, Inc. v. Entertainment Sports Programming Network, Inc., 215 U.S.P.Q. 755 (D.Mass. 1981); DC Comics, Inc. v. Reel Fantasy, Inc., 696 F.2d 24 (2d Cir. 1982).

23. Publications Int'l Ltd. v. Bally Mfg. Corp., 215 U.S.P.Q. 861 (N.D.Ill. 1982).

24. *See* Meredith Corp. v. Harper & Row, Publishers, Inc., 378 F.Supp. 686 (S.D.N.Y. 1974), *aff'd* 500 F.2d 1221 (2d Cir. 1974).

25. Gershwin Publishing Corp. v. Columbia Artists Management, Inc., 443 F.2d 1159 (2d Cir. 1971).

26. 17 U.S.C. §113(c); Italian Book Corp. v. American Broadcasting Companies, Inc., 458 F.Supp. 65 (S.D.N.Y. 1978).

27. Harper & Row, Publishers, Inc. v. The Nation Enterprises, 471 U.S. 539, 105 S.Ct. 2218 (1985).

28. Salinger v. Random House, Inc., 811 F.2d 90 (2d Cir. 1987), *cert. denied* 108 S.Ct. 213 (1987); New ERA Publications International, ApS v. Henry Holt & Co., 10 U.S.P.Q.2d 1561 (2d Cir. 1989), *rev'g* 695 F.Supp. 1493 (S.D.N.Y. 1988).

29. P.L. 101-650 §607, 104 Stat. 5132.

30. Berne Convention, Paris Text, Art. 10.

31. 131 F.Supp. 165 (S.D.Cal. 1955), *aff'd sub nom.* Benny v. Loew's, Inc., 239 F.2d 532 (9th Cir. 1956).

32. Columbia Pictures Corp. v. National Broadcasting Co., 137 F.Supp. 348, 350 (S.D.Cal. 1955).

33. Campbell v. Acuff-Rose Music, Inc., 510 U.S. 569, 114 S.Ct. 1164 (1994).

34. Liebovitz v. Paramount Pictures Corp., 948 F.Supp. 1214 (S.D.N.Y. 1996), *aff'd* 137 F.3d 109 (2d Cir. 1998).

35. Robert Stigwood Group, Ltd. v. O'Reilly, 346 F.Supp. 376 (D.Conn. 1972).

36. Time, Inc. v. Bernard Geis Associates, 293 F.Supp. 130 (S.D.N.Y. 1968).

37. Belmore v. City Pages, Inc., 8880 F.Supp. 673 (D.Minn. 1995).

38. Robart v. J. R. O'Dwyer Co., Inc., 34 U.S.P.Q.2d 1085 (S.D.N.Y. 1995).

39. Falwell v. Penthouse Int'l Ltd., 521 F.Supp. 1204 (W.D.Va. 1981).

40. Scherr v. Universal Match Corp., 297 F.Supp. 102 (S.D.N.Y. 1967).

41. Sony Corporation of America v. Universal City Studios, Inc., 464 U.S. 417 (1984).

42. H. Rep., p. 74.

43. *Ibid.,* p. 73.

44. Basic Books, Inc. v. Kinko's Graphics Corp., 785 F.Supp. 1522 (S.D.N.Y. 1991).

45. H. Rep., pp. 75–74.

46. American Geophysical Union v. Texaco, Inc., 37 F.3d 881 (2d Cir. 1994), *aff'g* 802 F.Supp. 1 (S.D.N.Y. 1992).

47. H. Rep., pp. 68–70.

48. *Ibid.,* pp. 70–71. The text as reprinted here, however, reflects a change in A.2 that was made after the House Report was printed. See remarks of Rep. Kastenmeier in the House Congressional Record for September 22, 1976, at p. 31980.

49. Library of Congress, Circular 21, "Reproduction of Copyrighted Works by Educators and Librarians," p. 26.

50. H.R. Conf. Rep. No. 94-1733, 2d Sess. 70, 1976 U.S. Code Cong. & Ad. News 5659, 5811.

51. 17 U.S.C. §108.

52. 17 U.S.C. §108(d).

53. Final Report of CONTU, pp. 54–55.

54. H. Rep., p. 77.

55. 17 U.S.C. §108(f)(1).

56. Sega Enterprises, Ltd. v. Accolade, Inc., 977 F.2d 1510 (9th Cir. 1993); Atari Games Corp. v. Nintendo of America, Inc., 975 F.2d 832 (Fed. Cir. 1992). *Cf.* Vault Corp. v. Quaid Software Ltd., 847 F.2d 255 (5th Cir. 1988).

57. Walt Disney Productions v. Filmation Associates, 628 F.Supp. 871 (C.D.Cal. 1986).

58. Sega Enterprises, Ltd. v. Accolade, Inc., *supra.*

59. A case pending in California has found that the plaintiff owner of linked text may have a cause of action, but the case is at too early a stage to be relied on. Futuredontics, Inc. v. Applied Anagramics Inc., 45 U.S.P.Q.2d 2005 (C.D.Cal. 1998).

60. 17 U.S.C. §1202.

61. 17 U.S.C. §1203.

62. 17 U.S.C. §1204.

63. 17 U.S.C. §1201.

64. 17 U.S.C. §1203.

CHAPTER 9

1. See discussion in Nimmer, *op. cit.*, at §7.12[D]. Considering that Congress has now acted to restore all foreign copyrights that were forfeited for noncompliance with U.S. formalities, you would be wise to assume forfeiture and take all actions available to owners of restored copyrights.

2. Former Title 17 of the U.S. Code, §§19, 21.

3. L & L White Metal Casting Corp. v. Cornell Metal Specialties Corp., 353 F.Supp. 1170 (E.D.N.Y. 1972), *aff'd* 177 U.S.P.Q. 673 (2d Cir. 1973); First American Artificial Flowers, Inc. v. Joseph Markovits, Inc., 342 F.Supp. 178 (S.D.N.Y. 1972).

4. Copyright Act of 1976, P.L. 94-53, §§103, 108.

5. The Statement of Administrative Action prepared by the U.S. Trade Representative, and explicitly approved in the statute (see P.L. 103-465 §101(a)(2)), states at §B.1(c)(2) that transfers by authors or original right holders are to be given effect according to their terms, "taking into account the expectations of the parties and relevant laws (including those concerning copyright, neighboring rights, contracts, descent and distribution, estates, and conflicts of law)."

6. The statute is so opaquely drafted that it could be read to impose a much earlier cutoff date where the source country is a Berne country. See §§104A(h)(3) and 104A(h)(4)(b). Such a result can hardly have been intended, however.

7. The drafters of the GATT implementing legislation neglected to repeal or qualify §405(b) of the Copyright Act, which could be read to provide a much broader defense to someone who relied on the absence of notice in a pre-1989 foreign work than is available to a reliance party who has received a "notice of intent to enforce." However, it is clear from the context that the new §104A was intended to override any such defense.

8. There is a theoretical gap here, of little practical consequence. The statute assumes that no country would join Berne or the WTO between December 8, 1994, and January 1, 1995. See §§104A(d)(3)(A) and 104A(h)(1).

9. Sheldon v. Metro-Goldwyn Pictures Corp., 81 F.2d 49 (2d Cir. 1946).

10. 17 U.S.C. §109(a), as amended by §514(b) of the Uruguay Round Agreements Act, P.L. 103-465, 108 Stat. 4809.

11. Goodis v. United Artists Television, Inc., 425 F.2d 397 (2d Cir. 1970). *See* Sanga Music, Inc. v. EMI Blackwood Music, Inc., 55 F.3d 756 (2d Cir. 1995), for an odd exception to *Goodis*.

12. Group Publishers v. Winchell, 86 F.Supp. 573, 576 (S.D.N.Y. 1952). However, this recordation requirement might well apply still to other types of works; see former Title 17 of the U.S. Code, §32.

13. Pushman v. New York Graphic Society, Inc., 287 N.Y. 302, 39 N.E.2d 249 (1942); Chamberlain v. Feldman, 300 N.Y. 135, 89 N.E.2d 863 (1949).

14. N.Y. Laws 1966, Ch. 688, §3; Calif. Civil Code §982(e).

15. Picture Music, Inc. v. Bourne, Inc., 457 F.2d 1213 (2d Cir. 1972). *Cf.* Shapiro, Bernstein & Co., Inc. v. Jerry Vogel Music Co., Inc., 221 F.2d 569 (2d Cir. 1955), *mod. on other grounds on rehearing* 223 F.2d 252 (2d Cir. 1955).

16. Shapiro, Bernstein & Co., Inc. v. Jerry Vogel Music Co., Inc., *supra;* Donna v. Dodd, Mead & Co., Inc., 374 F.Supp. 429 (S.D.N.Y. 1974).

17. White-Smith Music Publishing Co. v. Apollo Co., 209 U.S. 1 (1908).

18. *See generally* Nimmer, *op. cit.,* §2.10.

19. 17 U.S.C. §301(c).

20. H.R. 672 (P.L. 105-80); *see* La Cienega Music Co. v. ZZ Top, 53 F.3d 950 (9th Cir. 1995).

21. *Compare* Frederick Music Co. v. Sickler, 708 F.Supp. 587 (S.D.N.Y. 1989) *with* Marascalco v. Fantasy, Inc., 17 U.S.P.Q.2d 1409 (C.D.Cal. 1990).

22. Epoch Producing Corp. v. Killiam Shows, Inc., 522 F.2d 737 (2d Cir. 1975).

23. Miller Music Company v. Chas. N. Daniels, Inc., 362 U.S. 373 (1960).

24. Fred Fisher Music Co. v. M. Witmark & Sons, 318 U.S. 643 (1943).

25. Marks Music Corp. v. Borst Music Pub. Co., 110 F.Supp. 923 (D.N.J. 1953). For an excellent discussion of these rules and their many quirks,

see Nevins, "The Magic Kingdom of Will-Bumping: Where Estates Law and Copyright Law Collide," *Jrnl. Copr. Soc.* vol. 35, no. 2, January 1988.

26. De Sylva v. Ballentine, 351 U.S. 570 (1956); 17 U.S.C. §§304(a), 101.

27. Copyright Office regulations deal with the complicated problem of an author who leaves a will but has no executor actively serving: 37 C.F.R. §202.17(f)(3).

28. Rose v. Bourne, Inc., 279 F.2d 79 (2d Cir. 1960).

29. Edward B. Marks Music Corp. v. Jerry Vogel Music Company, 140 F.2d 266 (2nd Cir. 1944); *but see* Nimmer, *op. cit.*, §9.05[E].

30. Bartok v. Boosey & Hawkes, Inc., 523 F.2d 941 (2d Cir. 1975). For the mechanics of renewal of posthumous works, see 37 C.F.R. §207.17(f)(2).

31. H. Rep., p. 139.

32. Former Title 17 of the U.S. Code, §24; *see* Shapiro, Bernstein & Co. v. Bryan, 123 F.2d 1697 (2d Cir. 1941).

33. 17 U.S.C. §304(a), as amended by Copyright Amendments Act of 1992.

34. Stewart v. Abend, 110 S.Ct. 1750 (1990).

35. 37 C.F.R. Ch. II, §202.17(e), as amended on 11/24/92, 57 Fed.Reg. 60481.

36. *Ibid.*

37. 17 U.S.C. §408(c)(3).

38. 17 U.S.C. §304.

39. 17 U.S.C. §304(c).

40. *Ibid.;* 37 C.F.R. Ch. II, §201.10.

41. Maljack Productions, Inc. v. GoodTimes Home Video Corp., 81 F.3d 881 (9th Cir. 1996); Batjac Productions, Inc. v. GoodTimes Video Corp., 160 F.3d 1223 (9th Cir. 1998); Shoptalk Ltd. v. Concorde-New Horizons Corp., 49 USPQ 2d 1599 (2d Cir. 1999).

CHAPTER 10

1. Rev. Rul. 68-194, 1968-1 C.B. 87.

2. C. W. Churchman, 68 T.C. 696 (1977).

3. I.R.S. Pub. 334, Reg. §1.183-2.

4. Rev. Rul. 73-395, 1972-2 C.B. 87, as affected by P.L. 94-455, §2119. *See* Stern v. U.S.A., 1971-1 U.S.T.C. ¶86,491 (C.D.Cal. 1971).

5. Reg. §1.167(a)-1(b).

6. Rev. Rul. 60-358, 1960-2 C.B. 68.

7. *Ibid.*

8. Rev. Rul. 68-194, 1968-1 C.B. 87.

9. Reg. §1.167(a)-6(a); Rev. Rul. 73-395, 1973-2 C.B. 87, as affected by P.L. 94-455, §2119.

10. Heim v. Fitzpatrick, 262 F.2d 887 (2d Cir. 1959).

11. Rev. Rul. 55-706, 1955-2 C.B. 300.

12. This is by analogy to patents. See Reg. §1.1235-2(b)(2)(ii)

13. Cory v. Commissioner of Internal Revenue, 230 F.2d 941 (2d Cir. 1956), *cert. denied* 35 U.S. 828 (1956); for a patent analogy *see* Marco (1955), 25 T.C. 544.

14. I.R.C. §197, as amended by P.L. 103-66.

CHAPTER 11

1. For a compendium of U.S. copyright relations with foreign countries, see Copyright Office Circular 38a.

2. Berne Convention, Paris Text, Art. 7(8). For a detailed discussion of this, particularly as it affects works of the U.S. Government, *see* Ringer and Flacks, *op. cit.,* at pp. 157–204.

3. See, e.g., Wilhelm Nordemann, "The Term of Protection for Works by U.S.-American Authors in Germany," *Jrnl. Copr. Soc.* vol. 44, no. 1, Fall 1996.

4. Berne Convention, Paris Text, Appendix; U.C.C. Arts. Vter, V quater.

5. Itar-Tass Russian News Agency v. Russian Kurier, Inc., 153 F.3d 82 (2d Cir. 1998).

6. Nimmer, *op. cit.,* §17.07[B].

7. As noted in chapter 6, this treaty's definition of "performers" is quite broad and even includes (somewhat improbably) dancers.

Index